Praise for *An Audience of One* and for Jamie Turner and Chuck Moxley

One of the most important marketing books of the past decade. This should be required reading at every corporation and business school that wants to stay ahead of the curve.

—**Doug Busk**, former Global Group Director at
The Coca-Cola Company, US

Well researched and written in a fun, breezy style that makes this highly technical subject easy to understand and execute.

—**Kirsten McMullen**, Global Privacy Program Manager at
NortonLifeLock, US

An Audience of One provides a road map to how marketing is changing today and where it is headed tomorrow.

—**Doug Dichting**, former VP of R&D and Innovation at
Del Monte Foods, US

A blueprint for executives interested in using cutting-edge techniques to stay ahead of their competitors.

—**Desmond Martin**, former CTO of Harrods of London, UK

If you want to learn how to navigate the fast-changing world of marketing, then this book is for you.

—**Michael Brenner**, CEO of Marketing Insider Group and
former Global Director of Corporate Marketing at Nielsen, US

Everything you need to add the one-to-one secret weapon to your marketing today.

—**Bart Casey**, former SVP, International, at Ogilvy & Mather, UK

A must-have guide for marketers—beginners and pros—to take their game to the next level. This is the next step in marketing.
—**Emily Justin-Szopinski**, Director of Development and
Innovation at RedSaberes, Chile

Jamie Turner and Chuck Moxley are master storytellers. *An Audience of One* is the most captivating, comprehensive, and compelling book on how to market to each customer on a one-to-one basis, using large customer databases without the privacy issues.
—**Jagdish N. Sheth**, Charles Kellstadt Professor of Business at
Goizueta Business School of Emory University

The definitive guide on how to grow your revenues by narrowing your focus.
—**Ayman Itani**, CEO of Think Media Labs, Dubai

Effective marketing has shifted from one-to-many to one-to-one. Jamie Turner and Chuck Moxley understood that before most of us. Thanks to this book, we all have a chance to catch up.
—**Emeric Ernoult**, founder and CEO of AgoraPulse, France

Jamie Turner and Chuck Moxley have written the seminal book on how to send relevant, meaningful campaigns to individuals rather than mass audiences. This is the future of marketing.
—**Reshma Shah, PhD**, Associate Professor of Marketing at
Goizueta Business School of Emory University

There's a lot of buzz about one-to-one marketing, but up until now, there hasn't been a guidebook for it. Turner and Moxley have given us the keys to drive marketing success today and tomorrow.
—**Erik Qualman**, author of *Socialnomics* and *Digital Leader*

One-to-one marketing done right enables the holy grail of sales attribution. *An Audience of One* provides the framework to get you started.

 —**Carrie Schonberg**, CMO of Ashton Woods Homes, US

This is a book made especially for you, whoever you are. *An Audience of One* is a game changer.

 —**Jacques Meir**, Chief Knowledge Officer of Grupo Padrão, Brazil

Turner and Moxley have authored a book that not only provides big picture insights but also enables the reader to put together a one-to-one campaign that works. Definitely worth reading.

 —**Gary B. Wilcox, PhD**, John A. Beck Centennial Professor in
  Communication at The University of Texas at Austin

An Audience of One shows you how to shift from mass marketing to one-to-one marketing. It's a forward-looking guidebook with straightforward, practical advice.

 —**Siddharth Taparia**, Business Head at Emeritus Insights, Singapore

This book reveals how to set up, launch, and manage a successful 1:1 campaign.

 —**Frans Mahieu**, Director of Marketing at LeasePlan and
  former Global Marketing Director at Kimberly-Clark, US

The future of marketing has finally arrived. *An Audience of One* is a must-read on how to navigate the new marketing landscape.

 —**Robert T. Chin**, CEO of Aquilini Beverage Group, US

An Audience of One comes at a time when consumers expect brands to know them better and offer a seamless, personalized, and valuable experience. Essential reading if you want to survive the new normal.

 —**Ravi Raman**, Publisher of Martechvibe, Dubai

If you're interested in learning how to create cutting-edge marketing campaigns that can hypertarget consumers and follow them through to purchase, then *An Audience of One* is for you.

      —**Dave Kerpen**, *New York Times* bestselling author of
        The Art of People and *Likeable Social Media*

AN AUDIENCE OF
ONE

AN AUDIENCE OF ONE

DRIVE SUPERIOR RESULTS BY MAKING THE
RADICAL SHIFT FROM MASS MARKETING
TO ONE-TO-ONE MARKETING

JAMIE TURNER & CHUCK MOXLEY

NEW YORK   CHICAGO   SAN FRANCISCO   ATHENS   LONDON   MADRID
MEXICO CITY   MILAN   NEW DELHI   SINGAPORE   SYDNEY   TORONTO

1 2 3 4 5 6 7 8 9   LCR   26 25 24 23 22 21

ISBN   978-1-264-26854-2
MHID   1-264-26854-8

e-ISBN   978-1-264-26855-9
e-MHID   1-264-26855-6

This publication is designed to provide accurate and authoritative information in regard to the subject matter covered. It is sold with the understanding that neither the author nor the publisher is engaged in rendering legal, accounting, securities trading, or other professional services. If legal advice or other expert assistance is required, the services of a competent professional person should be sought.

>—*From a Declaration of Principles Jointly Adopted by a Committee of the American Bar Association and a Committee of Publishers and Associations*

Library of Congress Cataloging-in-Publication Data
Names: Turner, Jamie, author. | Moxley, Chuck, author.
Title: An audience of one : drive superior results by making the radical shift from mass
    marketing to one-to-one marketing / Jamie Turner and Chuck Moxley.
Description: New York : McGraw Hill, [2021] | Includes bibliographical references and
    index.
Identifiers: LCCN 2021026456 (print) | LCCN 2021026457 (ebook) | ISBN 9781264268542
    (hardback) | ISBN 9781264268559 (ebook)
Subjects: LCSH: Market segmentation. | Customer relations.
Classification: LCC HF5415.127 .T86 2021 (print) | LCC HF5415.127 (ebook)
    | DDC 658.8/02—dc23
LC record available at https://lccn.loc.gov/2021026456
LC ebook record available at https://lccn.loc.gov/2021026457

To our lovely wives, both cancer survivors,
who have fought and continue to fight
for each of us and for our respective families.

CONTENTS

FOREWORD

Our first book together, *The One to One Future: Building Relationships One Customer at a Time*, was finally published in August 1993. We had been working on it for more than three years, after meeting each other by chance at the Toledo Advertising Club in January 1990. Don was an advertising executive from New York, and Martha was a marketing professor in Ohio. We discovered that we each had been trying to work out how the advertising and marketing world might be changed by interactivity—whenever it arrived in full force.

The prevailing myth in those days was that when interactivity arrived, consumers would be able to watch a commercial on television, and if they liked it, they would push a button on their remotes and a coupon would print out of the set-top box. But we thought interactivity—*true* interactivity—would involve messaging that flowed both ways, not just from advertiser to consumer, but from consumer back to advertiser. The question was, how would that change the marketing discipline? Or would it?

So we undertook a thought experiment. What if, sometime in the distant interactive future, a child could be watching a Kellogg's Frosted Flakes commercial and talk back to Tony the Tiger—if the child could have an actual *conversation* with this cartoon character? What might Kellogg do differently because of the child's input? Would they treat the child any differently? Would they change their product in any way?

In answering this question, however, we realized that individual feedback was of no value at all to a mass marketer—not unless it was *representative* of a broader population or audience. A mass marketer learned about audiences and prepared its messages for them by conducting extensive market surveys. But the feedback of an individual customer? They called that "anecdotal." We wrote about the conflict between interactivity and the mass marketing discipline in Chapter 2:

> No one at Kellogg knows whether *you* prefer the added interest of nuts and raisins with high-fiber flakes. No one will wonder why *you* stopped buying Frosted Flakes after ten years as a loyal customer, or what they could do to get you back again. No one at Kellogg will know whether you personally replaced Frosted Flakes with another Kellogg brand or whether you started eating bagels every morning instead. No one in the marketing department at one of these companies really cares about you personally.[1] (Emphasis in the original.)

In conducting our thought experiment, however, we also realized that to be competitively successful in the interactive future, marketers would need to focus not on audiences of customers, but on *individual* customers, literally one customer at a time. Audiences of one. Instead of one-to-many communications and messaging, marketing in a truly interactive world would be competitively transformed into a one-to-one discipline.

We appreciated, of course, that this was a totally impractical idea. Absurd. Preposterous. But we consoled ourselves by visualizing our writing project as a work of business science fiction. We had no idea when or how interactivity would arrive in individual consumer households with full force, although we viewed it as inevitable. Sooner or later, we knew, the world *would* become fully interactive. We just didn't see how it could happen in less than the 10 or 20 years required to lay fiber-optic cables into residential neighborhoods.

But in 1994, just a few months after our book was finally published, the first commercial web browser, Netscape Navigator, became available. And the inevitable transformation of marketing that we had predicted began for real. Nearly three decades later, we're happy to report that many of the predictions we made in *The One to One Future* have now come true: e-commerce (Chapter 8: "Take Products to Customers, Not Customers to Products"); social media, remote workforces, and the gig economy (Chapter 10: "Society at Light Speed").

But one of our most significant predictions has not come true. At least not yet. We dedicated the entirety of Chapter 9 to this prediction, titling our chapter "Make Money Protecting Privacy, Not Threatening It." And given the plethora of interactive platforms that now trade in consumers' personal data, facilitated by all the free interactive services provided to them, protecting consumers' personal privacy has proved to be a daunting task indeed.

Until now. The interactive future as we imagined it in Chapter 9 would have protected individual consumer privacy through something we called "privacy intermediaries." These intermediaries would make extensive consumer data available to marketers, including not just family size, age, income, and so forth, but past transactions, expressed preferences, previous interactions, and other data. However, all this highly personal, consumer-specific data would be provided *without* any personally identifying information. A marketer would then be able to converse, one to one, with individual consumers, engaging each of them in highly personal, 1:1 interactions, but these consumers' privacy would still be completely protected unless and until they chose to engage personally with the marketer.

And this is, in fact, what Jamie Turner and Chuck Moxley are proposing in *An Audience of One*, with their idea of an identity graph. And why are they proposing it? Because, even though nobody in the mass marketing discipline even knows your name, much less whether you prefer nuts and raisins in your cereal, as Turner and Moxley describe it:

one-to-one (1:1) marketing . . . means that marketers treat each prospect and customer as a person who has a name, unique needs, distinct behaviors, and a desire to have some control over their relationship with the brand.

Indeed! We could not have said it any better ourselves. Read on . . .

Don Peppers and Martha Rogers, PhD

INTRODUCTION

The World of One-to-One Marketing

Imagine this—you're sitting in a conference room on the seventeenth floor of The Coca-Cola Company world headquarters. Across the table from you is the senior group head in Global Marketing. He's been put in charge of exploring new and emerging technologies that will drive revenue for The Coca-Cola Company, one of the world's most successful brands.

The conference room is spacious and elegantly decorated, but not overstuffed. It has a functional chic to the decor that has more in common with an Austin startup than a New York law firm. You notice that there's a look of mild skepticism on the executive's face, which is not surprising. After all, he travels the globe on behalf of the company looking for innovative technologies that can be used to stay one (or two) steps ahead of the competition. He's seen it all.

You've been invited to the meeting to share a new technology that can hypertarget personalized TV, desktop, mobile, and other ads to specific individuals who, according to the analytics running in the background, are statistically more likely to buy your product than if you used traditional marketing techniques. In other words, instead of using the spray and pray technique where ads are delivered to a broad audience in the hopes that a small percentage of them are prospective customers, you can use one-to-one marketing to send the ads to people who, based on data, are likely to buy your product.

The ability to connect the dots between massive amounts of data and the end consumer is a technique that has been the dream of marketers for decades. But what makes this even more appealing is that after the ad is delivered, marketers can watch to see which recipients went to the brick-and-mortar retailer and bought the product. In other words, marketers can use anonymized data to track customer data sets from the moment they see the ad all the way through their purchase at the retailer.

You look around the conference room and think of all the important decisions that have been made there—decisions about business strategies for dozens of brands, decisions about new facilities that would employ tens of thousands of people, and even decisions about whether an executive should be fired because they didn't deliver the results they had promised last quarter. With all that racing through your mind, you open your laptop and begin the presentation.

The story of the Coca-Cola executive isn't an imaginary one. It actually happened. And both of the authors of this book were either sitting in the conference room or working behind-the-scenes on the techniques that were being discussed.

The techniques involve one-to-one (1:1) marketing, which means that marketers treat each prospect and customer as a person who has a name, unique needs, distinct behaviors, and a desire to have some control over their relationship with the brand. The premise of 1:1 marketing is your customers don't want to be targeted with offers. Instead, they want to engage with brands in a dialogue and on their terms. In other words, they want to be treated as a *person*, not a *prospect*.

WELCOME TO A NEW FORM OF MARKETING

You might be surprised to learn that there are over 1,450 pieces of anonymized data that marketers can find out about the individuals in their target market. This data helps marketers fine-tune the campaigns they send to prospects and customers. Where do they get the information?

The starting point is frequent shopper card data. After all, when a consumer signs up to use a frequent shopper card at the grocery store, they're agreeing to allow the store to collect data about their purchases. But that's not the only place data is collected—your smart TV is collecting data, your smart speaker is collecting data, your car is collecting data, your laptop is collecting data, your favorite retailer is collecting data, your bank is collecting data, your mobile device is collecting data, and even your e-commerce store is collecting data. And that's not the half of it—Facebook, LinkedIn, Snapchat, TikTok, your fitness tracker, the photo editing app you just downloaded—they're all collecting data about you and your behaviors. And marketers can use that data to send you more relevant ads.

When the data is collected ethically and is put into non-personally-identifiable data sets, it helps marketers understand who you are, what your behaviors are, and what your propensities are. For example, if a marketer wants to target people who have recently put their house on the market and who are looking for new baby furniture—boom, that's a piece of cake. Or perhaps they want to target people living in an Atlanta suburb who are looking for left-handed, graphite golf clubs. Consider it done. They might even want to target doctors, living within five miles of the seashore, who own yachts, and who prefer red wine over white wine. Again, no problem.

There are two things that make this revolutionary. First, marketers who use 1:1 techniques can track whether or not their campaigns drive the prospects to the bricks-and-mortar stores to make the purchase. Tracking purchase behavior is easy if it was made on an e-commerce site—but now for the first time, marketers can deliver a TV, mobile, desktop, or other kind of ad and then connect the dots to see if the consumer who saw the ad made the purchase at the physical store.

The second reason this is so revolutionary is that action has been taken to ensure the consumer's privacy is protected every step of the way. In other words, marketers aren't targeting Barbie Thorne living on 123 Jones Street in Walton-on-Thames, Surrey, England. Instead, they're targeting #0019734756-9931, which is Barbie's anonymized ID number.

Said another way, because the data is held by a third party that is outside the reach of the brand running the ad, the marketer doesn't know that it's Barbie who is receiving their ad. They just know that they delivered an ad to #0019734756-9931.

DO WE HAVE YOUR ATTENTION YET?

If you're interested in how organizations are targeting and tracking consumers, while at the same time protecting their privacy, then you've come to the right place. This is a book about using information that has been *ethically* collected to design marketing campaigns that are then hypertargeted to consumers in an almost 1:1 fashion. But this is not a book that's just about technology. Instead, it's a book that's about a *technique*—one that any marketer can use to create meaningful, authentic dialogues with prospects and customers that can help build a bridge between your brand and the person who might buy your product or service.

Traditionally, marketers created a single campaign and blasted it out to a mass market in the hope that the message would resonate with some of the people who saw the ads. But for those who are willing to learn the new techniques outlined in this book, the future is very different. Instead of mass marketing, we'll show you how to do 1:1 marketing where you can create a meaningful, authentic, resonant campaign that speaks to individuals rather than audiences.

If that sounds like something you would like to do with your next campaign, then let's get started. There's a revolution going on and we don't want you left behind.

AN AUDIENCE OF
ONE

PART

1

THE ONE-TO-ONE MARKETING OVERVIEW

YOU ARE HERE... (NOT LITERALLY. BUT IN THE BOOK.)

| 1:1 OVERVIEW | DIGGING DEEPER | STRATEGIC THINKING | PUTTING IT ALL TO WORK | ADVANCED TECHNIQES |

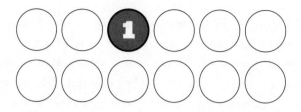

WHAT IS ONE-TO-ONE MARKETING?

We are reinventing brand building, from wasteful mass marketing to mass one-to-one brand building fueled by data and technology.
—DAVID TAYLOR, CEO, PROCTER & GAMBLE

If you're in marketing or sales, or work in any business trying to win new customers, then you already know the essential rule for growth, which is to get inside the mind of your customers and understand their motivations on a deep, nuanced level. In fact, executives who are serious about growing their business often know even more about their customers than they do about their product or service. As counterintuitive as that idea is, understanding your customer's needs and then acting on that knowledge will drive more growth for your business than understanding the inner workings of every last detail about your product or service.

The reason for this is because all humans share one thing in common: we all act in our own self-interest. As much as we would like to believe that we focus more on the needs of others than we do on ourselves, in the end, almost every decision we make is based on self-interest.

This inward, personalized focus is understood and leveraged by the most successful brands in the world. For example, Disney understands that the more personalized the experience is for their customers, the more likely those customers are to come back again and again. So when you enter into a Disney theme park, you're given a wrist band so Disney can personalize your experience. If a customer makes a dinner reservation on the Disney app, when that customer starts heading toward the restaurant, the wrist band lets the restaurant host know that the guest is approaching the restaurant. When the dinner party walks through the door, the host greets them by name and encourages them to sit anywhere, while the kitchen simultaneously gets an alert to begin cooking their meal.[1]

Personalization can go beyond live experiences at theme parks. It can be dropped right into your living room or office. Online retailer Very.com personalizes the web visitor's experience by creating weather-sensitive home pages tied to the visitor's weather in their neighborhood. So if the sun is shining where you live, you'll see a home page that says something like, "The sun is shining and it's 85 degrees outside. It's swimsuit season!" But your home page says something different from the one your cousin sees in rainy New York City. Your cousin sees a home page that says, "We're having a sale on rain gear today!"[2]

And when Marketo, a division of Adobe, invited prospects to their annual conference in Las Vegas, they distributed customized video invitations featuring each recipient's name in the iconic "Welcome to Las Vegas" sign. Imagine receiving a customized video that says, "Hey, Lily. Will you be joining us in Las Vegas?"[3] When you see a personalized marketing message that puts your name in lights, it's hard to resist clicking through to find out what it's all about, right?

When Don Peppers and Martha Rogers wrote *The One to One Future* in the 1990s, they predicted the kind of campaigns we're experiencing today. What they might not have predicted was that one-to-one marketing (or 1:1 marketing) would be available to both the largest brands in the world as well as the local coffee shop down the street.

In its simplest form, 1:1 marketing means engaging with prospects and customers using a one-to-one, personalized approach based on who they are, how they think, what they purchase, what their interests are, where they go, and how they prefer to be communicated with. It's the opposite of a traditional, mass-marketing approach where advertisers blast the same message to as many people as possible.

While the ability to hypertarget and personalize certain kinds of digital campaigns has been available for many years, 1:1 marketing is different because most of those campaigns existed in silos. In other words, the typical online display (i.e., banner ad) campaign existed in its own universe and didn't share data with the email campaign, let alone the TV, paid social, direct mail, and other campaigns.

What makes today's 1:1 marketing so revolutionary is that for the first time in history, those campaigns don't exist in separate silos—instead, we've been able to connect the dots across all channels. In other words, the data and information from each channel is "talking" to one another, so your campaigns can continuously become more relevant and meaningful to the prospect.

And it gets even better: because all of the data is interconnected, in many cases you can track whether or not the individual seeing the ad actually completed the purchase at the bricks-and-mortar retailer—not just online, *but at the physical retail location.* As an example, say you're the marketing director for Nike, Apple, or a small chain of restaurants. You can now watch to see if the specific group of people who saw your TV commercial actually visited your store and bought your product or service. That information is then looped around to continue to adapt and improve the results of your next series of ads.

1:1 marketing gives you the ability to deliver messages via TV, online display, email, direct mail, paid social, and other channels, and then know who is seeing and acting upon the ads. Because of this, you can have a more wholistic understanding of who your customers are, what they know about your product, what they want from brands in your category, and how much they're worth to you. You'll still run "campaigns," but they are orchestrated moments of contact with the customer that cumulatively result in the customer's loyalty, which increases over time. This is *circular momentum*, which is when a 1:1 campaign builds upon itself to get better and better results and add more and more value.

Practicing 1:1 marketing means treating each prospect and customer as a person who has a name, has a unique set of needs and desires, and wants some control over their relationship with a brand, instead of being treated as a target on a list. Audiences of one don't want to be targeted with offers. They want to engage with brands in a dialogue or two-way exchange of information and on their terms. In other words, they want to be treated as a *person*, not a *prospect*.

Chances are, you've created many personalized communications or experienced the two-way communication common with social media. To understand the difference between personalized communication and 1:1 marketing, let's review a brief history of marketing and advertising. By doing so, it will become obvious how advances in technology enable a level of precision marketing never before possible.

Later chapters will discuss why 1:1 marketing is the "new black" due to changes in consumer behavior that are rendering mass marketing techniques less effective. And you'll get some examples of brands embracing 1:1 marketing to drive superior results.

IN A NUTSHELL

What makes 1:1 marketing so revolutionary is that for the first time in history, we can connect the dots across channels and track the results all the way through to purchase (even if the purchase was made at a bricks-and-mortar retailer). As a result, a 1:1 marketer isn't interested in blasting out mass marketing campaigns to as many people as possible. Instead, they're interested in narrowing their focus and delivering the ads to a smaller group of individuals who are more likely to buy their products or services in the first place.

EVERYTHING OLD IS NEW AGAIN

The concept of 1:1 marketing actually isn't new. For decades, local butchers, grocers, shop owners, milk delivery men, and paper boys practiced 1:1 marketing. They knew most of their customers by name, recognized a new customer who'd not been in before (and treated them differently than someone who'd been a customer for years), and communicated with customers based on how each customer preferred to communicate—long conversations with one person and short, to-the-point discussions with the people who simply wanted to transact business and get back to what they were doing.

But then the world of *Mad Men* burst onto the scene in the 1950s, and the concept of slogans, television commercials, promotions, snipes (the little starburst on an ad shouting "new and improved" or "best value"), and other mass marketing approaches grew in popularity. Advances in technology made it possible for brands to talk to hundreds, thousands, or even millions of prospects at the same time. All it took was finding the right hook and jingle to create a memorable, funny, or dramatic TV commercial, and use broadcast media such as television or radio to get an advertiser's message to the masses. A good commercial running on national television alone could make a brand an instant hit.

In the 1960s and 1970s, social scientists got involved and began to identify, formulate, and measure approaches that could cause masses (or herds) of people to buy a certain product or stampede a brand's stores. Of course, taken too far these social science experiments lead to some unethical mass marketing approaches.

One such technique was known as subliminal advertising, where images were inserted in a commercial for a fraction of a second—so fast that the unsuspecting consumer had no idea they'd even seen the image. The premise, since disproven, was that exposing the right image subliminally would cause viewers to crave something and purchase the product to satisfy the craving. For example, a photograph of popcorn inserted in a commercial at a theater would, in theory, bump popcorn sales at the concession stand.

During these golden years of advertising, direct marketing also took off as marketers found ways to obtain mailing addresses of customers and prospects. Mailers were blasted to thousands or hundreds of thousands of households, with the goal of procuring purchases via mail order or a visit to the brand's local store. Mailers expanded into catalogs, and catalogs expanded into bigger catalogs—remember getting the three-pound Sears *Wish Book* in the mailbox every fall?

ADVANCES IN COMPUTING TECHNOLOGY CHANGED MARKETING FOREVER

The advent of computers in the 1960s and 1970s made it possible to capture and use data for marketing. Initially, the concept of "database marketing" (sending a message to a database compiled of prospects or customers) was practical only with direct marketing, since it was the only "addressable media" at the time. By combining customer, census, and other compiled data into mailing lists, marketers could narrow offers to the households most likely to make a purchase.

Early adopters of data-driven direct mail provided a glimpse into what the future of people-based marketing could be. But only a glimpse. Mailing lists were maintained using mainframe computers. The significant cost and time involved in updating databases and mailing lists limited how often and how quickly direct marketers could create and change offers or segment lists. By today's standards it was quite rudimentary.

As computing power improved (while the size of computers shrank), the level of sophistication with targetable direct mail improved, too. Minicomputers were introduced that were a fraction of the size of mainframe computers. They didn't need to be housed in data centers requiring massive cooling systems. Microcomputers, dubbed personal computers, arrived later that were small enough to be placed on desks in offices.

These innovations in technology allowed more data to be captured and updates made more frequently, all at a much lower cost. However, direct mail pieces were still printed on large, production-printing presses, limiting the extent to which they could be personalized and messages varied. At best, a marketer could print a handful of different versions and send each version to a different mailing list.

Once digital printing processes were invented and refined enough to make personalizing individual mailers practical, it became possible to change the direct mail pieces to target more finite groups of prospects. And in theory, a unique mailer could be printed for each recipient, with variables such as names, headlines, and offers customized to each recipient. Nevertheless, collecting data from customers or purchasing lists and creating variations in direct mail pieces remained a time-consuming, sequential process, limiting the ability to truly personalize offers and mailers.

By the 1990s, with the explosion of personal computers democratizing the collection of data, the notion of 1:1 marketing emerged. In 1993, Don Peppers and Martha Rogers published their seminal book *The One to One Future.* They predicted a future where brands would have a "dialogue with customers" instead of just blasting them with ads, where measuring share of market would be replaced by measuring "share of customer," and why brands should invest as much or more in retaining customers than acquiring new ones.

The ideas that Peppers and Rogers espoused were so revolutionary in the marketing world that *Inc. Magazine*'s editor in chief called *The One to One Future* "one of the two or three most important business books ever written," while *Businessweek* called it the "bible of the new marketing." For people working in the emerging field of database marketing, whose companies were investing heavily in the ability to personalize communications to prospects and customers, *The One to One Future* became their bible, the promise of an entirely new world in which data fueled 1:1 marketing.

TWO DECADES LATER, 1:1 MARKETING IS NO LONGER A FUTURE STATE

The book was called the *One to One Future* because in 1993 technology simply hadn't evolved to the point to make all of Peppers and Rogers's predictions a reality. But the creation of the World Wide Web changed everything, making it possible to interact with prospects and customers in real time.

The World Wide Web started as an idea by Sir Tim Berners-Lee, a software engineer working for CERN, to solve the challenge of data being distributed on siloed computer systems. He laid out his vision in a 1989 proposal, and the very first "web server" came online in December 1991. Initially, use of the web was limited primarily to the scientific world, and by late 1993, more than 500 web servers were operating.

In 1994, Berners-Lee moved from CERN to the Massachusetts Institute of Technology and founded the World Wide Web Consortium (W3C), an international community devoted to developing open web standards that he still leads today. As the media picked up on this radical new idea revolutionizing information sharing, usage took off. By the end of 1994, the web boasted more than 10 million users and 10,000 servers, 2,000 of which were commercial. See Figure 1.1.

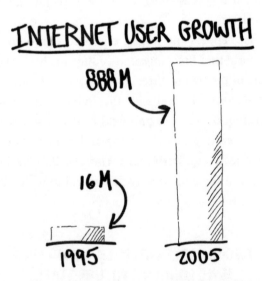

Figure 1.1 Internet penetration grew nearly 900 times in the first decade after its commercialization.

In the early days of the World Wide Web, forward-thinking marketers and agencies spent countless hours explaining to CEOs why a company should even care about the people using the internet. In the early days of the web, after all, internet users tended to be scientists, technical folks, or teenage boys. In December 1995, there were only 16 million internet users in the entire world, which equaled less than one-half of 1 percent of the world's population. A decade later, 888 million people had access to the internet. And today, more than 4.7 billion people—or more than 60 percent of the world's population—use the internet.[4]

The World Wide Web made it possible to move from data stored on a handful of mainframe computers to a completely interconnected world that defies time and space. It makes virtually everyone in the world accessible 24/7 and enables billions of data points to be collected every hour across more than 1.6 billion websites.

And it's not just a privileged few who have access to the internet but 90 percent of the US population—which means virtually all of your prospects and customers can be reached with one-to-one marketing via the internet. The internet enables unlimited dialogues with prospects, and not just via text but through just about any medium—text, images, videos, live chats, webinars, even taking control of a remote user's computer—thanks in large part to 73 percent of US households accessing the internet via a fast broadband connection.

Moving from dial-up, low-speed internet access to always-on, high-speed connections made it possible and easy for people to be accessible and engaged during all waking hours and addressable across a variety of devices. More than 250 million people in the United States use email,[5] 97 percent of Americans own a mobile phone,[6] and 73 percent of Americans use social media.[7]

With the technology advances over the past two decades, marketing has been forever altered. It's not only possible but affordable for every business to leverage 1:1 marketing to create and connect with audiences of one. If we were to compare the advances in marketing to transportation, mass marketing would be akin to the ocean liner, computers and digitized printing akin to jetliners, and today's connected world akin to a teleporter!

The 1:1 future is here, now.

THE PARADIGM SHIFT: FROM MARKETING TO ANONYMOUS MASSES TO 1:1 MARKETING

As discussed throughout this book, 1:1 marketing isn't just about data or technology. It truly represents a paradigm shift for marketers. After all, many of the practices of mass marketing haven't changed in decades and are used still by the majority of consumer brands.

> ### IN A NUTSHELL
>
> It's not only possible but affordable for every business to leverage 1:1 marketing to create and connect with audiences of one.

The chief marketing officer (CMO) of a large quick-service restaurant chain was discussing recently how it's possible to leverage 1:1 marketing with the chain's millions of customers who opted in to receive weekly text messages featuring offers and promotions. The executive, whose career had spanned numerous consumer brands that relied largely on mass marketing, argued that the effort and cost to communicate with such a relatively small audience didn't make sense. After all, she could run a television commercial on the Olympics and reach two hundred million consumers. Wouldn't that be far more efficient?

Marketers whose careers were built on mass marketing techniques are likely to resist changing what's worked for so many years to adapt to the new reality of consumer behavior and technology-powered possibilities. Fundamental to embracing this new paradigm is understanding that we've moved from marketing to masses of anonymous consumers to engaging with *audiences of one.*

When the words "addressable" and "advertising" are mentioned in the same sentence, many people think the conversation is about addressable television, which is the ability to show different ads to different people who are watching the same TV show. Make no mistake—the addressable consumer is about much more than addressable television.

It's now possible to reach specific individuals or households with your message across all of their devices. And instead of measuring campaign performance based simply on how many people viewed a specific ad, advertisers can now measure campaigns based on more meaningful metrics the CEO really cares about.

For example, CEOs care far more about incremental sales lift than they do how many people were exposed to a TV ad or clicked on digital ads. And yet 1:1 marketing practices, such as targeting individuals and measuring sales lift, are relatively recent developments not embraced by all marketers. Some don't fully understand the capabilities available in marketing today. Others don't see a reason to change from the tried-and-true practices of mass marketing, despite their inherent limitations.

> In the end, the only thing the C-Suite cares about is whether $1 spent in marketing generates more than $1 in profit for the business. One-to-one marketing is perfectly suited to help marketers accomplish that goal.
> —DESMOND MARTIN, FORMER CIO, HARRODS OF LONDON

Since the days of the *Mad Men*, ad targeting has been limited because ads traditionally have been delivered using one-dimensional, mass distribution technology: broadcast television, radio, newspapers, magazines, and outdoor billboards. These technologies allowed for a single message to be transmitted to a massive audience all at once. The audience is composed entirely of anonymous individuals: whoever happened to be within the broadcast area, reading the publication, or driving past the billboard.

As noted earlier, the advent of direct mail in the 1960s represented the first "addressable advertising" option for marketers. The ad—a direct mail piece—was literally targeted based on the home address of an individual or household and hand delivered via the US Postal Service. This new method of one-to-one targeting ushered in an entirely new industry, with many companies collecting data about people and households mapped to a home address, including tax and parcel records, purchase data, warranty registrations, surveys, and more. But direct marketing—as the industry came to be known—was a unique discipline held apart from traditional advertising. Direct marketing was often siloed into a specific department at an advertiser or into specialized teams in agencies who served as the experts in the approach.

Because of the high cost of delivering ads physically, however, the practice was limited primarily to categories and advertisers that could afford to use direct marketing for customer acquisition and growth. The cost of reaching people via direct mail was and remains significantly higher per person than mass marketing methods, such as television and radio advertising. Therefore, relatively few brands marketed to their audiences of one. And even if they did, it was simply one of many channels they used to promote their brand and products.

To be clear, ad targeting has been used in some mass marketing. It's just that rather than hypertargeting on a household or individual basis, marketers have relied on less-granular tactics such as demographic targeting. In other words, they targeted people likely to be of a certain age or income as a proxy for people most likely to purchase a particular item or category. A marketer targeting consumers most likely to purchase his product—for example, a premium brand of orange juice—would employ a decade-specific demographic proxy (e.g., adults 25 to 34) and hope it reached mostly buyers of premium orange juice.

IN A NUTSHELL

Traditionally, one-to-one marketing was used primarily by the direct response industry. Mass marketers had to rely on other methods, like demographic targeting, for their campaigns.

But demographic targeting itself is relatively new. It wasn't even possible until companies like Nielsen and Arbitron began calculating an estimate of the number of people who tuned into a show, station, or network. They started doing this in the 1940s for radio and in the 1950s for television. It was done by paying a large panel of people (typically at least 100,000 people across the United States) to maintain a detailed diary of every program they watched or radio station they listened to. Panel members also reported demographic information, such as age, presence of children, address, and other information that allowed Nielsen to report what type of people were watching a particular show. For example, the audience for a show like ABC's *The Bachelor* would comprise a higher percentage (or "over index" in research terms) of women ages 25 to 34 and comprise a small percentage (or "under index") of men ages 45 to 54.

Meanwhile, brands conducted their own market research to determine what types of consumers were most likely to purchase their product. For example, women ages 25 to 34 are more likely to shop at Macy's. Therefore, Macy's could target their advertising to reach the people most likely to buy their product, women ages 25 to 34, by buying ads that ran during television shows most likely watched by women ages 25 to 34 (e.g., *The Bachelor*), as measured by Nielsen ratings. In theory, advertisers are being more efficient with their advertising budgets by placing ads only on the shows watched by people likely to buy their products.

But there are numerous problems inherent with this approach—the data used by Nielsen and other platforms sampled only a fraction of the total population. In fact, just 40,000 people determine what shows make it on television and which shows are cancelled or not renewed. In the world of research, a sample size of that many people is statistically large enough to predict the behavior of all American television viewers.

But that means that the 120 million people watching TV in the United States are controlled by the programming decisions TV networks make based on this sampling of a few individuals. And while it may be true that women ages 25 to 34 are the people most likely to watch *The Bachelor*, it's also true that millions of people not in that demographic enjoy watching that show.

Furthermore, the demographic characteristics captured by product research, such as age, are just one factor in who buys a product. While it's true that women ages 25 to 34 are the most likely people to shop at Macy's, it is also true that there are many women aged 25 to 34 who never shop at Macy's.

Similarly, 70 percent of Macy's shoppers are female. That means it's also true that nearly a third of Macy's shoppers are male. To target advertising primarily toward women ages 25 to 34 means ads will be reaching people who aren't Macy's shoppers. Meanwhile, Macy's will miss large groups of people who shop there, but may not be aware of a current promotion because they aren't seeing the ads promoting it.

THE INTERNET ENABLED A PARADIGM SHIFT FOR ADVERTISERS

It wasn't until broad internet use emerged in the mid- to late 1990s that the paradigm shifted. The internet wasn't just a broadcast medium, like television, but instead enabled two-way communication between brands and consumers. Furthermore, each website a consumer visits is hosted at a unique address (called an internet protocol address, or IP address). Similarly, each device must also connect to a network, and each network has a unique IP address. This method of assigning unique addresses provides a means for identifying each unique device accessing the internet as well as each media property carrying advertising.

And while it isn't quite as easy to address an ad to a person using the internet as it is to address a direct mail piece to a person, transitioning from targeting an anonymous mass of unknown people to targeting specific individuals radically altered the potential for marketers both large and small.

Additionally, because the internet enabled two-way communication, it became possible to do more than simply blast a message to consumers; marketers could now create one-to-one dialogues with their customers and prospects. Eventually, the same technology that enabled internet access for desktops and laptops made smartphones and tablets addressable. And more recently, internet-connected televisions and other television devices (e.g., a Roku or Fire TV Stick) have made television viewers fully addressable across all of their connected devices.

This means that in today's world of addressable consumers, a marketer who wants to target ads to premium orange juice buyers can use past-purchase data to target people with a history of buying premium orange juice. For example, Minute Maid Orange Juice can take purchase data acquired from people's frequent shopper cards, sort out the people who buy a lot of orange juice, and target just those people in a 1:1 ad campaign. By using the past purchase data as a targeting tool, the campaigns are much more effective because they eliminate wasted ad impressions. See Figure 1.2.

ONE-TO-ONE MARKETING IS 3 TIMES MORE EFFICIENT

VIEWER #1: BUYS GENERIC ORANGE JUICE ⟹ THE BACHELOR → DOES NOT GET O.J. AD ✗

VIEWER #2: BUYS PREMIUM ORANGE JUICE ⟹ THE BACHELOR → DOES GET O.J. AD ✓

VIEWER #3: DOESN'T BUY ORANGE JUICE ⟹ THE BACHELOR → DOES NOT GET O.J. AD ✗

BY USING PURCHASE DATA INSTEAD OF JUST DEMOGRAPHIC DATA, A 1:1 MARKETER NARROWS THE FOCUS WHILE INCREASING REVENUES.

Figure 1.2 All three groups in this illustration watch *The Bachelor*—(1) people who buy generic orange juice, (2) people who buy premium orange juice, and (3) people who don't buy orange juice. A 1:1 campaign will collect data on who is buying the premium juice and use that data to target only those consumers on *The Bachelor*. The other two groups don't see the ad even though they're watching the same show at the same time.

Addressability also changes the game when measuring the success of ad campaigns. Previously, advertisers had no way of knowing who actually saw their ads. Campaigns were measured using ratings to estimate how many people in the targeted demographic saw an ad. This, as was pointed out earlier, only loosely correlates to the people actually buying the advertised orange juice.

Since consumers are now addressable, advertisers can see which non-personally identifiable individuals saw the ad and then use transaction data from point-of-sale systems, frequent shopper data, or online purchases to measure whether $1 spent in advertising generated more than $1 in profit for the business.

For example, in the case of the Minute Maid Orange Juice campaign, an ad platform working in partnership with a data company, such as NCSolutions or IRI, could measure orange juice purchases as a result of the ad campaign. They do this by comparing sales from the people reached by the advertising to an identical control group who didn't see the ads.

By comparing the test and control groups, the advertiser can determine how much additional Minute Maid Orange Juice was purchased by the people seeing the ads versus the people who didn't see the ad. In the end, the measurement company would provide data that shows actual incremental dollars generated and a return on ad spend (known as ROAS) for every dollar spent on the ads. For example, the data would show that when a brand spends $1 on a campaign, it generates $1.50 in incremental revenue. Measuring advertising based on real-world results, such as in-store sales, is a game changer for advertisers.

Here's a curveball for you—purposely reaching *fewer* consumers with an ad campaign probably sounds crazy to a traditional marketer who is accustomed to measuring campaign success based on what percentage of the audience the ad reached. Their goal was to reach the maximum audience size for the fewest dollars possible. The perspective isn't wrong; it's simply out of sync with the new reality created by the ability to market to audiences of one.

IN A NUTSHELL

With 1:1 campaigns, your goal isn't to blast out a bunch of ads to a group of anonymous consumers. Instead, the goal is to send targeted, relevant ads to *fewer* people who are more likely to buy your product or service. This is a radical shift in the way marketers have done business in the past.

If you buy into the idea that *how* brands are able to reach consumers has changed dramatically enough to consider a paradigm shift, your next question is likely "*Why* should we change what's worked so well for so many years?" After all, just because you *can* market differently isn't justification alone that you *should* market differently. The next chapter will cover how dramatically consumers have shifted in how they think, buy, and consume media, which is the reason why you should consider a radical shift in how you market your brand, products, and services.

KEY TAKEAWAYS

Here are some things to keep in mind as you reflect on the concepts in this chapter.

- **Traditional versus mass marketing.** Traditional mass marketing prioritizes reach and recall, whereas 1:1 marketing prioritizes reaching just the right people with the right message at the right time.
- **Transitioning to 1:1.** Some experienced marketers may be reluctant to transition from mass marketing to 1:1 marketing. After all, if it ain't broke, why fix it, right? Well, it is broke. And it's being replaced by a technique called 1:1 marketing. ,
- **Metrics and measurement.** Not only is targeting possible at a 1:1 level, but so is campaign measurement, allowing data to drive who to target and prove the value of marketing investments.

YOUR CONSUMERS ARE CHANGING. ARE YOU KEEPING UP WITH THEM?

Our data management platforms now have over one billion
consumer IDs worldwide. We're using that data to accelerate
performance analytics, hiring our own data scientists,
reducing media waste by 20% while increasing media reach 10%
and pivoting to more relevant and effective one-to-one marketing.
—MARK PRITCHARD, CMO, PROCTER & GAMBLE[1]

Ever had one of those dreams where you are in a familiar situation
but suddenly everything works differently than it did before? The rules
seemingly changed, people's responses to your questions aren't how they
typically respond, you find yourself in unfamiliar places, and your head is
spinning as you try to make sense of your situation.

That's kind of how it is today with marketing and advertising to consumers. Things seemed more predictable a few years ago. The formulas,
strategies, and tactics marketers used for decades worked so consistently
that marketing was almost as simple as, well, following a formula. But
today, marketers will tell you that reaching consumers, convincing them

to purchase, and cultivating brand loyalty has evolved into a constantly changing game. At times it feels to many marketers as if we've woken up in a new reality where few things seem familiar and repeatable.

Truth is, advances in technology, evolving social values, and shifting cultural priorities are rewriting the rules of marketing to consumers. The way people consume media, entertain themselves, and keep up-to-date with the world around them has turned upside down in less than a decade. (See Figure 2.1.)

Consumers can now research, prepare for, and even negotiate prices on purchases long before they ever talk to a salesperson. They complete purchases without ever setting foot in a store or talking to a company representative, even for major considered purchases such as a car or a boat. The power ratio between brands and consumers has irreversibly shifted.

What's more, people's fundamental thinking about the world around them and how they decide to spend their money is radically different from just a few years ago. A newly "woke" perspective on biases and ethics informs every purchase decision and influences brand loyalty in ways most brands weren't prepared for.

THREE BIG CONSUMER SHIFTS

Figure 2.1 The rules on how to market and advertise
to consumers have dramatically changed.

NEW CONSUMER REALITY #1: CONSUMERS ARE NOW IN CONTROL OF WHAT, WHEN, AND WHERE THEY DIGEST CONTENT

If you are older than 40, you likely remember how television used to work. Programs were broadcast on a specific day at a set time and typically played only once live and once in rerun. It was up to you to keep track of which night and time your favorite shows appeared, and you scheduled your evening plans around the network's schedule. If you missed the original showing, you waited months to catch that episode in a rerun.

For the most popular shows, people often would host "viewing parties" where friends gathered to watch each week's episode while eating, drinking, and chatting about the characters and plotlines. People even created drinking games around certain idiosyncrasies of a show, ordering everyone to drink a shot when an actor uttered a specific, often-uttered phrase.

Networks were in control and commanded huge premiums for commercials on the most popular shows because those were the shows that could deliver the highest audience reach against a target audience. In fact, the NBC network created what they called a "Must See TV" night with a blockbuster Thursday evening lineup of their most popular shows. NBC literally owned that night of television viewing for years.

Contrast that with how television programming is consumed today. Virtually any show is available "on demand" and can be streamed on a viewer's device of choice, from connected televisions to laptops to tablets or mobile phones. People have access to the internet from pretty much anywhere. People under the age of 25 have no idea what day and time a program is scheduled, since they choose to watch a show whenever they wish and on their terms.

Remember when television networks used a "cliffhanger," where characters were left in peril or doubt as to what the outcome would be to their predicament during the final show of a season? Pop culture followed famous cliffhangers, such as whether villain J. R. Ewing (from the show *Dallas*) died during that season's cliffhanger episode. Networks used this technique to generate buzz among fans that would last for days and guarantee a strong rating when the next season premiered months later.

The concept of a cliffhanger season finale holds little value in today's viewer-driven experience, where viewers demand instant gratification and binge-watch multiple seasons of a show over a few days. They only have to wait a minute to get the answer to the cliffhanger between season one and season two. In fact, with many of the burgeoning entertainment networks created by technology companies, including Netflix, Amazon, and Hulu, an entire season of shows is typically released all at once, allowing consumers to binge-watch all the episodes within a day or two.

Changes in media consumption extend beyond entertainment. Take a look at news programming. A couple of decades ago, people consumed most of their news through analog methods, including network television, radio, and newspapers, which simultaneously distributed news updates to everyone at preset times. People tuned into morning TV news shows and read their newspaper over breakfast as they prepared to leave for work. Then in the evenings, they sat in their living rooms to catch the national news show. That was often followed by their local affiliate station's local news show.

Contrast that with how news is consumed today. People listen to news updates over morning coffee that are read by digitized assistants named Alexa and Google, both of which communicate through a kitchen smart speaker. People receive constant push notifications of breaking news throughout the day on their smartphones. Later that evening, they'll surf their iPad and catch up on the news while simultaneously flipping through TV shows on a streaming television.

Hardcore news junkies tune into one of the 24-hour news networks when they get home, catching up on the entire day's stories compressed into less than 30 minutes. Or they can view one of dozens of livestreamed news shows or news-clip videos shared by friends via social networks, all from the comfort of their bed and streamed on their smartphone, tablet, or Wi-Fi-connected television.

So, what are the common threads of change found in how consumers are entertained, informed, and consume media? First, networks and news organizations are no longer in control of their content and programming. Consumers are. They control when, how, where, and how long they are going to get their updates and be entertained.

Second, most content is consumed via digital devices versus the analog, mass-broadcast media channels of the past. That's why newspapers are struggling, and many of the few remaining newspapers have ceased distributing printed copies in favor of their digital properties. And it's why Netflix spent $17 billion in 2020 to create original content.[2] (Which, by the way, was more than double what CBS spent on content in 2019.[3])

The impact on marketers is nothing short of a game changer, especially when trying to serve ads to their target consumers at scale. Consider this: in 1950, the average household had just three channels to choose from. Forty years later, in 1990, consumers could choose from 27 channels. Today, less than 30 years later, the number of available channels has ballooned to more than 1,000!

Keep in mind that doesn't include the 130-plus video streaming services available to watch shows and content. In fact, 25 percent of television viewing happens through on-demand streaming,[4] which only happens when each individual consumer chooses to view a particular piece of content.

Remember, traditional television media buyers target consumers who are of the demographics likely to buy a brand's product. They place commercials on television shows those same consumers are most likely to watch. In the highly fragmented streaming-television world of today, targeting ads based on the shows people watch is as challenging as finding a needle in a haystack.

What's more, not every streaming session includes commercial breaks, and some commercials are skippable by the viewer. For example, Netflix comprises more than a third of all US video streaming.[5] But Netflix doesn't sell ads. Their business model is based on consumers paying for subscriptions, which means advertisers cannot buy commercial time to reach Netflix viewers.

For marketers, the growth of content streaming upends everything they've traditionally practiced. Not just how they plan campaigns but also in how they measure a campaign's success. After all, gross rating points (the measure applied to broadcast television) can't be easily calculated against streaming audiences of one.

Fortunately, it's not all bad news for marketers. Remember, the evolution of technology and media consumption has resulted in the fully "addressable consumer." Sure, most people are no longer sitting down at eight o'clock every night to catch their favorite show or read the newspaper. But these consumers are reachable across a nearly limitless plethora of addressable devices and can be addressed as easily as sending a direct mail piece to their residence.

> **IN A NUTSHELL**
>
> Consumers can be reached across a wide variety of addressable devices. And hypertargeting them on their TV, mobile, desktop, and other devices can be every bit as specific and nuanced as a direct mail campaign.

With addressability comes an entirely new level of targeting and personalization never before possible in the broadcast era. And addressability changes the game when it comes to measuring campaign success, making possible advanced measurement techniques not possible in the old broadcast world where advertisers had no way to know which households actually viewed their ad.

Media planning, buying, and measurement in an addressable world are night-and-day compared to how media was planned, bought, and measured in a broadcast, nonaddressable world. Yet a surprisingly large percentage of marketers still approach media planning and buying based on the old tenets. Although the old tenets still can work, they are far less effective than newer techniques.

If advertisers stick with the tried and true, they risk missing many consumers who simply don't ever view entertainment on traditional media channels. In a world where 34 percent of US adults are streaming-only consumers[6] (often referred to as "cord cutters"), a third of a brand's target customers become unreachable to a marketer who adheres to traditional broadcast tactics.

The 1:1 marketer embraces the brave, new world with all of its possibilities and takes advantage of the ability to more precisely target ads, personalize messages, and know what's actually driving sales and by how much. 1:1 marketers lean in and rethink many of their assumptions, such as reaching *more* people is better than reaching only the *right* people. Or that everyone should be reached in the same way and at the same time.

And while we've given examples primarily from television advertising, the reality is all media and marketing channels have been impacted by changes in media consumption. Which means not just the large, national advertisers are affected—all marketers are affected. Even smaller advertisers, who rely on local television, radio, and newspaper ads, struggle with the percentage of their target customers that can be reached via these media vehicles.

Later chapters will discuss exactly how to approach your planning and buying to leverage the new, brave, addressable world to reach your brand's audience of one. Applying these techniques and principles will ensure you adapt to the new world order of consumer media consumption and continue to achieve your revenue goals.

NEW CONSUMER REALITY #2: POWER IN THE PURCHASE PROCESS HAS SHIFTED FROM BRANDS TO CONSUMERS

The second new reality for marketers is the 180-degree shift in power between brands and consumers. Forrester Research identified this shift in its pivotal 2015 research titled *Winning in the Age of the Customer*.[7] Forrester noted in its report that technology used to favor companies. Brands could leverage closely held product and price information and controlled how and where consumers could transact with them. That gave brands tremendous control over every aspect of product delivery, pricing, and purchasing, allowing brands to call the shots.

But not anymore. Today, the power has shifted to the consumer, as shown in Figure 2.2. Technology empowers people to research products in-store and online, compare products and vendors, and read hundreds and thousands of opinions from others who've purchased and used the product. Without ever setting foot in a store, people are able to compare prices among dozens of sellers, and ultimately buy on their own terms—when, where, and how they want to. Brands now compete harder than ever for fickle consumers, and nearly every brand faces margin pressure in the age of the customer.

Figure 2.2   Power has shifted from brands to consumers.

For the first time in marketing history, customers are taking control of the consumer-brand relationship. As the demographics of the United States shift, and millennials rise into primary purchasing phases, the demands of consumers will also rise. To win going forward, marketers must seek to better understand consumers, to reach them more efficiently, and to engage them in the ways they want to be engaged.

A 2017 Catalina study found that major brands in consumer packaged goods (CPG) have *not* been the beneficiaries of this shift. Rather, smaller brands are the winners. In fact, 90 of the top 100 CPG brands lost market share over the last decade. And the 25 largest food and beverage companies in the United States drove only 3 percent of total category growth from 2011 to 2015, while companies below the top 100 drove nearly half of the growth.[8]

The only saving grace for the established CPG brands, ironically, may have been the impact of stay-at-home orders resulting from the Covid-19 pandemic. A study from NCSolutions based on shopper data from 51 million US households measured an unprecedented 34 percent growth of CPG sales between March and May, giving CPG brands an opportunity to grow market share.[9] The research revealed that consumer brands with high levels of brand equity and consumer trust, and which consistently advertised through the market disruption, were the major beneficiaries of consumer loyalty and expanded market share. However, in the end, while growing brands grew more, the data shows that declining brands still lost share.

Consider how many choices consumers have today for where to buy products, what products to buy, and how to get them. A by-product of limitless choices is shifting loyalty with consumers asserting more independence in how and why they buy. For example, consider consumers who demand authentic, pure, natural ingredients and shun the traditional consumer packaged brands their parents bought that come with a long list of chemicals no one can pronounce.

We also see it through the complete disruption of categories, such as with the emergence of a new type of brand: "direct to consumer" (DTC) brands. DTC brands bypass traditional distribution and sales methods, and sell and deliver their products directly to consumers.

The poster child for the DTC disruption is one the earliest entries: Dollar Shave Club (DSC). Founded in 2011, this upstart upended its entire category. Gillette's share of the men's razor market in the United States fell from 70 percent in 2010 to just 54 percent in 2016. Which not coincidentally was the year that DSC was bought by Unilever, a leading traditional CPG company, for more than one billion dollars. DSC and the hundreds of DTC brands created in the past decade in virtually every category—from CPG to mattresses to eyewear to financial products—proved that no traditional brand or category is safe from disruption.

The key takeaway for 1:1 marketers: data is the linchpin to survival in the radically shifting of power between brands and consumers. DTC brands leverage their direct customer relationships to amass a treasure trove of valuable first-party data and use this same purchase data to measure advertising performance in their quest to disrupt traditional brands.

IN A NUTSHELL

Data is the linchpin to survival in the radical shifting of power between brands and consumers.

These brands bypass the decades-old, multitiered retail distribution structure that formed a fissure between manufacturers and consumers. Selling direct to consumers gives them the irreplaceable advantage of a 1:1 relationship with customers. They use this advantage to shape everything they do, from brand communications to sales transactions to product development.

But even if a brand sells through a multitiered distribution system, like many traditional consumer goods do, it doesn't mean the brand can't be a 1:1 marketer. They simply need to find ways to bridge the gap. For example, they could collect warranty data, offer enhanced services and benefits that consumers must sign up for, or build media channels using social media, email, or text messaging that consumers opt into to receive discounts and exclusive early access to products. Or a brand could use its own brand power to sell direct to consumers in addition to selling products via retailers, as a number of consumer packaged goods have begun to do.

PepsiCo created Snacks.com, an e-commerce site that offers many of Pepsi's snack brands such as Doritos, Cheetos, and Ruffles shipped direct to consumers for free with a minimum $10 order. It provides consumers with access to flavors and varieties they might not be able to find in their local stores. But more important, it gives Pepsi valuable customer data that enables the company to build a 1:1 marketing relationship with the brand's biggest fans and adapt quickly to evolving interests. "We need to stay very reactive, living in the moment, planning on a much shorter cycle than we've been used to planning,"[10] said Karen Scott, senior innovation director of future brands at PepsiCo.

NEW CONSUMER REALITY #3: BRANDS STRUGGLE TO ADAPT TO THE NEWLY "WOKE CONSUMER"

As if marketing hadn't been challenging enough with the rapid changes in technology and power shift between brands and consumers, there's a third challenge of selling to the new consumer. Consumers make decisions about what brands they will buy from based on rapidly shifting attitudes about social values and cultural priorities, attitudes that were catalyzed by the twin seismic disruptions of the Covid-19 pandemic and Black Lives Matter movement.

The pandemic also forced consumers who otherwise might have been technology luddites to adapt to new ways of transacting with brands, and in many cases advanced so far ahead of sellers that they are now playing catch-up. In fact, according to data by Forrester Research,[11] an astounding 62 percent of US online adults performed some kind of online transaction for the first time as a direct result of the Covid-19 pandemic. From ordering groceries on an app and having them delivered to their home, to visiting a doctor via telemedicine, people who otherwise had not converted from analog to digital behaviors were compelled to do so as a result of the contagion lockdown.

Through extensive research, Forrester identified three specific shifts among empowered consumers that will shape the future of consumption:

1. Consumers Will Buy from—or Avoid—Brands Because of Perceived Company Values

Already, over 60 percent of US and European consumers say they regularly purchase from companies that align with their personal values. From Chick-fil-A to Danone, consumers seek out brands that demonstrate an ongoing commitment to certain values across their brand strategy, manufacturing practices, supplier partnerships, employee experience, and corporate partnerships.

2. Product and Service Experimentation Will Proliferate

Ten years ago, 39 percent of US online adults said that they were always willing to try out new brands and products; today, 53 percent agree. As more brands feed consumers' appetite for experimentation—for example, by pivoting to product trials or sending shipments of new products through subscription boxes—they condition consumers to expect an element of experimentation before and during the purchase experience.

3. Consumers Will Demand Both Traditional and New Buying and Delivery Methods

The recent launch of Walmart+, the subscription service that offers benefits like delivery, discounts, and scan-and-go purchasing in physical stores, is not an isolated event—it signals that consumers are demanding better experiences of every kind. At the same time, as consumers experiment with e-commerce variations that promise new modes of product discovery and acquisition, shoppers still hold fast to the tried-and-true channels that have become engrained in their routines. In Forrester's research, the most empowered consumers said they were likely to buy more from retailers online *and* spend more time in physical stores as distancing restrictions lifted.

• • • • • • • • • •

The good news is that these trends align with the transition to 1:1 marketing. In fact, it's only by leveraging the data-driven, personalized fundamentals of 1:1 marketing that brands will adapt and prosper in a world where many brands reported experiencing two years of digital transformation in just a few months during 2020.

A Tragic Killing by Police That Ignited a Movement

In the midst of the pandemic, a Black man named George Floyd was killed while in Minneapolis police custody, with his death caught on eyewitness video and replayed for months on national television and online. Violent protests erupted in cities across America, and a new movement emerged with consumers declaring Black lives matter and that they would no longer tolerate violence against minorities or anyone. Research from Pew Research Center found that consumer support cut across all ethnic groups, with two-thirds of US adults saying they support the movement, and 38 percent strongly supporting it.[12]

Consumer brands, already reeling from unprecedented business impacts from the pandemic, attempted to address changing consumer sentiment with mixed success.[13] Brands donated money to Black Lives Matter and other organizations supporting equality, took stands against racial inequality, hired senior executives whose sole job was to ensure ethnic diversity and racial parity, and discontinued products used by the government and other organizations to surveil citizens.

Several major CPG brands, including Aunt Jemima, Mrs. Butterworth's, Uncle Ben's, and Cream of Wheat, were renamed or discontinued completely[14] due to racist stereotypes perpetuated by the brands' names and/or mascots/imagery. Major league sports teams, including the Cleveland Indians and Washington Redskins, agreed to change their names under pressure from fans and sponsors.

For 1:1 marketers, understanding customer sensitivities and values is critical to earning trust and building loyalty. It's critical to avoid being tone deaf, making politically insensitive statements, or employing insensitive humor or terminology that could be insulting or demeaning to customers in brand communications. Brands can use 1:1 approaches to understand consumers' cultural and political sentiments, and engage and respond according to their preferences and perspectives.

IN A NUTSHELL

For 1:1 marketers, understanding customer sensitivities and values is critical to earning trust and building loyalty.

The bottom line for the 1:1 marketer: today's consumer is unlike the consumer that the world of mass marketing was built for. Failure to recognize this monumental shift in how consumers consume media, research products, make purchases, view the world, and evaluate brands puts a brand at risk for being perceived as irrelevant or outdated in this brave new world of the empowered consumer.

KEY TAKEAWAYS

Here are some things to keep in mind as you reflect on the concepts in this chapter.

- **Shifting habits.** Television viewing and information access have shifted from traditional, analog channels controlled by media companies to a world where consumers are in control of where, when, and how they are entertained and informed. Traditional mass marketing methods, such as broadcast television buying based on demographics, are less effective in this new consumer reality. Fortunately, consumers are now addressable on a 1:1 basis, and that evolution is powering the transition to 1:1 marketing.

- **Shifting power.** Thanks to technology, the power in purchase transactions shifted from brands to consumers. With access to pricing, reviews, and limitless ways to purchase, consumers now call the shots. Brands are adapting by building and leveraging first-party data—now more readily available than ever—to build and maintain a direct connection to consumers.

- **Shifting values.** World events have resulted in a newly woke consumer with evolving social values and cultural priorities. Failure to recognize this and respond accordingly can land a brand in hot water with its own customers. Brands can use 1:1 marketing approaches to uncover key attitudes and perceptions of customers that will help them to navigate the rapids of consumer sentiment effectively and build loyalty from customers.

PART

2

DIGGING
DEEPER

YOU ARE NOW HERE. (MOVING RIGHT ALONG!)

1:1 OVERVIEW | DIGGING DEEPER | STRATEGIC THINKING | PUTTING IT ALL TO WORK | ADVANCED TECHNIQES

DISSECTING 1:1 CAMPAIGNS VERSUS MASS MARKETING CAMPAIGNS (THE WHO AND THE WHAT)

It's hard to target a message to a generic 35-year-old, middle-class, working mother of two. It's much easier to target a message to Jennifer, who has two children under four, works as a paralegal, and is always looking for quick but healthy dinners and ways to spend more time with her kids and less time on housework.
—ELIZABETH GARDNER, FOUNDER AND PRESIDENT, GARNISH MEDIA

Hopefully, by this point, you understand how advances in technology have made the vision that Peppers and Rogers espoused in *The One to One Future* possible. And you agree that marketers have to adjust their practices based on changes in how people consume content, are entertained, research products, make purchases, and think about the world around them.

If so, then your next logical question is likely, what exactly does a 1:1 marketing campaign look like? And is it really that different from what you're already doing today? After all, if you're reading this book, you've no doubt attended numerous conferences and sat through presentations of "new" concepts and ideas that once you peel back the layers and really understand the underlying principle are little more than age-old ideas repackaged by the speakers as unique and different ideas. At best, the differences between the ideas amount to simple nuances of distinction.

The good news is 1:1 marketing is different. It's not just personalized or segmented marketing repackaged. At its core, 1:1 marketing is about a fundamental change in mindset. Instead of viewing prospects as audiences or masses you market to, the 1:1 marketer views his target audience as a collection of numerous audiences of one. He or she understands that each audience of one views the company's products and services differently, has different motivations, and wants to learn about and purchase the company's products in the way that works for that individual.

As a result of this profoundly different mindset, every aspect of a 1:1 campaign is transformed. From the approach the 1:1 marketer uses to engage her target prospects, how she educates them about the company's products, and ultimately how she convinces prospects to buy.

First, we'll explore the characteristics of a 1:1 campaign from the tried-and-true framework of the five Ws: Who, What, Where, When, and Why. And of course, the sixth question: How. Then we'll compare and contrast a traditional mass marketing campaign to a 1:1 marketing campaign for the same product. Our goal is to make it crystal clear how 1:1 marketing is fundamentally different from traditional approaches. And more than likely, how it's different from how your company is currently marketing its products and services.

FUNDAMENTAL CHARACTERISTICS THAT MAKE A 1:1 CAMPAIGN DISTINCT FROM TRADITIONAL MASS MARKETING CAMPAIGNS

There are two huge differences in 1:1 marketing versus traditional marketing, namely, who is being targeted and, as consequence, how the marketing message is researched, crafted, delivered, and analyzed.

Who You Are Targeting

You're probably wondering how on earth a shift to 1:1 marketing could change *who* you are targeting: After all, the people who buy your products are the same, regardless of how you market to them. And you would be correct. In the end, the buyer remains the same. But how you target messages and reach your target audience with your message is vastly different. Especially when it comes to the data you'll use for targeting.

The term *mass marketing* might suggest that mass-market ads aren't targeted, but simply delivered to the masses. In truth, some form of targeting has been applied for decades. But ad targeting in traditional advertising mediums, such as broadcast and print, lacks the granularity and precision that's possible with 1:1 marketing.

As discussed in Chapter 1, it's because mass mediums lack the ability to know precisely who is seeing an ad. Therefore, television campaigns typically are limited in targeting to simple demographics. And how exactly is the ad targeted to a specific demographic group? That's accomplished by buying ads on television shows most watched by people in that demographic, as determined by Nielsen surveys.

The fact that Nielsen panel data made it possible to target television ads to specific demographics was, at one point, revolutionary. Once proven and adopted, demographic targeting became the de facto standard practice for ad buying and measurement, despite its limitations. After all, some level of targeting is better than no targeting at all, don't you agree?

But now marketers can know exactly who is exposed to their ads. And they can use platforms to target people on a 1:1 basis rather than doing mass marketing campaigns segmented simply by demographics such as gender, age, and income. As discussed earlier, demographics alone aren't necessarily the pivotal factors that differentiate buyers.

What's more, the way ads are actually targeted in television—buying commercials on shows viewed by people in target demographics—is fundamentally flawed, since only a portion of the viewers match the target demographics. The result: some impressions are inevitably wasted by reaching the wrong people. Meanwhile, people who are likely to buy your product are missed altogether and never see your ad. In traditional television advertising, you take what you know about customers (their demographics) and then match it to the programs that those people watch. It's a two-step process, and with each step, a certain amount of accuracy is lost.

Conversely, the ability to target people based on data and then to actually track whether or not those people see the ad is known as addressable advertising. Technology makes it possible to target ads to actual people.

> **IN A NUTSHELL**
>
> Addressable advertising helps you reach the individuals you want to reach, regardless of what network and television program they are watching. This creates new possibilities for advertising precision and effectiveness—possibilities that the 1:1 marketer enthusiastically adopts.

For example, 1:1 marketers often use one or more of these characteristics to help them decide who to direct their campaigns toward:

How Do People Think About Purchases in Your Category?

For example, people think about buying a home in a vastly different way than they think about buying a car. Both represent large, considered, infrequent purchases. However, a person buying a car might prioritize safety and convenience. But when the same person is buying a house, she might prioritize finishes and style.

Understanding how prospects think—in other words, understanding their needs and desires—provides far more insight into their likelihood to purchase than basic demographics. Jerry Brown, the former managing director at BBDO South, calls this "thinking backward," which means you're getting inside the mind of your prospects and customers and then working backward from there. That way, the fact that your car buyer and your home buyer might have the same demographic makeup makes no difference at all because you're basing your campaign on a more nuanced profile of your prospects and customers.

Which Products Have They Historically Purchased in Your Category?

Anyone who has watched TV psychologist Dr. Phil McGraw's show *Dr. Phil* is familiar with one of his favorite phrases: "The best predictor of future behavior is past behavior." He's typically referring to a person with a history of dishonesty and cheating on his spouse: the fact that he cheated before means he's likely to cheat again in the future. You can apply this same philosophy to predict if a consumer is likely or unlikely to purchase your product. For example, a consumer who historically purchases premium toilet tissue isn't likely to purchase a low-cost store brand, regardless of the advertising they are exposed to.

Where Do Prospects Go During Their Day?

Thanks to mobile phones being attached to the majority of Americans' hand or ear, 1:1 marketers can tap into the location signals emanating from their mobile devices to gain insight into whether they might be a good prospect for a specific product. For example, people who attend concerts and other live spectator events are more likely to have an interest in music or experiential purchases. (If targeting based on where people go sounds creepy, don't worry. 1:1 marketers can't actually identify and target you based on your device's location history. Rather, they employ ad platforms that identify groups of anonymous individuals with similar location patterns and target them with ads. How to be a 1:1 marketer and not be creepy is discussed in Chapter 12.)

These are just a few examples of precise insights into prospects that can be used to transition from less precise, mass marketing to 1:1 marketing. Additional data you should consider is covered in Chapter 15. The takeaway: chances are your current marketing practices are based on less granular, more general data, which is different than the data you'll use when you make the shift from mass marketing to 1:1 marketing.

IN A NUTSHELL

The 1:1 marketer's mindset is to zero in on the meaningful factors that drive likelihood to purchase, with the goal of wasting few dollars targeting people who aren't likely to ever buy their product.

. . . .

1:1 MARKETING IN ACTION

Midas is one of the world's largest providers of automotive services, offering brake, tires, exhaust, and other services at more than 1,300 US locations. The brand turned to its ad agency for a campaign designed to convince previous customers to come back and have their cars serviced at Midas. The brand also wanted to target its competitor's customers and get those prospects to switch from the competitor to Midas. The agency tapped 4INFO, a cross-channel advertising company (since acquired by Cadent, an advanced TV platform company) to send ads to these prospects while they were using mobile apps or browsing the web on their smartphones.

While Midas likely has data on its customers, it didn't have a way of identifying its competitors' customers. So 4INFO worked with Nielsen Buyer Insights (NBI) and tapped into the data on 12 billion transactions from 125 million different cardholders (approximately 80 percent of all credit and debit transactions). They looked at all the people who had used their cards for automotive service in the past year and created two subcategories. The first subcategory consisted of Midas's previous customers, and the second subcategory consisted of its competitors' customers.

4INFO used a privacy-safe method to connect the dots between smartphones and the households that used those smartphones. Those individuals were then served ads from Midas. After the campaign, NBI examined purchases from the households that saw the Midas ads and compared their purchases to a group of identical households that didn't see the ads during the campaign.

By specifically targeting ads to households based on past purchase data, Midas saw an increase in total spend per buyer of 11 percent; saw an increase in its share of market from these households by more than 8 percent; and generated $562,668 in incremental sales dollars from that single campaign. After accounting for the cost of the campaign, NBI determined that the campaign produced a respectable $10.42 return on ad spend (ROAS). In other words, for every dollar spent on the targeted media, the 1:1 advertising campaign generated more than $10 in incremental sales lift![1]

· ·

What Approach You Use to Build Your Messaging

In traditional mass marketing, the marketer's mindset is focused on achieving marketing efficiency. Efficiency is achieved by reaching the largest target audience possible with a memorable message.

Take a typical ad running on network television programming, such as the game-changing commercials that debut during a broadcast of the Super Bowl. What is the goal of marketers who shell out millions of dollars to debut a television commercial during the Super Bowl? They want to achieve maximum impact by showing an ad that will reach the most prospects possible—something they can accomplish by buying ads during the Super Bowl.

Success often depends more on the shock and awe attained than whether or not the spot delivered the right message for the audience. Typical mass marketing centers around interrupting people to get their attention. Campaigns are measured by a combination of audience *reach* (how many people saw the commercial) and *recall* (how many people remember the ad after they've seen it).

But marketers who practice 1:1 marketing turn that paradigm upside down. First, it's more important in 1:1 marketing to reach the *right* people than the *most* people. Which is why 1:1 marketers employ far more precise targeting than mass marketers. They only want to show ads to the people most likely to buy—which in the end often results in reaching smaller audiences than can be reached with mass marketing. But that's a good thing!

Second, the goal of 1:1 marketers is to engage with prospects and customers, delivering a message that is meaningful based on the consumer's needs and interests at that moment, instead of interrupting them to garner attention. Which means instead of deploying a single ad blasted to an audience of millions, 1:1 marketers prefer to deploy millions of ads unique to each *audience of one* receiving it to ensure the message is relevant.

Ad delivery technology makes this possible today. Marketers can start with relatively simple approaches, such as swapping out one or more elements of an ad to personalize the message to the recipient. This is often referred to as A/B split tests, where two different versions of headlines, visuals, and/or offers are tested with each alternate ad display. By analyzing clicks or some other type of conversion, marketers can gradually arrive at the best-converting version of each.

Over time, 1:1 marketers employ more advanced techniques where hundreds of ads are created and continuously improved and perfected over time. To determine how to improve and perfect ads, they measure based on actual purchases made by the people receiving hundreds of unique ads built dynamically from combinations of elements. Elements are removed from the ads that resulted in lower sales and replaced by elements from ads that produced higher sales.

IN A NUTSHELL

Instead of deploying a single ad blasted to an audience of millions, 1:1 marketers prefer to deploy millions of ads unique to each *audience of one* to ensure the message is relevant.

The latter approach uses a concept called dynamic creative optimization (DCO), in which the advertiser creates a number of different possibilities for each element of the ad. For example, you might create half a dozen different headlines, a dozen hero images, and five offers. The ad delivery platform assembles each ad on the fly, inserting the numerous possible combination of elements to painstakingly create thousands of ads, or experiments in industry parlance, in seconds.

It's a lot like a Mexican restaurant. If you think about all of the different dishes you could order in a typical Mexican restaurant, each consists of just a handful of common ingredients: shell (a tortilla or taco shell), protein (beef, pork, or chicken), cheese, beans (black, pinto, or refried), salsa, sour cream, and guacamole. Whether you order a burrito, taco, enchilada, or tamale, the cook simply assembles a specific combination of ingredients to create the tasty dish you requested. While the ingredients vary little, the specific combination creates distinctly different dishes.

A platform employing DCO does the same thing, but in a fraction of a second. And unlike a Mexican menu where certain combinations are curated to create a specific flavor and texture, the combinations produced in DCO are initially randomized to create the maximum possible ads to show each prospect. The ads are tested across millions of people to determine the most effective combination.

To determine the most effective ads, sales data is analyzed continuously to find which experiments yield the highest sales conversions at the lowest cost. Less efficient combinations are gradually dropped from the campaign to achieve the optimal versioning of ad for each target segment.

As noted in Chapter 1, you won't likely start your 1:1 marketing journey deploying complex DCO ad creation. Instead, most marketers start out with simple A/B testing, and over time, as your organization builds its capabilities and your team gains the skills needed, they will naturally want to push the envelope on what's possible.

As marketers start to see the data rolling in and the resulting gains each step yields as they move closer to advanced 1:1 marketing practices, most will naturally be motivated to continually improve and optimize their approach to maximize value for their organization. And as they do, they will find a plethora of tools and technology solutions available to automate complex processes and make it possible for even smaller marketing organizations to accomplish.

And while we've discussed message delivery in terms of ads, 1:1 marketing goes far beyond ads to influence every communication across every channel throughout the customer's purchase journey. Ads by their very nature are one-directional. The most accomplished 1:1 marketers strive for achieving 1:1 engagement, by creating two-way dialogues with customers. Remember, today's audience of one is less interested in being marketed to than in interacting and engaging with brands they find relevant and important to their life. Engagement builds stronger bonds with customers, and over time can help brands learn from their customers to make their products better, service delivery more effective, and the customer experience more delightful.

. . . .

1:1 MARKETING IN ACTION

Metadata.io is an account-based advertising platform that helps business-to-business (B2B) marketers create a predictable pipeline of inbound leads. At the core of the Metadata platform lies patented technology that performs DCO, executing thousands of B2B campaigns in a matter of hours, automatically optimizing campaigns for pipeline impact at a velocity not humanly possible.

But Metadata also conducts its own marketing to build a customer base. The company employs its own technology to create a high-performing ad campaign that drives a predictable pipeline of inbound leads.

By loading multiple headlines, images, and copy into the Metadata platform, hundreds of ads were created on the fly and tested. Two ads emerged through the process (see Figure 3.1).

Which ad do you think performed better? A common evaluation marketers use to measure digital ad performance is which ad produces the most clicks at the lowest cost. The goal is to achieve the lowest cost per click (CPC). In the previous test, the ad on the left produced a CPC of $15.32, while the ad on the right produced a CPC of $25.69, a nearly 70 percent higher CPC (see Figure 3.2). Clearly, the ad on the left was the winner, at least based on CPC.

Figure 3.1   Two ads created dynamically by the Metadata platform.

Impressions	33,231	20,546
Clicks	164	142
CPC	$15.32	$25.69

Figure 3.2   The ad on the left produced a cost-per-click
of 70 percent less than the ad on the right.

But an even better metric to measure is the cost per lead (CPL),
which takes into account what happens after the click. In this campaign,
the ad on the left resulted in 46 leads, while the one on the left only
produced 29 leads (see Figure 3.3). Once again, the ad on the left
outperformed the one on the right by 63 percent! And when Metadata
factored in the cost of the clicks to get the lead, the ad on the left
resulted in a CPL of $54.63, less than half the $126.80 CPL the ad on the
right racked up.

Leads	46	29
CPL	$54.63	$125.80

Figure 3.3   The ad on the left resulted in
a cost-per-lead half of the ad on the right.

But this is where the differences between mass marketing and 1:1
marketing shine through. The metrics of CPC and CPL are more akin
to mass marketing, since the marketer is simply evaluating a mass of

anonymous clicks and leads without regard for who they come from and whether those people are ideal customers.

Remember, the Metadata platform, like most DCO platforms, evaluates performance based on the actual revenue produced from each ad. This requires the marketer to go beyond anonymous clicks and leads, matching each lead one-to-one to a person who either purchases or doesn't.

What did Metadata learn when it matched people to purchases for true 1:1 attribution? The ad on the left ultimately converted to a pipeline of $440,000, of which $97,000 in revenue resulted from the prospects who purchased. The ad on the right? It produced $700,000 in pipeline, and $187,000 in revenue resulted—or double the revenue!

Wait a minute, you might argue: the CPC and CPL were significantly higher with the ad on the right. Fortunately, since Metadata was able to tie sales 1:1 to each ad, it determined after dividing the revenue by the costs for each ad that in the end, the return on investment (ROI) from the ad on the right was 51 times versus 39 times for the ad on the left (see Figure 3.4)! Guess which ad Metadata continued running after the test?[2]

Pipeline	$440,000	$700,000
ClosedWon	$97,000	$187,000
ROI	39x	51x

Figure 3.4   The ad on the right resulted in a return on investment (ROI) 30 percent higher than that of the ad on the left.

Most companies only launch with a single campaign variation, assuming they got it right. The reality is you almost never hit the efficient frontier with a single experience. DCO and tools like Metadata allow marketers to find the point of diminishing returns on experimentation without deep resource commitment.

—JASON WIDUP, VP OF MARKETING, METADATA.IO

That's how 1:1 marketing campaigns compare to traditional mass marketing campaigns from the standpoint of Who you are targeting and What you are communicating when reaching them. Next up: the Where, When, Why, and How of 1:1 campaigns.

KEY TAKEAWAYS

Here are some things to keep in mind as you reflect on the concepts in this chapter.

- **Hypertargeting.** Traditional mass marketing campaigns are limited in their targeting precision because traditional broadcast media don't know who actually is reached by a campaign. But now that virtually all media provide addressable options (where individual consumers are reached on a 1:1 basis), campaigns can now be hypertargeted using data that is closely linked to a consumer's likelihood of purchasing a specific product or brand. Data such as past purchase data, attitudinal data, historical location data, and more can be used.

- **Creative opportunities.** The creative and message options in traditional mass marketing campaigns are also naturally limited. But when individual consumers are reached based on data tied to them, ads and other messages can be personalized using the same data used for targeting of ads. And in nonbroadcast methods, ads can be built dynamically. Various elements, such as the headline or visual, can vary by recipient. This presents game-changing opportunities for marketers to transition from blasting the same messages to the most consumers to delivering unique messages to each audience of one.

DISSECTING 1:1 CAMPAIGNS VERSUS MASS MARKETING CAMPAIGNS (THE WHERE AND WHEN)

The world is now awash in data and
we can see consumers in a lot clearer ways.
—MAX LEVCHIN, COFOUNDER, PAYPAL

Now that the Who and What of 1:1 marketing campaigns versus mass marketing campaigns have been covered, it's time to tackle the Where and When.

WHERE YOU REACH AND ENGAGE WITH PROSPECTS AND CUSTOMERS

Given mass marketers' goal of achieving maximum reach with their campaigns, they tend to favor media channels that deliver the greatest audience scale. These include broadcast media, such as television and radio, and print advertising. With TV, they favor advertising on blockbuster events and top-rated shows to get the maximum reach. With print advertising, they seek the magazines with the largest circulation, like *Better Homes and Gardens* and *People* magazine.

Given the consumer shift to digital media, mass marketers have also shifted significant media dollars to digital publications. Following the paradigm of more is better, they concentrate their ad spend on the largest aggregators of audiences in digital, including Facebook and Google.

Conversely, 1:1 marketers operate on the paradigm that reaching the right audience is better than reaching the largest audience. They would rather reach just the right people with the right message at the right time. Remember, *their intent isn't to interrupt but to engage.*

Which is why 1:1 marketers favor addressable channels that enable them to target the right individuals. In the early days, that would've meant direct mail. Fortunately, most communication channels have advanced to enable 1:1 engagement with prospects and customers—including the traditional channels chosen by mass marketers for their large reach.

IN A NUTSHELL

The 1:1 marketer wants to reach just the right people with the right message at the right time.

Most 1:1 marketers are likely to invest heavily in digital advertising, the second medium that lets them address ads to individuals. They run paid social media ads on Facebook. They'll also advertise on Instagram and YouTube to target consumers and LinkedIn and Twitter to target businesses. They can also reach and engage consumers 1:1 using online display ads on ad platforms, such as The Trade Desk, that place ads on thousands of different sites and mobile apps. All of these media offer some form of 1:1 ad targeting based on data about the viewer, such as topics liked, purchases made, previous ads clicked on, or any data that can be tied to personally identifiable information about the viewer.

And with the advent of streaming television, the most advanced 1:1 marketers are targeting prospects using television ads seen only by the households that match the specific targeting criteria they use, such as people who have a history of purchasing single-serve coffee pods. Unlike traditional broadcast advertising, where ads are targeted by running on shows popular with specific demographics, addressable television ads are delivered only to the households matching the data used for targeting, irrespective of the particular show the household is viewing at the time the ad is run.

Conversely, in both digital and streaming television advertising, it doesn't matter what content is being viewed at the time the ads run, as long as they appear on high-quality, advertiser-approved websites and apps. After all, why should Starbucks care if their single-serve coffee ads are viewed while a consumer is watching a comedy or a drama television show? Or while the person is playing a game, checking sports scores, catching up on news, or watching TikTok videos on a mobile phone? They only care that people who see the ads have a history of buying that product and thus are likely to purchase their brand.

· ·

1:1 MARKETING IN ACTION

A stock brokerage was able to use 1:1 data to create a segment of its customers who (1) had a small amount of money invested through that brokerage, but who (2) had large assets not currently invested with that brokerage. In other words, they wanted to target their own customers who were wealthy, but who invested only a small amount of their wealth with their brokerage. Their goal was to get those customers to increase the assets under management. The brokerage also wanted to target noncustomers who have substantial assets, in hopes of getting them to place some of those assets in the brokerage.

Their agency turned to 4INFO,[1] an identity company that can reach people on their connected devices by targeting based on home addresses (since acquired by Cadent, an advanced TV platform company). 4INFO partnered with IXI/Equifax, a data company specializing in financial assets, to build target groups. They created a total of six segments for each of the two target audiences (customers and prospects), using a combination of wealth estimates, investment propensity, household income, and spending using aggregate credit and debit card transaction data.

4INFO ran ads across their own network of mobile apps and simultaneously worked with several of the largest cable television operators to target the same households with TV commercials via addressable television cable boxes. Remember, the campaign was using the home addresses of customers and prospects for targeting. So instead of buying commercials on shows watched by the people being targeted (the tactic typically used with mass marketing television campaigns), these ads were targeted to specific set top boxes in target households regardless of the shows the consumer was watching. And instead of running ads on specific apps or publishers the target audience typically uses, the ads were targeted to specific mobile phones, regardless of what app the consumer was using at the time the ad was served.

After the campaign, IXI/Equifax could measure the impact of the campaign using the brokerage's customer data, assets invested through the brokerage, and impression data supplied by 4INFO and the addressable TV operators. Existing customers exposed to the ads on both their smartphones and televisions increased their assets under management by a whopping 462 percent! Meanwhile, the opening of new customer accounts increased by nearly 200 percent. In fact, for every dollar the brokerage invested in media for this campaign, the brokerage gained eight dollars in increased assets under management.[2]

WHEN YOUR MESSAGE IS DELIVERED

Timing is everything, as they say. And that's also true in advertising. But how mass marketers view the timing of ads compared to 1:1 marketers is dramatically different. Because mass marketers favor scale with maximum reach, ads run at the same time for all viewers. On television, for example, they buy based on reaching people who watch a particular show, so the ad runs at that day and time the program is shown. After all, a brand that advertises during the Super Bowl has only a five-hour window on one day of the year in which to place its ad.

Therefore, mass marketers tend to approach timing of messages based on windows of time, such as seasons. Holiday ads run in December, back-to-school ads in August and September, and Memorial Day ads, well, just before Memorial Day.

Not true for 1:1 marketers, who happily trade large reach for more precise, lower-scale targeting of individuals. And instead of producing outrageous ads to interrupt consumers, 1:1 marketers favor engaging with consumers with the right message that will resonate with that particular person at the time they view the ad. And with a message that ideally causes them to take action (such as making a purchase) as a result of timing the ad perfectly.

To be as relevant as possible, 1:1 marketers often time messages based on where the consumer is at the time the ad is delivered. By leveraging addressable media, it's possible to deliver even the same ad to different people at different times for the ad to be delivered at the optimum time for each person.

For example, a quick-service restaurant brand can deliver promotional offers via text message to customers who've opted in to receive weekly text messages. If messages are sent in a single batch, a customer in New York would receive the lunch promotion text message around 11 a.m. (just before lunch), but a customer in California would receive the message at 8 a.m. By the time that consumer is deciding where to eat lunch, the 8 a.m. lunch-promo text has long been forgotten.

IN A NUTSHELL

The 1:1 marketer knows that careful timing makes messages more relevant. And increasing impact by communicating immediately relevant messages increases the likelihood consumers will take action on the message, such as making a purchase for the product advertised.

So instead of sending promotional texts at the same time to everyone, 1:1 marketers stagger the batches based on time zone. That enables them to deliver the message within an hour of the consumer eating lunch, regardless of where in the country they live. Ideal timing improves conversion rates, making the campaigns far more effective.

"In a world where consumers are willing to engage with brands on their most personal device, it just makes sense to use data to better target messages instead of blasting the same offer or promotion to everyone," noted Dennis Becker, CEO of Mobivity, a company that helps brick-and-mortar brands, including Subway, Sonic Drive-In, and Checkers/Rally's, connect digitally with their customers using text messaging tied to digital offers and promotions. Becker went on to say, "By segmenting consumers using the information you already know about your customers—when they last purchased, what menu items they purchase frequently, what daypart they most often visit during—messages really hit home. Not only will engaging with consumers 1:1 make the message the consumer receives a whole lot more useful and relevant, we've proven that it drives meaningful return on a brand's marketing spend, making it a win-win for both brands and their customers."[3]

Timing of messages can also vary based on the actions taken by a target prospect in 1:1 marketing. Suppose you work in marketing for an e-commerce clothing company that sends emails with the same promotional offer to three different customers. A marketer practicing 1:1 marketing might vary the follow-up email based on the action or inaction the customer took with the initial promo email. For example:

- Customer A opens the email but doesn't click on the link to visit the retailer's site. The marketer might send an email designed to create a sense of urgency and get the customer to visit the website, perhaps by warning that the sale ends at midnight.
- Customer B opens the email and clicks on the link, browsing several items on the retailer's website and adding one to the shopping cart. But the customer doesn't complete the purchase. The marketer might send that customer an email with a bonus incen-

tive, such as an extra 5 percent off, to return and purchase the item left in the cart.

- Customer C doesn't even open the email. The marketer might simply resend the first email, hoping this time the customer chooses to open and clicks to shop.

By varying the follow-up email based on the level of engagement with the first email, the brand can maximize impact by making the message more relevant to each customer.

· ·

1:1 MARKETING IN ACTION

A major quick service restaurant (QSR) sought to reach mobile audiences at the most relevant times and locations to increase interest and consideration in the brand's various fresh meal options, including its selection of hot soups, sandwiches, and salads. The goal of the campaign was to increase foot traffic to the QSR's physical locations during the heavy lunch rush hours in areas that were experiencing lower sales due to aggressive competition.

The QSR brand turned to Groundtruth, a location targeting company, whose SmartFence™ technology combines consumer location, time of day, and location-specific weather triggers to target ads on consumers' mobile devices. The QSR ran a campaign with ads based on the theme "It's a soup kind of day" to their target audience just before the heavy lunch rush.

The campaign used geo-fenced ads that were served within a one-mile radius around the brand's location as well as top competitive locations and large business parks in the area. One hour prior to the lunch rush, consumers were served ads with meal options generated based on local weather conditions. When temperatures dropped below 60 degrees, ad creative promoted the restaurant's hot selection of fresh soups. But when temperatures were above 60 degrees, consumers were shown ads focused around the brand's cafe salads and sandwiches. Soups-focused ads were also served when and where weather events such as snow or rain appeared. The different ads are shown in Figure 4.1

The campaign exceeded the client's benchmarks by 124 percent, generating an above-average click-through rate (CTR) and measurable sales lift from the target audience, as a result of delivering the right message given the time of day, weather, and proximity of the consumer to the QSR.[4]

Figure 4.1 Different ads were deployed depending on outside temperature.

This chapter covered a lot of important information relating to the Where and When aspects of a successful 1:1 marketing campaign. The next chapter dives deeper into the Why and How.

Let's keep going, shall we?

KEY TAKEAWAYS

Here are some things to keep in mind as you reflect on the concepts in this chapter.

- **Using data to target.** Traditional mass marketing focuses on reaching people based on broad measures, such as demographics, and by buying television shows people in the target market are more likely to watch. But 1:1 marketing focuses on reaching the right consumers, based on who they are and what's known about them, using data such as customer data or past purchase data. Therefore, while 1:1 marketers want their ads to run on high-quality content, in the end, they don't focus on *where* the ad runs as much as *who* the ad is shown to. It really doesn't matter what show, website, or app the person is on at the time ads are served; it only matters that the message is seen by the person they want to reach.

- **Timing is everything.** Timing of mass marketing campaigns is usually governed by general timeframes, such as dayparts or seasons. But 1:1 marketers know that where a person is and at what time the message is delivered can have a big impact on the effectiveness of the message. Therefore, they use the more precise methods of 1:1 marketing to carefully deliver specific ads to certain people at a precise time with the message most likely to resonate, such as an ad for warm soup just before lunchtime when the weather outside is cold.

DISSECTING 1:1 CAMPAIGNS VERSUS MASS MARKETING CAMPAIGNS (THE WHY AND HOW)

Every trackable interaction creates a data-point,
and every data-point tells a piece of the customer's story.
—PAUL ROETZER (FOUNDER AND CEO OF PR 20/20)[1]

Now that the Who, What, Where, and When of 1:1 marketing campaigns versus mass marketing campaigns have been covered, it's time to tackle the Why and How.

WHY YOU ARE MESSAGING A PROSPECT

Because mass marketers maximize reach and impact, their efforts must be big and wide. A single campaign is expected to drive new customers, as well as remind existing customers to return and buy again.

But thanks to the precision of 1:1 marketing, brands can launch many campaigns with different purposes and target audiences. A 1:1 marketer is more likely to have very different campaigns targeting prospects who've never bought versus campaigns targeting existing and past customers.

One reason for the difference in mindset, beyond the precision of marketing approaches, is how campaigns of mass marketers tend to be measured compared to campaigns by 1:1 marketers. Mass marketing efforts often are judged on short-term impact: how did same store sales last week compare to the same week last year?

Conversely, 1:1 marketers tend to think longer term. The most advanced 1:1 marketers seek to measure and impact *customer lifetime value*, the cumulative value customers bring the enterprise when viewed in the entirety of their lifetime as a customer. Some customers may buy just once, while others may become regular customers and buy for years. Those two customers represent radically different value to the brand and ideally should be treated and marketed to differently.

In fact, 1:1 marketers understand there are five essential tactics a brand can employ to increase their customers' lifetime value:

1. Get customers to purchase more frequently
2. Get customers to spend more when they do purchase
3. Get customers to remain a customer for a longer period of time
4. Get a customer to refer friends
5. Get a customer who has lapsed to come back again

Each of these objectives require different tactics and involve different target audiences. This is why collecting and leveraging customer data becomes a secret weapon for 1:1 marketers. The more data a company can amass about its customers, including every purchase they make over their lifetime, increases the effectiveness of its 1:1 marketing. After all, a brand that doesn't know when its customers purchase won't know when they don't. This means customers can lapse and the brand won't even know it happened.

> ### IN A NUTSHELL
>
> Campaign goals often are a distinguishing factor between 1:1 marketing campaigns and mass marketing campaigns. Whereas mass marketing campaigns tend to be focused on driving short-term results, such as sales during a promotion, 1:1 marketers typically view their customers as having greater value over a longer period of time. Thus, campaign goals often revolve around increasing the lifetime value of customers, such as specific campaigns designed to increase purchase frequency or obtain referrals.

The value of customer data (or *first-party data* in industry parlance) is discussed later in the book when you dive deeper into the data you'll need to be an effective 1:1 marketer. The key takeaway is that 1:1 marketers adjust their marketing approach based on why they are marketing to a person and what they want to achieve.

Mass marketers tend to place emphasis on acquiring new customers. In part, that's because many mass marketers don't actually know who their customers are. For example, manufacturers who sell products through distributors, who in turn sell products through mass market retailers, are two steps removed from their customers. They often lack a way to obtain first-party data from or link purchases to their customers. Which means they have no way to distinguish who is a new purchaser, a repeat purchaser, or a lapsed purchaser.

While 1:1 marketers certainly value acquiring customers, they also understand that it costs five time as much to acquire a new customer as it does to keep and make a current customer more valuable over time.[2] This means investments made to engage 1:1 with customers return far more profit than investments made to acquire new customers.

. . . .

1:1 MARKETING IN ACTION

Every year, over 75 million passengers travel through Heathrow on their way to and from 185 cities. The airport—Europe's busiest—also runs Heathrow Express trains to London and features over 100 retail and restaurant brands across its terminals. Working to make "every journey better," the airport prioritizes a customer-centric initiative that goes well beyond actual flights to include travel to and from the airport, foot traffic inside terminals, the airport's facilities such as free Wi-Fi, and the online experience.

Over the last decade, Heathrow built a marketing database with data on more than 25 million consumers. With a continued aim to improve customer satisfaction, Rewards membership, and revenue growth for Heathrow and its retailers, Heathrow needed to implement a digital transformation strategy that put both data and technology at the center of its business to build deeper relationships with its existing passengers, as well as grow its base through new passenger engagements.

Heathrow, who has partnered with Acxiom for more than a decade to host and manage its marketing database, asked Acxiom to help it gain greater intelligence from its data so it could trigger personalized messages at the ideal time to travelers coming through its terminals. Acxiom is a leader in customer data management, identity, and the ethical use of data; it helps thousands of clients and partners around the globe work together to create millions of better customer experiences. Acxiom enhanced Heathrow's passenger database with second- and third-party data to better understand those passengers. The airport's goal was to grow the value of each customer, acquire new Rewards members, and provide valuable information to each passenger to ensure a smooth journey through the airport and back.

Heathrow provided travelers with tools and personalized prompts to help them plan ahead for things such as parking, terminal navigation, dining, and shopping. A family planning a holiday might receive several touches tailored to their specific journey, for example:

- Reminders to complete a parking reservation or join the Rewards program
- Special offers for shops and restaurants in the departing terminal
- License plate recognition in the car parks, automatically prompting the barrier to open, simultaneously triggering a communication to welcome a passenger to the airport

With each interaction and transaction, the airport gathers more data about customers, enabling ever more personalized communications.

Acxiom is also able to measure the impact from Heathrow's programs. By implementing finely tuned 1:1 marketing informed by data, Heathrow saw significant gains year on year from CRM-related activity, including:

- 22 percent increase in Rewards retail spending
- 19 percent growth in total membership
- 20 percent growth in active membership
- 23 percent increase in spending per visit
- 34 percent increase in reactivated members

"1:1 marketers, like Heathrow Airport, are data-driven customer problem solvers," noted Chad Engelgau, CEO of Acxiom.[3]

HOW YOU MEASURE CAMPAIGN SUCCESS

The final characteristic that differentiates mass marketing from 1:1 marketing is how campaigns are measured. Mass marketing's focus is on reach and recall, which means those are the things that get measured.

As mentioned in Chapter 1, mass marketing television campaigns are planned and measured based on rating points, which represent the percentage of a target or total target audience the campaign reaches while it's running. In other words, how many people saw the ads.

Mass marketers sometimes also use a longer-term form of measurement: awareness, which is based on surveys of consumers in the target audience to measure whether they recall the ads and the advertiser. More memorable ads are likely to increase consumer awareness and recall, which the marketer hopes in turn translates into a lift in sales for the brand.

But that's not always the case. Let's face it, no CEO or CFO is measured on how well the company's ads are recalled. This is especially true if the brand's sales don't grow or worse, go down. In the end, boards and investors measure brands on the revenue and profit they produce. Period.

Which is why 1:1 marketers prefer to measure campaigns the same way. Therefore, 1:1 campaigns and efforts are judged primarily on the revenue they produce and how much it costs to produce that revenue. It's possible to measure these factors because 1:1 marketing techniques and technology enable brands to know who actually sees or engages with ads and other marketing efforts. The same technology and data also can be employed to measure whether consumers exposed to the marketing ultimately make a purchase.

IN A NUTSHELL

Measuring success for 1:1 marketers is more likely to relate to metrics the CEO values, such as sales, versus typical metrics used by mass marketers, such as message reach and frequency. Long-term views, such as customer lifetime value, also guide 1:1 marketers, whereas mass marketers are more likely to focus on short-term results, such as sales lift.

Mapping those two datapoints together enables marketers to determine if people who were exposed to ads ultimately purchased more than an identical group of people who weren't exposed to the ads—which then allows them to calculate precise returns on their marketing investment, often expressed as return on ad spend (ROAS). Crosswalk IDs are typically employed to match these datapoints and maintain data privacy.

. . . .

WHAT ARE CROSSWALK IDS?

When an advertiser decides to run a campaign targeting customers on a publisher's platform, it typically works with a data or identity company that manages the customer's data for campaigns. The data company matches the customer data to its own identity graph, which contains a file of people and unique IDs for each one.

When it's time to run a campaign, the data company and selected publishers or demand side platform (DSP) establish a unique set of anonymous Crosswalk IDs that will be exchanged between them. In essence, a Crosswalk ID provides a privacy-safe framework for matching customer data to subscriber data for targeting and impression data for measurement, without revealing the identity of the customer.

They perform a onetime match of publisher data to the data or identity company's identity graph, creating a table that contains each party's unique ID mapped to an anonymous Crosswalk ID. Then when campaigns begin and end, the only ID passing between the two parties is this anonymous Crosswalk ID. Crosswalk IDs are meaningless to anyone besides the data company and publisher, who hold the secret mapping table on their own servers behind firewalls.

When a campaign begins, the data company selects the customers the advertiser wants to target during the campaign and sends the specific Crosswalk IDs for the people the publisher should target. The publisher uses its table to decipher the anonymous IDs and match to its subscribers. As the campaign runs, the publisher knows exactly which subscribers to target with the advertiser's ad.

When the campaign ends, the publisher uses its table to map impressions from known subscribers to the anonymous Crosswalk ID and sends those back to the data company. The data company uses the table to map those impressions back to the advertiser's customers. That allows the data company to measure the impact of the campaign by tying purchase data to ad impressions.

The beauty of using anonymous Crosswalk IDs is that it allows your treasured and proprietary customer data to be used for targeting without sharing your customer data with publishers. Conversely, publishers never have to share their valued subscriber data with advertisers. The data or identity company sits between advertisers and publishers, and thanks to the anonymous Crosswalk IDs, plays the role of cipher between the two. It's a win-win-win for everyone involved.

* *

Why ROAS versus ROI? Because marketers may not know all of the costs involved in product delivery, which are needed to calculate return on investment (ROI). To calculate the ROAS, the marketer simply takes the cost of the advertising divided by the incremental sales lift (the incremental amount spent by the control group versus the test group). Marketers have access to both pieces of information, so calculating ROAS is easy. ROAS and other measurement methodologies are discussed in more detail in Chapter 18.

* *

1:1 MARKETING IN ACTION

A voice over internet protocol (VOIP) platform needed help determining exactly how new customers were finding it and what that journey looked like on their path to buying its unique services. The company had its doubts about radio, and after a month using paid ads on radio, it was left unimpressed. Its marketing agency asked LeadsRx for help in assigning attribution for an impartial view of the company's advertising campaigns. The data from a month-over-month attribution report showed what was working and what was not, giving the agency and the business insights into how to increase its ROAS.

The company was struggling to see any sort of return on paid advertising, including the new radio spots and existing paid search ads. Its paid search campaigns were typically running at an uninspired 0.92 ROAS, as shown in Figure 5.1. The company was lacking data to show where best to spend ad dollars to increase its overall conversions.

THE DETAILS – BEFORE (AUGUST 2019):

STARTING ROAS	0.92
BUDGET	$64,000 for Aug.
REVENUE	$59,100 for Aug.
6 CHANNELS	Radio Ads, Unpaid Social, Google: Paid and Organic, Direct, Referrals
KPI	Increased ROAS and Revenue Growth

Figure 5.1　Details and ROAS for the company's campaigns before applying multitouch attribution.

The business also had a lack of understanding of attribution and the insight it could provide into its marketing channels. LeadsRx worked with both the company and the agency to understand where advertising dollars were being spent and how to improve that allocation across each channel.

Attribution examined radio dayparts, days of the week, and specific content being fed to campaigns, and the ROAS attributed to each of those metrics. By cutting lower-performing ads and increasing spend toward better-performing ads—along with homing in on the best delivery schedule—LeadsRx could to guide the agency to optimization solutions for the communications company.

By following the attribution insights from LeadsRx, the company achieved a nearly 50 percent improvement in ROAS (and a 27 percent increase in revenue), depicted in Figure 5.2. Radio broadcasting, at first

THE RESULTS – AFTER (SEPTEMBER 2019):

NEW ROAS	1.38
BUDGET	$54,500 for Sept.
REVENUE	$75,100 for Sept.
CHANNELS OPTIMIZED	Existing channels; no new channels added
KPI	ROAS improved 58.6%; revenue increased 27%

Figure 5.2　Details and ROAS for the company's campaigns after applying the recommendations based on multitouch attribution.

a choice received with skepticism by the company's marketing team, proved to be a low-cost paid-advertising solution. It continues to show promise for increased ROAS.[4]

. . . .

THERE'S NO CLEAR LINE OF DISTINCTION BETWEEN MASS MARKETING VERSUS 1:1 MARKETING

Much of this chapter and book contrasts mass marketing with 1:1 marketing approaches as though they are polar opposites where a marketer is either practicing one or the other. In truth, most marketers practice some combination of both.

For example, a national consumer brand might leverage the scale and impact of broadcast television, such as ads appearing during the Super Bowl, to raise or maintain brand awareness and drive trial from new customers. And if they have amassed a treasure trove of first-party data about their customers, they also will employ 1:1 marketing to increase their share of customers' wallets over time.

Even a brand that decides to go all in on 1:1 marketing will have to start from where they are, which likely involves more mass marketing than 1:1 marketing approaches. It's impossible for a brand to throw a switch and in one day, one month, or even one year go from practicing mass marketing to 1:1 marketing. The methodologies are so dissimilar and require different assets, tools, skillsets, and tactics that marketing teams must transition over time. In fact, Chapter 13 talks about how you should expect to employ a crawl-walk-run approach to this transition and manage senior management's expectations accordingly that over time the organization will incorporate more effective 1:1 marketing techniques.

The *1:1 framework* (shown in Figure 5.3) approach to visualizing where various channels, techniques, data sets, and tactics fall in the spectrum between mass marketing and 1:1 marketing will help illustrate this principle throughout the book. By seeing in which of the four quadrants

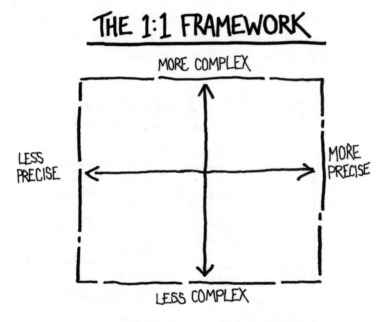

Figure 5.3 The 1:1 framework highlights the differences between various 1:1 tactics that marketers use.

a particular approach fits, you can start to plot where your marketing is currently and set goals for which quadrant you want to ultimately move your marketing to.

The horizontal x-axis indicates the amount of precision involved in what's being measured. For example, if you are plotting broad demographic targeting versus targeting individuals using in-store purchase data, the former would rank low (to the left) and the latter would rank high (to the right) on a scale between low and high precision. (The x-axis could also also represent effort or cost as well, since those things increase the more precisely one markets.)

The y-axis indicates the relative complexity of the element being used in the campaign. For example, measuring your 1:1 marketing campaigns with a marketing automation campaign is not all that hard to do, so it would fall toward the bottom of the y-axis. But using sales enablement solutions to engage via email and phone would fall higher up on the y-axis.

With that understanding of the 1:1 framework, here are some examples of the tactics you might use in a 1:1 campaign and where they might fall on the following framework. Check this out:

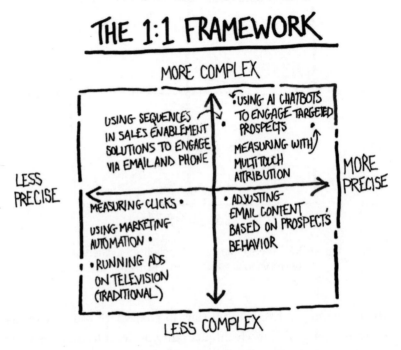

Figure 5.4   Example of different types of marketing and where they fit in the 1:1 framework.

In Figure 5.4, you'll notice that "Running Ads on Television (Traditional)" is in the bottom left quadrant. That's not to say that creating, developing, and placing a TV spot doesn't require a good amount of time, energy, and budget. Instead, it's that running an ad on traditional TV doesn't provide you the precision that other 1:1 techniques will provide, nor is it all that complex to execute.

In the upper right-hand quadrant, you see "Measuring with Multitouch Attribution" as both more complex and more precise. Implementing a robust, dynamic, constantly evolving multitouch attribution campaign is not easy to do, but it's a lot more precise than a traditional TV campaign.

KEY TAKEAWAYS

Here are some things to keep in mind as you explore the concepts in this chapter.

- **Customer lifetime value.** While mass marketers tend to focus more on customer acquisition, 1:1 marketers take a more holistic approach and often focus as much if not more effort on increasing the value of their customers over time versus trying to get new customers. Even within customer campaigns, 1:1 marketers know they have multiple ways to increase lifetime value and apply different techniques, targeting, and methods based on the specific goal of each campaign.

- **Measurement.** Mass marketers tend to focus on short-term results, such as sales lift, but 1:1 marketers are more likely to take the long view to marketing, seeking to increase the value of customers over time. They are also more likely to measure metrics that directly relate to the bottom line, such as sales. Mass marketers tend to measure less granular metrics, such as how many people their ads reach and how often, which typically don't directly correlate to sales or profit.

- **Evolution not revolution.** No company can flip a switch and go from being a mass marketer to a 1:1 marketer overnight. And some marketers use multiple techniques, turning to mass marketing for customer acquisition and 1:1 marketing for increasing the value of customers. Throughout the book you'll find specific ideas as to where on the spectrum between mass marketing and 1:1 marketing your organization belongs to help you gauge the level of effort involved as well as the potential ROI.

PART

3

STRATEGIC
THINKING

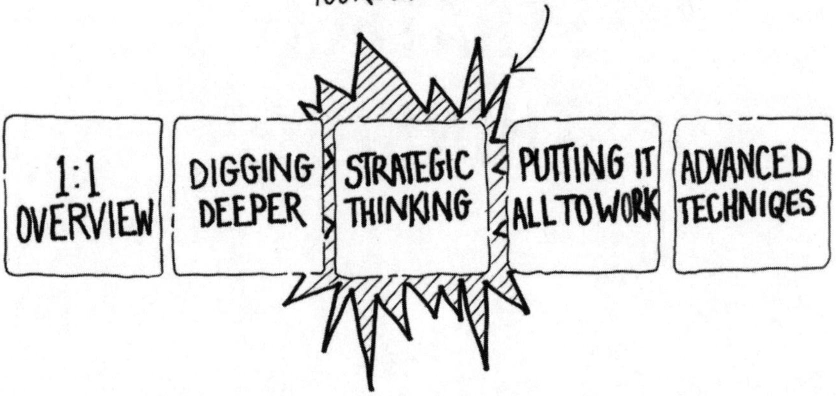

YOU'RE ZIPPING RIGHT THROUGH THE BOOK.
1:1 OVERVIEW
DIGGING DEEPER
STRATEGIC THINKING
PUTTING IT ALL TO WORK
ADVANCED TECHNIQES

THE SALES FUNNEL ISN'T DEAD. IT JUST NEEDS A KICK IN THE BUTT.

The marketing funnel can give marketers funnel vision. In focusing on the transaction over the relationship, marketers can lose sight of the actual consumer the funnel was designed to reach.

—TOM FISHBURNE, FOUNDER AND CEO, MARKETOONIST[1]

OK, the first few chapters of the book covered a lot of ground. Part 1 discussed what 1:1 marketing is and how it differs from mass marketing. Then Part 2 discussed how your consumer is changing and that you need to keep up with those changes. And it also discussed what a 1:1 campaign actually looks like.

This chapter discusses the sales funnel and how it is evolving. If you've been in marketing long enough, you're already familiar with the sales funnel framework. It was invented in 1898 by Elias St. Elmo Lewis, an advertising executive who was trying to develop an explanation that described how prospects engaged with brands and ultimately became customers. There were four stages to Lewis's model—awareness, interest, desire, and action. Using Lewis's framework, marketers could discuss how prospects become *aware* of a product/service and then gain *interest* in the product/service. At a certain point, that interest turned into *desire*, which ultimately resulted in *action*, where they converted from prospect into customer.

In 1961, Robert Lavidge and Gary Steiner wrote an article titled "A Model for Predictive Measurements of Advertising Effectiveness" for the *Journal of Marketing*.[2] They added a few new wrinkles to Lewis's model and called it the hierarchy of effects theory. Instead of just awareness, interest, desire, and action, Lavidge and Steiner went a bit deeper and created a model that included awareness, knowledge, liking, preference, conviction, and purchase. As a result, the sales funnel looked like the illustration in Figure 6.1.

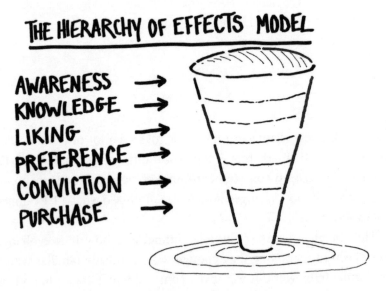

Figure 6.1   The hierarchy of effects model was created by Robert Lavidge and Gary Steiner in 1961.

The six behaviors tied to the hierarchy of effects theory (i.e., awareness, knowledge, liking, preference, conviction, purchase) can be sorted into three categories—think, feel, and do. The awareness and knowledge stages (i.e., the *think* stages) happen when a prospect gets information about a product or service and then processes that information cognitively. The liking and preference stages (i.e., the *feel* stages) happen when a prospect starts to feel emotions about the product or service. And the conviction and purchase stages (i.e., the *do* stages) focus on action, which is when the prospect buys the product or service and becomes a customer.

> One-to-one marketing is about understanding how people move from being a prospect to being a customer, in a targeted and personalized manner. The foundation for that is research—doing your homework to understand what drives a purchase and how to optimize that process— and robust inference, e.g., via holdout experimentation.
>
> —JULIAN RUNGE, PHD, VISITING RESEARCHER[3]

Lewis's model and the hierarchy of effects model are both fine and dandy—they do a good job explaining the theory behind the consumer journey. The problem is that these models imply that there is a *linear* journey for your prospect. In other words, they assume all prospects start at the top of the funnel and then gradually work their way down each stage until they convert at the bottom. That was fine if you were a mass marketer working in the twentieth century. But that process, outlined in Scenario 1 of Figure 6.2, isn't always accurate. As you can see in Scenario 2 of Figure 6.2, sometimes people start in the middle of the funnel and then work their way back to the top before moving back down through the funnel.

At other times, prospects might follow the path in Scenario 3 of Figure 6.2—they might start at the bottom of the funnel with an impulse purchase without having gone through any of the other stages. After making the purchase and consuming the product, they might jump back up to the top of the funnel where they go through the awareness and knowledge

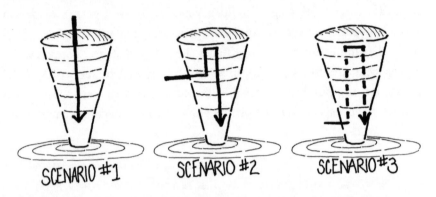

Figure 6.2   Customers take a variety of paths to making a purchase decision.

stages, then skip down to the preference and conviction stages before making a repeat purchase.

The truth is that it's almost impossible to map how consumers move through the decision-making and response process. A "journey" implies that someone goes from top to bottom in some logical, orderly fashion. But as we all know, consumers may start in one place, go to another, come back to the first, and then skip all the steps in between on their way to a purchase.

In addition, some decisions are made rapidly (within seconds) and others may take months or longer. Given this nonlinear and unpredictable behavior, 1:1 marketers have to rethink not only how they communicate with customers, but also what types of interaction, engagement, and persuasive techniques will make a difference.

RETHINKING THE SALES FUNNEL WITH A 1:1 MINDSET

Mass marketing was all about interrupting a consumer's life with a message about your product or service. The consumer would be enjoying a TV show, radio program, print magazine, or any other form of mass media. The brand would interrupt that experience to force its message into the consumer's mind.

There were two primary drivers behind traditional mass marketing—frequency and engagement. If you pushed your message on consumers frequently enough, they would remember your product or service and (hopefully) purchase it. The alternative was to engage consumers with a message that made them laugh or cry. When consumers engage emotionally with an ad, a memory is created. When a memory is created, a consumer is more likely to purchase your product or service.

In some cases, larger brands could achieve high frequency and high engagement. Global brands like Nike, Apple, and BMW leveraged the one-two punch of frequency and engagement in a way that drove significant awareness (and revenue growth) around the globe. But most brands don't have the marketing muscle of these large, well-established brands. Furthermore, no matter how much marketing muscle you have, if consumers are resistant to commercial interruptions, they won't respond to the messages anyway.

It's also worth noting that mass marketing lacked relevance for most of the consumers who saw the messages. One of the strengths of a 1:1 marketing campaign is that they're more relevant to the person who sees the ad. Here's an example of the waste that happens with a traditional mass marketing campaign.

Say you're the marketing director for Ralph Lauren Blue, a fragrance that appeals to a subset of the larger population as a whole. Traditionally, you would run a TV campaign to build brand awareness and drive people to online or brick-and-mortar retailers who sold the product. Your TV campaign would run during prime time on a show that might have a higher than average female viewership. Despite running on a show targeting women, there's still waste—perhaps 40 percent of the viewers might be men who aren't necessarily in the market for perfume. Out of the 60 percent remaining, you could argue that half of those wouldn't have the demographic or psychographic makeup to purchase a Ralph Lauren fragrance. And out of the 30 percent of those remaining, perhaps two-thirds had plenty of perfume already and didn't need any more.

That leaves you with a TV campaign that's reaching 10 percent of the intended audience. In other words, to reach that 10 percent, you have to waste 90 percent of your budget, as illustrated in Figure 6.3. Can you imagine walking into your CFO with any other business expense and trying to justify that kind of waste? "Hi Barbara, can you approve this expense? We're going to buy light bulbs for our office building, but 90 percent of the light bulbs we buy won't work. Can you just sign right here so I can make the purchase?" It's mind-boggling. And it's why the solution that 1:1 marketing offers is not only necessary, it's imperative.

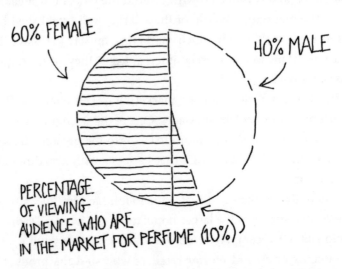

Figure 6.3 A TV spot for Ralph Lauren Blue perfume on a TV show with 60 percent female viewership and 40 percent male viewership resulted in 90 percent inefficiency.

WHAT 1:1 MARKETING IS AND WHAT IT ISN'T

1:1 marketing isn't a tactic or a series of tactics. Instead, it's a strategic approach that brands use to create a more meaningful and personalized campaign for the consumer. You can think of 1:1 marketing as a mindset.

It's an approach you can use to build a better and more meaningful relationship with your prospects and customers. To execute a 1:1 marketing campaign properly, you'll need three things—the mindset, the techniques, and the technologies.

If traditional marketing was all about using mass marketing to create a linear sales funnel, then 1:1 marketing is about creating meaningful, relevant campaigns that are as personalized as possible. Instead of interrupting a passive experience with generic mass marketing campaigns, 1:1 allows a brand to weave itself into the fabric of the prospect's life in a more relevant and meaningful way.

One of the best examples of a brand that successfully used 1:1 marketing is Airbnb, which has avoided running large-scale, traditional mass marketing campaigns throughout most of its existence. What kick-started Airbnb's growth was a bit of sophisticated programming and innovative problem solving. The team found a way to cross-publish Airbnb listings on Craigslist so that whenever someone searched the Craigslist classified site for a vacation rental, listings for properties on Airbnb popped up. They didn't run generic mass marketing campaigns. Instead, they figured out a way to create hypertargeted, relevant, and meaningful ads that popped up right when an individual was searching for, say, a short-term rental unit located in downtown Denver. The result was that Airbnb was seamlessly woven into the fabric of the consumer's life, not in a loud, traditional, mass marketing approach, but through a quiet, more intimate, 1:1 approach.[4]

Fisher-Price used 1:1 marketing to reverse the decline in sales they were experiencing in France.[5] They dug into a pile of data and derived insights about that segment's demographics, media affinities, purchase intentions, and purchase behaviors. They also created microsegments of their ideal customers so they could create and deploy remarketing campaigns along with a personalized call-to-action for each e-commerce site. To make the campaign even more efficient, they uploaded a list of their existing customers to their online display ad network and excluded those existing customers from the campaign. In other words, since the goal for the campaign was to attract new prospects and convert them into customers, they excluded existing customers from the campaign as a way to improve efficiencies.

What were the results? Fisher-Price experienced 95 percent aided awareness immediately following the campaign (number one in their category). Their cost-per-view was 25 percent lower than anticipated and their cost-per-click was 66 percent lower than anticipated. Most important, sales increased 10 percent during the first two weeks of the campaign.

The key for Fisher-Price was that they shifted their mindset from a traditional mass marketing campaign, which might entail buying a generic Thursday evening prime-time advertising slot on network TV, to a more targeted, nuanced, 1:1 campaign that used cutting-edge technology to hypertarget ads to precisely the right prospects.

Unilever in Thailand used a similar 1:1 campaign to increase sales of their fast-moving consumer goods (FMCG) 5 percent to 10 percent over the course of the campaign.[6] They acquired consumer data via Line, which is Thailand's biggest chat platform. As prospects engaged with the platform, automated chatbots asked a series of questions specific to that prospect's previous online behavior.

As an example, a single male who has a propensity to shop online and who was asking Line for a quick, easy dinner recipe would also likely be a candidate for products that require a minimum of fuss and are simple to use. Unilever used customer data to derive insights about the prospects who were using the Line platform. Then based on those insights, they delivered customized, personalized campaigns for specific products that might be particularly appealing to the prospect. In this example of the single male who shopped online and was asking about an easy dinner recipe, Unilever delivered an ad with a special offer for a simple-to-use laundry detergent that would appeal to that user's personality traits. The result was a campaign that drove a 5 percent to 10 percent increase in sales during the course of the campaign.

Not bad for a day's work, right?

McDonald's ran a 1:1 marketing campaign in Indonesia that generated sales results that were 18 percent better than projected.[7] The campaign used TV and the McDonald's app to give the appearance that the app and the prospect's TV were connected to one another. During a commercial break featuring McDonald's, the prospect was asked to open the McDonald's app and select which fruit they wanted in their next fruit smoothie. The TV commercials and the app both created a countdown effect at exactly the same time. Once the countdown reached zero on the TV commercial and the app, the "winning" fruit was revealed. If the fruit on the TV matched the selection the prospect made on their app, then they were sent a coupon to receive a free fruit smoothie using that fruit flavor.

THE 1:1 FRAMEWORK

The 1:1 framework presented earlier is used at various points throughout the book to help you gain a better understanding of the complexity and precision of various 1:1 techniques (Figure 6.4). For each of the campaigns

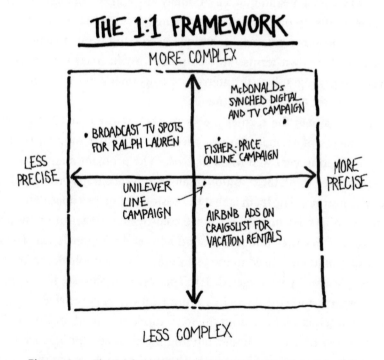

Figure 6.4 The 1:1 framework is designed to help you understand the complexity versus precision equation for different kinds of campaigns.

in this chapter—McDonald's, Fisher-Price, Airbnb, Unilever, and Ralph Lauren—you'll see where the campaigns fall on the matrix. Take a spin through the graphic, and think through why each of the case studies is plotted the way it is. Over time, you'll be able to make judgments on the campaigns you're considering based on the complexity and precision required to execute them.

1:1 ISN'T ABOUT A TECHNOLOGY, IT'S ABOUT A MINDSET

The key for each of these campaigns wasn't the use of a complex, new technology. These campaigns used technology that is readily available to any marketer working at just about any corporation. Instead, the key was that these marketers each had a 1:1 mindset and decided to use 1:1 techniques to create a meaningful, emotionally engaging campaign that drove superior results. In other words, they treated each prospect and customer as a person who has a name, has unique needs, and wants to engage with brands on their own terms. This is in contrast to mass marketers who simply use demographics to interrupt a consumer's life with an ad that may or may not be relevant to them.

Frans Mahieu, the former global marketing director for Kimberly-Clark (makers of Huggies, Kotex, Kleenex, and other brands) summed up 1:1 marketing very well when he said, "The problem many marketers face is that they think the traditional sales funnel accurately represents the customer journey. The truth is that the customer journey doesn't just start at the top of a sales funnel and move step-by-step down to the bottom. The customer journey bounces around a lot and is a non-linear journey. As a result, marketers need to use techniques and technologies to connect with people in a hyper-targeted, 1:1 capacity. By doing so, they connect with prospects and customers in a more relevant, personalized, engaging manner, which is a far cry from the mass marketing used previously."[8]

For many executives, understanding the nuances and application of 1:1 marketing takes time. One way to wrap your mind around the concept is to observe and analyze other brands to see if they're implementing a 1:1 marketing strategy. Another way is to study Table 6.1, which provides a snapshot of what 1:1 marketing is and what it isn't.

Table 6.1   Marketing in a Nutshell

WHAT IT IS	WHAT IT ISN'T
A strategy	A tactic
Based on an individual's preferences	Based on a mass market's demographics
Based on the desire for a long-term relationship with the prospect	Based on a desire for a transaction with the prospect
A technique	A technology
An approach designed to engage fewer people with more meaningful, relevant messages	An approach designed to deploy massive amounts of ads against an anonymous group in the hopes that some of the ads will stick
One-to-one focused	One-to-many focused
About increasing lifetime value	About driving short-term sales
About reaching the right people	About reaching the most people

When thinking about your customer's journey, remember that the sales funnel isn't dead, it just needs to be viewed as a framework rather than a specific set of occurrences. In other words, understand that the sales funnel is useful as a way to describe where your customer is in the purchase process, but it's not a linear process. Your prospect can be anywhere in the sales funnel at any given time.

With that in mind, understand that traditional mass marketing was about targeting audiences based on the hope that your prospect would be interacting with a particular medium at a particular time. 1:1 marketing is about targeting individuals by meeting them where they are with campaigns that are relevant to their specific needs and desires. 1:1 isn't about a specific technology (although later chapters go deeper into some advanced techniques that will take 1:1 to an entirely different level). Instead, 1:1 is about changing the way you look at the sales funnel, the customer journey, and the media you can use to connect with those prospects.

KEY TAKEAWAYS

Here are some things to keep in mind as you explore the concepts in this chapter.

- **Sales funnel.** The traditional sales funnel is a good framework that helps highlight the customer journey, but the customer journey should not be thought of as a linear process. Instead, it's a nonlinear process where prospects jump around, skip over, and bypass some of the specific points on the funnel. 1:1 marketing can help you engage with those individuals no matter where they are in the sales funnel.
- **Mass marketing.** The old approach to mass marketing was to deploy campaigns that were highly inefficient but had enough volume to overcome their inefficiencies.
- **1:1 marketing.** The new approach is to use 1:1 techniques and technologies that can help you have more meaningful and relevant conversations with your prospects. 1:1 is about having the mindset that you're going to move away from mass marketing and move toward having a dialogue with your prospects on your way to converting them into customers.

REINVENTING THE WAY YOU THINK ABOUT MARKETING

Pretty much everything that's been written and theorized
about our field over the last 20 years is being questioned,
refined, or flat out demystified as we speak.
—GREG CREED, FORMER CEO, YUM! BRANDS

The previous chapter discussed how the sales funnel is a good framework for marketers to understand, but it has its limitations because most people's journey from prospect to customer is nonlinear. It also discussed how 1:1 marketers use techniques to create more relevant campaigns rather than just blasting out ads to masses of anonymous prospects.

This chapter is going to ask you to reframe how you think about marketing so that you can become an expert at the 1:1 techniques outlined in the book. Speaking of which, you'll notice there are two kinds of chapters in the book—those that explain how to *do* 1:1 marketing and those that explain how to *think* about 1:1 marketing. This chapter discusses ways to think about 1:1 so you can do a better job when you get down to executing your campaign.

So with all that said, let's get started.

When you sit down to develop a marketing campaign for your company, the first thing you probably do (after getting your morning cup of java) is list your goals and objectives. Then you move on to developing a strategy. From there, you develop a set of tactics you'll use to accomplish your goals. And then you develop an executional plan to launch and manage the campaign.

We've been doing it that way for more than a century, and there are aspects of that approach that are as good today as they were when they were invented. But part of the purpose of this book is to help you reimagine some of the traditional approaches to marketing so you can come at it from a different angle. You'll still start your campaign by defining your goals, objectives, strategies, and tactics. The difference will be in how you think about your marketing campaign. After all, 1:1 marketing is about understanding your prospects and customers at such a nuanced level that you're almost speaking to them as individuals rather than audiences.

Later this book takes a deeper dive into the tactics and technologies you'll be using to create a 1:1 campaign. At this stage, you're still looking at 1:1 from a 30,000-foot level so you can understand it conceptually before getting into the more granular stuff.

. . . .

GOALS, OBJECTIVES, STRATEGIES, AND TACTICS

Some people confuse the difference between goals, objectives, strategies, and tactics. So to clear that up:

- **Goal.** The desired end result (e.g., "to win World War II" or "to retire in Hawaii")
- **Objective.** A specific, measurable, time-bound outcome that leads to the goal (e.g., "to defeat Hitler in Europe before the end of 1945" or "to have a nest egg of $1 million before I'm 65")
- **Strategy.** The approach you use to accomplish your objectives (e.g., "to open a two-front war on Hitler" or "to own my own business and to invest 100 percent the annual profits into my retirement account")

- **Tactics.** The action-steps or techniques you use as part of your strategy (e.g., "to mount a surprise attack on Hitler's troops at dawn on June 6, 1944" or "to open a restaurant specializing in high-end Mexican cuisine by this time next year")

• •

Perhaps the best way to understand 1:1 is to describe how it can be used by the organizations that choose to embrace it. After all, 1:1 isn't only about tools, technologies, and techniques, it's also about a mindset. In other words, it's about how you think about marketing.

The traditional way people thought about marketing was all about interruption. A brand created an ad and then interrupted the audience with a message that was, oftentimes, irrelevant or unwanted. But 1:1 is about using data, analytics, and insights to create and then place meaningful messages in front of people who are likely to purchase your product or service and engage them.

In a true 1:1 scenario, you've gathered data on your prospects, then created anonymized data sets of those prospects with an identity resolution partner, then delivered the message to those specific individuals using an ad agency and/or an ad-buying platform, then tracked whether or not the prospect purchased your product/service at the retail level, and then calculated the ROI of your campaign based on your ability to track the campaign and tie it to the specific purchase. See Figure 7.1.

As you move through the book, you'll go deeper and deeper into the 1:1 tools, technologies, and techniques. But you don't need a ton of new tools to create a 1:1 campaign. Yes, it helps to have all of the tools at your disposal, but as was said, 1:1 isn't just about the tools, it's about a mindset. In other words, it's about thinking about marketing in a new and fresh way.

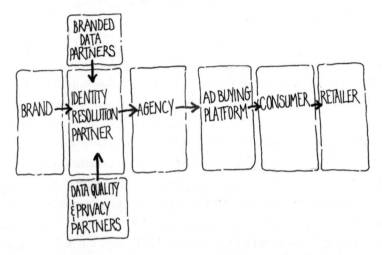

Figure 7.1   In a true 1:1 campaign, tools and technologies are used to target anonymized prospects and track whether or not they made the purchase at the retail level.

IN A NUTSHELL

With 1:1 marketing, you're not speaking to audiences, you're speaking to individuals. We call this speaking to *me* instead of speaking to *we*.

Take a look at a basic 1:1 campaign. At the most fundamental level, 1:1 can be accomplished with a good marketing automation platform like GetResponse, Mailchimp, or HubSpot. When you combine marketing automation with, say, a good e-commerce platform like Shopify, BigCommerce, or Wix, then you can do a basic 1:1 campaign. For example, if you publish a newsletter, your approach would be to break your e-newsletter subscribers into nuanced, granular subsets. If you're the chief marketing officer (CMO) of Nike and you're selling running shoes via the Nike e-commerce website, then you'd want to be able to identify your customers based on demographics like age, sex, and geographic location.

To take things a little deeper, you'd want to create a subset of those customers based on certain behaviors—for example, how often they purchase, what kind of shoe they buy, and how much they spend on each purchase. If you do this properly, then you might have dozens or even hundreds of categories for your email marketing campaigns.

One category might be "men, living in Oregon, who buy expensive trail running shoes a minimum of four times a year." By creating an email marketing campaign that specifically targets that group, you can improve your conversion rate. Remember, if 1 percent of the recipients of a generic running-shoe email make a purchase, but you improve that conversion rate to 1.2 percent when you create a personalized, relevant, 1:1 email campaign, then you've increased your revenues by 20 percent simply by speaking to individuals rather than audiences. That's the power of 1:1.

Of course, the preceding scenario is not all that revolutionary. If you have an e-commerce website and an e-newsletter list, then you've known about doing this for quite some time. But at a fundamental level, it constitutes a 1:1 campaign because you're speaking (as much as possible) to *me* rather than *we*. You're crafting messages that are hypertargeted for specific groups of individuals and then tracking their journey through the sales funnel all the way to their purchase on the e-commerce store.

If you were doing a more advanced 1:1 campaign, then you'd create anonymized data sets of prospects; then hypertarget TV, online display, social media, and other ads to those individuals; and then track the behaviors of those individuals all the way from first contact to purchase at a physical retail store. Ultimately, that's the level a 1:1 marketer is shooting for. But as you're moving toward that goal, it's helpful to understand that 1:1 campaigns are on a spectrum ranging from simple campaigns like the Nike example mentioned earlier to more advanced campaigns referenced throughout the book.

DIGGING DEEPER

Now dig a little deeper into another example so you can see a 1:1 campaign that's a little more complex. In this example, you're the CMO of a national chain of convenience stores that sells gasoline. It could be BP, 7-Eleven, Speedway—it doesn't really matter. The CEO has come to you and asked you to find a way to grow incremental revenue by 4 percent over the next six months.

The CEO wants you to grow incremental revenue for your chain of convenience stores by 4 percent over the next six months. What would you do?

Well, since you're good at your job, you know that the easiest way to generate incremental revenue is not by trying to acquire new customers but by getting your existing customers to come back more frequently and/or increase the amount they spend when they're at your store. In other words, if you want a quick bump in incremental revenue, your first step is to do a campaign to your existing (and loyal) customers before you move on and target people who are not currently your customers.

IN A NUTSHELL

The easiest way to grow incremental revenue is to get existing customers to come back more frequently and to get them to spend more while they're at your store. Once you've exhausted that approach, it's time to move on to your next easiest source of revenue, which is to target people who are buying your competitor's products or services. But always start by focusing on your existing customers first before you move on to acquiring new customers.

Now that you have your marching orders from the CEO, you're ready to dive in. Your goal is to increase incremental revenue by 4 percent. Your objective is to get customers to come back more frequently and to spend more when they're in the store. Your strategy is to focus on existing customers who are members of your frequent shopper card program. And your tactic is to send those customers hypertargeted promotions based on their previous purchase behaviors.

With all that in mind, you start to analyze some of the frequent shopper card data you have at your disposal. Shopper card data is a terrific way to gain insights into your customers. With the right technology, you can analyze what they buy, where they live, how frequently they visit, and how much they spend while they're there. When you analyze your customers at a deep, nuanced level—in other words, when you derive insights about their behaviors—then you're on your way to creating a 1:1 campaign.

So jumping back to the scenario, your CEO has asked you to increase revenues from existing customers by 4 percent over the next six months. It's a tall order, but by putting some of the 1:1 techniques into place, it's doable. Your first step is to take your frequent shopper card data and create clusters of customers based on previous purchases. In doing so, you realized there are five distinct behaviors exhibited by people living within a five-mile radius of your stores, as shown in Figure 7.2.

Figure 7.2   By analyzing customer data, 1:1 marketers can break customers into nuanced segments based on demographics, purchase patterns, and other behaviors.

Now that you've created clusters of customers, you can develop meaningful, relevant, hypertargeted promotions for each group that are designed to change their behavior. What you're trying to do is get people to behave slightly differently than they're currently behaving. In other words, if they currently stop by once a week to buy gas, you want to train them to stop by once a week and buy gas as well as coffee. Your goal is to nurture their behavior in such a way that they deepen their relationship with your brand, which lets you hit the incremental revenue targets your CEO has asked for.

Take a look at what you want to accomplish for each of the clusters of customers:

- **Customers who purchase gas only.** This cluster's default behavior is to just stop by and fill up for gas. Nothing else. Your 1:1 marketing goal is to get them to change their regular behavior by providing them a discount only available if they come into the store. With consistent effort, a certain percentage will change their default behavior from just purchasing gas to purchasing gas and stopping in for a store visit. That's money in the bank.
- **Customers who purchase gas and coffee.** This cluster is already coming into the store, so your objective is to get them to add more items into their basket. Since you know they typically purchase coffee when they buy gas, you can provide them a coupon with a discount for an item that goes well with coffee—a donut, a breakfast burrito, a biscuit—something that's a natural with a cup of java.
- **Customers who purchase gas and cigarettes.** For this cluster, your goal is the same as with the previous cluster, which is to get them to buy something in addition to their default purchase of gas and cigarettes. Discounts for energy drinks, soft drinks, or other items that go well with cigarettes are the order of the day here.
- **Customers who purchase gas, drinks, and a snack.** This cluster is a high-value group because they're spending more on each visit than other clusters. Your goal here would be to drive non-gas-

dependent visits, so you'll want to promote the fact that you also have grocery items—bread, toothpaste, aspirin, and other items of that nature. By reframing your convenience store into a mini-grocery store in the mind of your customer, you can increase their frequency of visits, which adds revenue to your bottom line.

- **Customers who purchase gas and miscellaneous.** Your goal with this cluster is the same as the previous one—to reframe their thinking so they view your store as more than a convenience store. Instead, you want them to think of you as a mini-grocery store so they stop in even when they don't fill up for gas.

For some marketers, the preceding example is the kind of promotional effort they've been doing for some time. But most marketers aren't thinking that way. Instead, they segment based on demographics rather than behaviors, which is what traditional mass marketers have been doing for years. By changing the way you think of your target audience—in other words, *by thinking about the behaviors of customers rather than just the demographics of customers*, you can open up a more relevant, meaningful 1:1 conversation with them.

> 1:1 marketing is like the game of chess. Most of your competitors
> have the same set of tools at their disposal, so your goal is
> to figure out how to use the tools in the most imaginative fashion.
> By understanding the tools conceptually as well as tactically,
> you'll put yourself in a position to win the game.
> —AJ BROWN, CEO, LEADSRX

SHIFTING FROM A MASS MARKETING MINDSET TO A 1:1 MARKETING MINDSET

Several years ago, one of the authors' clients was working as a marketing executive at TransUnion, the large credit reporting agency based out of Chicago. The executive was smart, hardworking, and eager to do a great job, but she was also thinking about marketing using a mass marketing mindset. She said, "Our target market visits news websites with some regularity, and so please place these banner ads on Time.com, Yahoo.com, CNN.com, and FoxNews.com."

We explained to her that that was the wrong way to go about running the online display campaign. The approach she wanted to use was based on the old TV model developed in the twentieth century where you would buy a certain TV program so you could (hopefully) capture your target audiences' attention. But with the introduction of 1:1 marketing techniques, we didn't need to buy campaigns that way anymore. And we don't want to because they're highly inefficient.

We had already established that her target market was midlevel managers working at mid- to large-sized business located in the 35 largest markets in the Southeast. If we simply ran the ads on the websites she suggested, there would be huge amounts of waste. Only a small fraction of the people visiting those websites matched her target market exactly.

So instead, we used an online display network, which is a company that has access to hundreds of thousand or even millions of websites, and asked them to deploy the ads only to the people in our target market. Said another way, we were buying eyeballs rather than websites. We didn't care if our prospect was on Yahoo.com or if they were on BobMakesStuff.com. Instead, what we cared about was that the ad was served to the specific individual in our target market no matter what website they were visiting.

The TransUnion scenario provides an example of how to shift your thought patterns from a mass marketing mindset to a 1:1 mindset. Instead of using the traditional approaches that have been leveraged for more than 100 years, we need to step back, look at things from a different angle, and create campaigns that are more meaningful, more impactful, and more effective.

KEY TAKEAWAYS

Here are some things to keep in mind as you explore the concepts in this chapter.

- **1:1 is on a spectrum.** At its most advanced level, 1:1 involves connecting the dots with large data sets and then using that data to hypertarget ads and track the prospect's journey through the sales funnel. At a more fundamental level, 1:1 can be accomplished with an email marketing campaign that targets customer segments based on their previous behaviors and then tracks their purchase on an e-commerce site. Essentially, both those examples are 1:1, but the purpose of this book is to show you how to move toward the more advanced side of the spectrum, which will help you generate campaigns with a better ROI.

- **It's about a mindset.** 1:1 isn't only about tools, technologies, and techniques. It's also about having a 1:1 mindset. With the tools you have at your disposal, how are you using them to derive customer insights, create relevant and meaningful conversations, and track your customer's journey through the sales funnel? Doing that is about a mindset, not just about a set of tools.

- **1:1 targets individuals, not audiences.** As mentioned in this chapter, 1:1 is about focusing on *me*, not on *we*.

- **Focus on existing customers first.** The easiest way to start your journey on the 1:1 spectrum is to focus your initial efforts on your existing customers. The odds are you have data about those individuals, and as a result, you can begin deriving insights, creating segments, and then hypertargeting meaningful, relevant messages to them. Once you've developed campaigns focusing on existing customers, you'll be ready to take the next step, which is to do campaigns focused on your competitor's customers.

KEY CONCEPTS AND DEFINITIONS EVERY 1:1 MARKETER MUST KNOW

Marketing is no longer about the stuff that you make
but about the stories you tell.
—SETH GODIN, AUTHOR AND ENTREPRENEUR

Are you thinking: "Oh, my gosh, an entire chapter that's just a bunch of definitions. And in the middle of the book? That's bizarre."?

Well, that might be true on one level. But if you want to cut it as a 1:1 marketer, you absolutely must understand the nomenclature and underlying concepts. If you've come this far, you appreciate that 1:1 marketing is a sea change away from traditional mass marketing. Guess what? The language is completely different, too.

The remainder of the book tosses around the terms defined in this chapter quite a bit. As you learn about (and hopefully begin to apply) these terms, you'll find yourself becoming much more insightful about how 1:1 marketing works and how you can use it in your organization.

While these are important concepts, the book tries to make the definitions meaningful yet fun to read. (Not too fun, but just a *little* fun, so don't get your hopes up. It's not like we're comedians or anything.)

These definitions are organized in alphabetical order (surprise, surprise). You might be familiar with some of the concepts. If that's the case, you can skip over them. If you're not familiar with the concept, then read the definition because it'll be referred to throughout the remainder of the book.

A/B split testing. Good marketers do more than just track their results—instead, *they test their way to success.* This is accomplished by running one ad (version A) and a second ad (version B) with a single variable that is different (e.g., a different headline, a different call-to-action, a different illustration, etc.). An A/B split test is when you compare the results generated by version A versus the results from version B. The winning ad becomes the "control." As you move forward with your A/B split test, you continue to test against the control to see if you can improve the results. If you're interested in an advanced form of testing called randomize controlled testing, then keep reading. The end of this chapter has an explanation of that concept from marketing experiments guru Guy Powell.

Above the fold. This is a term from traditional marketing that has been adopted for digital marketing. In traditional terms, above the fold meant that your ad ran on the top half of the newspaper page. In digital terms, above the fold means that your content can be seen immediately when someone lands on your web page. Be careful about being charged for ads that run below the fold since most of those ad impressions aren't seen by the web visitor (see Figure 8.1).

Ad fatigue. You know how sometimes you see the same banner ad over and over and over again? Doesn't that drive you nuts? That's ad fatigue. (A related term is *banner blindness,* which is where you start ignoring banner ads because you're suffering from ad fatigue.)

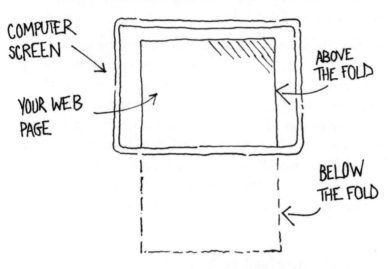

Figure 8.1   Ads that run above the fold are more likely to engage prospects and customers than those that run below the fold.

Addressability. To target a prospect in a 1:1 campaign, you need a way to identify and target them. In other words, you need an address. In its simplest form, this can be an email address, or for direct mail, a postal address. In its most sophisticated form, addressability involves collecting data from a wide variety of sources and then cleaning up that data so you can use it for your 1:1 marketing campaign.

Addressable TV. Imagine two neighbors next door to one another. They're both watching the same 6 p.m. network news program. But one is 75 years old and the neighbor is 35 years old. With addressable TV, you can deliver an ad for diabetes medicine to the 75-year-old at the same time you're delivering an ad for a Honda Civic to the 35-year-old—even though they're both watching the same TV show at the same time.

Advanced TV. This is slightly different from addressable TV. With advanced TV, you can reach your prospects and customers regardless of how they watch TV—whether it's addressable TV, over-the-top, or digital video.

Anonymous/anonymized ID. One of the most important things you can do as a 1:1 marketer is to be sure you protect the privacy of the prospects and customers you're targeting with your ad campaigns. This is accomplished by working with an identity resolution partner (IDR). IDRs specialize in cleaning up your data and anonymizing it so you (the brand) don't have access to any personal data. Instead, you have what looks like a random set of numbers so you protect the privacy of the individuals for whom you have data (see Figure 8.2).

Figure 8.2 Your customer looks different in real life versus how they look as a data point.

Attribution. Say your customer prospect saw a banner ad for your product but didn't click through on it. The next day, they saw another one of your banner ads and decided to click through on it, but they didn't buy your product. A week later, they saw another one of your banner ads, clicked through, and finally bought your product. Even though all three ads contributed to the final sale, only the last ad would get credit (which is called last-click attribution). Attribution models allow you to assign weights to each ad along the customer journey. In the preceding example, it might be 25 percent for the first ad, 25 percent for the second ad, and then 50 percent for the final ad. It's kind of up to you how you distribute the weights. A later chapter discusses attribution in slightly more depth.

Backlink. When a website points a link to your home page or a page deep within your site, they're essentially endorsing your site. That's called a backlink. If you have a large number of backlinks, you can improve your website's performance in search engines such as Google and Bing.

Bid. The price you will pay an advertising platform to run your ad. It's primarily used in pay-per-click (PPC) advertising and paid search advertising.

Bing. Microsoft's alternative to Google. Ads purchased on this platform will run on Yahoo and Bing. Bing is a worthy alternative to Google—if your prospects are traditional consumers or non-tech-savvy, they just might be using Bing instead of Google.

Bounce rate. The percentage of users who visit your website and then leave after visiting only that single page. If a user lands on a page of your website and then bounces off without clicking a link or visiting other pages on your site, it's a signal to you (and to search engines), that *that* page isn't as engaging as you might want it to be.

Call-to-action (CTA). A word or phrase used by marketers to get your prospects to convert to customers. Common CTAs include "Learn More," "Buy Now," "Subscribe Now," and "Contact Us." CTAs that have proven to be entirely unsuccessful include "Don't Click Here," "We Don't Want Your Business," and "Go Away."

Click-through-rate (CTR). The percentage of prospects who see your ad and then click on it. If one million people see your ad and 5,000 click on the ad, the CTR is 0.5 percent. According to SmartInsights, the typical CTR of a paid search ad on Google is 1.55 percent. The typical CTR on an online display (banner) ad is 0.47 percent.[1]

Connected TV (CTV). A subset of over-the-top TV (OTT) that is delivered through smart TVs or any TV that is internet-enabled. Samsung, Vizio, and other manufacturers have interfaces that allow users to directly log in to the OTT apps on their connected TVs to view content. (If you've bought a TV in the past several years, it's probably a CTV.)

Conversion rate (CR). The percentage of your prospects who clicked on or saw an ad and then bought your product or service based on their engagement with your ad. If 1,000 prospects see your ad and 10 of them buy your product or service based on that ad, then your CR is 1 percent (10/1,000).

Cookies. There are two kinds of cookies. The kind you eat. And the kind marketers use to track web visitor behaviors. Cookies are going away (not the kind you eat, thank goodness, but the web browser kind). In essence, a web browser cookie is a small file created by a website that is stored in the user's computer. Cookies provided a way for brands to recognize you, keep track of your preferences, and retarget ads to you. Google and other platforms are eliminating support for third-party cookies, but that's OK—1:1 marketers can still use first-party data and cookies to enable their campaigns to reach the right prospects at the right place and at the right time.

Cost-per-acquisition (CPA). Also known as cost-per-conversion, this is the amount a marketer will spend on a campaign to convert one customer. If a brand spends $500,000 on an online display (banner) ad campaign and they gain 20,000 new customers as a result of the campaign, then the CPA is $25 ($500,000/20,000).

Cost-per-click (CPC). The amount a marketer is spending to generate one click on an ad. If you spend $250,000 on an ad campaign and 100,000 people click on your ad, your CPC is $2.50 ($250,000/100,000).

Cost-per-lead (CPL). The amount a marketer is paying for one lead from an ad campaign. If you're spending $500,000 on an ad campaign and you generate 10,000 leads, your CPL is $50 ($500,000/10,000).

Cost-per-thousand (CPM). The amount a marketer is paying for 1,000 impressions of an ad. As an example, if you're spending $1,000 to run an online display campaign and 400,000 people see your ad, then your CPM is $2.50 ([$1,000/400,000] × 1,000). (Do you know why they use M in CPM? Because the Roman numeral M equals 1,000.)

Cross-channel marketing. This is when you reach the same customer on different marketing channels with a single campaign. As an example, say Michael sees a sponsored post on Instagram letting him know about a new tennis racket. The next day, he sees an ad on TV for the same tennis racket. The day after that, he sees a banner ad for the tennis racket and decides to click through to the website where he makes the purchase. That's cross-channel marketing in a nutshell.

Customer data platform (CDP). It's like a big computer that collects your customer data, cleans it up, and then makes it available for you to use in CRM, email marketing, SMS messaging, direct mail, and other channels, as shown in Figure 8.3. The benefits of a CDP include improved marketing ROI, simplified customer data, real-time web personalization, and data mining for consumer insights. A CDP is different from a data management platform (DMP) in that a CDP uses your customer data only. DMPs use a different set of data (a full definition of DMP follows in this section).

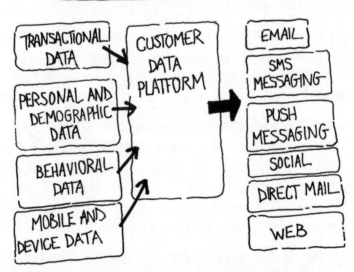

Figure 8.3 A customer data platform cleans and organizes data and keeps it in a central depository so you can use it for email, SMS, push, direct mail, and other forms of marketing.

Customer ID. If you have a database of 100,000 customers, you need a way to identify them. A CDP, CRM, and other customer management systems organize your database and then assign a customer ID to each individual. That way, you don't know the individual's specific name. Instead, you just have a customer ID, which helps protect the individual's privacy.

Data hygiene. Also known as data cleansing, it is the process of cleaning up the data you have and making sure it complies with US Postal system standards. Duplicate records are merged, data elements standardized, and other data inconsistencies are resolved for maximum accuracy and performance.

Data management platform (DMP). Essentially, it's a data warehouse that contains information about people you might want to target in your campaign. A DMP has information on people's demographics, household income, past browsing behavior, purchasing information, location, device, and so on. Advertisers use DMPs to help target prospects and customers across a variety of different channels.

DMPs and CDPs are similar but different. Take a look at the following differences.

A DMP:

- Uses third-party data
- Uses anonymized data from cookies, IDFAs, and so on
- Can create look-alike audiences for use by marketers
- Lets you segment customers based on demographic and behavioral information

A CDP:

- Uses your first-party data
- Uses personally identifiable customer information such as full name, email address, customer ID, and so on.
- Cannot create a look-alike audience without using a DMP
- Allows a 360-degree customer view using all the information about a customer

Daypart. Traditional radio and TV networks divide up time segments for scheduling purposes. These segments include prime time, daytime, late night, early morning, and total day.

Demand side platform (DSP). A platform used by marketers to buy online display, search, and video ads from a marketplace on which publishers (websites) list advertising inventory (i.e., space for banner ads), depicted in Figure 8.4. As an example, a DSP analyzes a web visitor's demographics, interests, and behaviors and compares that information to a group of advertisers' bids for those prospects. After that, the DSP makes a real-time decision on who gets to purchase that ad placement. Together with supply side platforms (SSP), DSPs enable programmatic advertising.

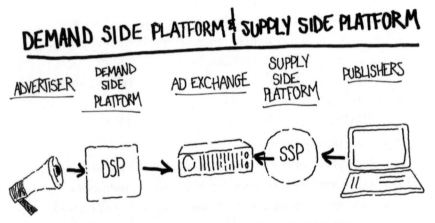

Figure 8.4 Demand side platforms work together with supply side platforms to enable programmatic advertising.

Display advertising. Also known as a banner ad. You see them all the time—and you ignore most of them. Despite that, they're an effective tool for marketers because they have a lowish CPM and enough of their prospects click through on the ads to justify their expense.

Dynamic keyword insertion (DKI). A feature in Google AdWords that allows marketers to customize ads based on keyword searches. If a person types in a keyword and that keyword is included as part of your Google paid search campaign, Google inserts that keyword into the text of your ad.

So imagine a person types "Best Restaurants in Atlanta" in a Google search. If a restaurant is using DKI, then the restaurant's paid search ad might read, "Are you looking for the best restaurants in Atlanta?" Boom, you've got an ad that exactly matches your customer's search term.

Frequency. The number of times an ad is seen by a prospect or customer. Roughly speaking, an ad performs best when it is seen more than 3 times but fewer than 15 times by your prospect. Once your prospect sees an ad about 15 times, they reach ad fatigue, which was discussed earlier.

Google Analytics (GA). Google's platform that tracks and measures various metrics on a website. You want to be sure you have GA tracking code installed on your site so you can follow visitors' behavior when they're visiting your site.

Hypertargeting. This can be as simple as cookie-based retargeting (which has been phased out by most web browsers), or as complex as using first-party customer data, past purchase data, location data, demographics, behavioral data, and other data to hypertarget ads to specific groups of prospects or customers.

Identity resolution. OK, say you have a ton of data at your disposal. You have existing customer data, you have old customer data, and you've also collected some data from third-party vendors. Now that you have this massive wall of data, you want to clean it up and create a single set of data that you can use for your 1:1 campaign. Identity resolution helps you do that in a way that's ethical and respects the privacy of the individuals in your database.

Impressions. This term is related to frequency mentioned earlier. One impression is an ad seen by a potential customer.

Key performance indicator (KPI). Technically speaking, it's a measurable value determined by a company to indicate how well that company's efforts are performing. Want that in plain English? Here it is—a KPI is a metric you use to see if what you're doing is working.

Landing page. A web page designed to get a prospect or customer to take action. In other words, it's the destination for people who have clicked on your paid search ad, your online display ad, your paid social media ad, or just about any other campaign you're running.

Look-alike audience. When you're running an ad campaign on some platforms, you can upload your existing customer data into their platform. Once you've uploaded your data, the platform finds other profiles that match the profiles of the ones you uploaded. Essentially, you're saying, "People love our tennis rackets! I'm going to upload my customer database into Facebook so Facebook can find me more tennis players. That's a win/win all the way around, right?"

Marketing automation. Basically, marketing automation is email marketing on steroids. With marketing automation tools like GetResponse, Mailchimp, and HubSpot, you can segment your subscriber base, personalize your messages, and track the subscriber's engagement with your campaign. Cool stuff.

Media mix. The different media that you use to run your campaigns. As an example, say you're using paid search, online display, addressable TV, and radio for your campaign. That's your media mix. (Not all that complex, right?)

Net reach. The number of individual people that your ad reaches at least one time.

Online display ad network. Say you want to advertise to people who are interested in buying golf clubs. There are 100,000 websites that might be a match for you. So you can either reach out to all 100,000 websites to run your ads, or you can contact an online display ad network and have them do the work for you. (Hint: Save yourself the time. Contact an online display ad network or your ad agency and let them do the work for you.)

Over-the-top video (OTT). You know how your kids don't watch TV anymore? Instead, they bypass cable channels and get their content via Hulu, Apple TV, YouTube, Roku, or some other service. That's called "going over the top," and it's basically the way a growing percentage of the population watches content nowadays.

Page speed. The amount of time it takes for the content on your web page to load into a desktop, tablet, or mobile browser. There are a lot of great page speed tools out there. Visit tools.pingdom.com to test how fast a specific web page loads on a typical browser or speed.cloudflare.com to measure the speed of your computer's connection to the internet. Both are pretty nifty tools.

Paid search. OK, so you've gone into Bing or Google and conducted a search for "life insurance." At the top of the search results, you see a bunch of ads. Those are paid search ads, and they're placed above the organic search results for the same search term. In most cases, a brand doesn't get charged for a paid search ad until a prospect clicks on the ad. (Before you go out and start clicking on your competitor's ads as a way to deplete their marketing budget, remember—that's called click fraud and Google and Bing don't like that kind of stuff. Neither does the FBI.)

Pay-per-click advertising (PPC). Ads that are paid for on a per-click basis. In other words, you don't pay for the ad until someone clicks on it.

Pixel. A small piece of software code that's used to track conversions or form fills on your website.

Programmatic advertising. This concept sounds complex but it's really not all that difficult to understand. Imagine three boxes. The box on the left is your brand. The box on the right is your prospect. The middle box (i.e., a programmatic advertising platform) is a computer that auctions off banner ads to you and your competitors so you can show your banner ad to the right prospects. In other words, programmatic is just a way to connect the dots between your prospective customer and your brand. (Side note: Programmatic can actually get a little more complex than that, but if you just want to understand the key concept . . . boom, you're done.)

Quality score. Used by Google, Yahoo, and Bing to measure the quality of your ads. None of those companies want bad ads shown to their audiences, so they track your ad's CTR, your website load times, the copy on your landing pages, and other metrics to give you a quality score. You want your quality score to be as high as possible.

Reach. The percentage of your total target audience that is exposed to an ad at least once during your campaign.

Remarketing. This is often confused with retargeting, but it's actually something different. Say you have an e-commerce site that sells jewelry. One of your previous customers visits your site and plans on buying a new necklace. That customer selects a necklace and gets to your checkout page. But before they buy the necklace, they get distracted and never make the purchase. If that happens, since you have that customer's email address (from a previous purchase), you have an opportunity to remarket to them by sending them a reminder email to finish their checkout process. There are a lot of other forms of remarketing, but that's it in a nutshell.

Retargeting. When ads for your product or service are shown to prospects who have visited your website in the past, that's retargeting. It's no more complex than that.

Return on ad spend (ROAS). A metric that measures the amount of incremental revenue your business earns for each dollar it spends on advertising.

Return on marketing spend (ROMS). It's pretty much the same thing as ROAS mentioned previously, except that it's the amount of incremental revenue your business earns for each dollar it spends on marketing (not just advertising).

Return on investment (ROI). A metric that measures the amount of *profit* (not revenue) generated by an ad campaign relative to the cost of those ads. ROI is important because you can go out of business if you just use ROAS or ROMS, which uses only the incremental revenue in the calculation. Here's what we mean—if you spend $100 in advertising to generate $200 in gross revenue, you might think that you're doing a great job. But if it costs you $125 to manufacture the product and you spent $100 in advertising to sell the product, then your costs to make the product and run the ad amount to $225 ($125 in manufacturing costs + $100 in ad costs = $225). So you actually lost $25 when you sold the product for $200. ROI uses *profit* in the calculation rather than *gross revenue*, so it's a much more accurate way to measure whether or not your campaigns are contributing to the bottom line. (ROI is discussed in depth in Chapter 18. It's a great chapter, if we don't mind saying so ourselves, so don't miss it.)

Search engine optimization (SEO). Google and Bing each use over 200 different metrics in their algorithm to decide how to rank your site. When you use *white hat* tools and techniques to get your site to rank well, that's called SEO. (Don't use black hat techniques to try to increase your rankings because you'll never outsmart Google and Bing. Instead, just create content that engages your reader and keeps them coming back for more.)

Supply side platform (SSP). It's the publisher equivalent of a demand side platform (DSP). Where DSPs are used by marketers to buy ad impressions from exchanges as cheaply and as efficiently as possible, SSPs are designed by publishers to maximize the prices their impressions sell at.

Variable. Say you're running a banner ad with a blue "Buy Now" button. You want to test whether or not a red "Buy Now" button will give you a better conversion rate. That's your variable—the green/red button. Capisce?

· · · · · · · · · ·

So there you have it. A bunch of terms you'll be using with some regularity on your journey to become a 1:1 marketing expert. That wasn't so painful, was it?

But wait, there's more!

The very first definition about A/B split testing mentioned that marketing metrics expert Guy Powell was going to explain what RCT is. It's an advanced concept, so buckle your seatbelts and turn it over to Guy.

Guy, over to you.

· ·

OPTIMIZING A 1:1 CAMPAIGN WITH
A RANDOMIZED CONTROLLED TRIAL
by Guy Powell

For most marketers, a simple A/B split test is the go-to methodology for learning whether or not version A of an ad outperforms version B. But there are new analytic methods that use machine learning to help marketers improve upon the typical A/B split test. Randomized controlled trial (RCT) is one of the advances that help marketers improve their 1:1 campaigns to generate more revenue at a lower cost.

RCT, which is often referred to as *experimental design on steroids*, uses machine learning to analyze past marketing activities to learn where improvements can be made. In a recent study by the Kellogg School of Management at Northwestern University and Facebook, researchers analyzed true advertising lift as judged by RCTs compared to the lift calculated by using more common testing strategies.

"The degree of variation was stunning," said Florian Zettelmeyer, a marketing professor at the Kellogg School.[2] According to Zettelmeyer, the more common testing methods dramatically inflated the true incremental lift. In one case, lift was reported at 416 percent, while the RCT proved it was actually closer to 77 percent.

The differences between RCT and traditional testing methods allow marketers to connect the incremental impact of each marketing activity and sequence. RCT analyzes campaigns from complex environments to determine the most effective mix and sequence of activities to improve results. Response can include conversion to sales, web visits, unsubscribes, retention, or upsell/cross-sell.

Data requirements for RCT include marketing activities such as emails sent, direct mails sent, social messages delivered, outbound calls made. For response analysis, data can include sales conversions, inbound calls, calls to customer service, retention, upsell/cross-sell, web visits, and many others where the individual making the response is known.

An RCT study that results in a better mix and sequence of marketing activities can be very valuable. For example, a client of ours wanted to improve their overall retention of customers. They used RCT combined with a machine learning approach to improve their retention rates by over 15 percent, leading to an increase in sales of over $20M per year.

. . . .

KEY TAKEAWAYS

Here are some things to keep in mind as you digest and reflect on this chapter.

- **New vocabulary.** 1:1 marketing involves changing your mindset as well as changing your vocabulary so you can understand the new ideas.
- **New concepts.** Many of the concepts used in 1:1 marketing will be new. Others will be familiar to many people. Having a good grasp on both old and news concepts is important as you move forward on your 1:1 journey.
- **Putting it all into action.** It's one thing to understand the concepts. It's another thing to put them into action. So don't just sit there—let's get going!

WHAT'S REQUIRED TO BECOME A 1:1 MARKETER?

In God we trust. All others must bring data.

—ATTRIBUTED TO W. EDWARDS DEMING, STATISTICIAN, PROFESSOR, AND AUTHOR

If you recognize the benefits of transitioning from mass marketing to 1:1 marketing, then the natural question will be what's required to become a 1:1 marketer? After all, 1:1 marketing represents a radically different approach from what you're accustomed to. It's much more than just having a new marketing strategy—it's a fundamental reframing of how you go to market.

The good news is that the transition can and should be a process. It's not like flipping a switch and a day later your team is using 1:1 marketing—especially if your brand has always relied on traditional marketing and media practices.

To be an effective 1:1 marketer, you'll invest in infrastructure, technology, and data, both in the capturing of first-party data (your brand's customer data) as well as incorporating third-party data (data collected by companies who sell the curated data sets to marketers). There will be changes in processes and approaches and a learning curve for your team. Plus, you may discover your team is missing critical expertise that you must recruit new players to fill.

The most important first step is to decide that you're ready to take the leap. Once you've made that commitment, there are three components that will be critical to your success as a 1:1 marketer:

- Customer data
- An identity graph
- The 1:1 marketing plan

1. CUSTOMER DATA: THE FOUNDATION OF 1:1 MARKETING

One of the best examples of using data to engage prospects and customers is Amazon. Did you know that Amazon's market value is larger than the value of Walmart, Target, Macy's, Best Buy, Kohl's, Nordstrom, JC Penney, and Sears combined? As depicted in Figure 9.1, in 2016, Amazon's market capitalization was more than $600 billion larger than these eight venerable retailers combined.

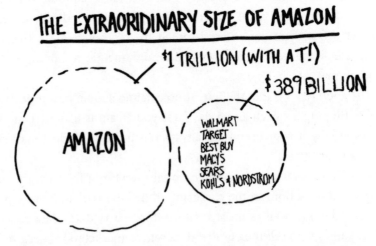

Figure 9.1 The market capitalization for Amazon dwarfs its competitors.

When Amazon crossed the rare threshold of being worth one trillion dollars later that year (only the second company to do so, after Apple crossed the one-trillion-dollar threshold a month earlier), Amazon's market capitalization had grown to two and a half times the size of Walmart. Amazon achieved this feat despite ringing up only one-third of the revenue of Walmart. (Amazon's revenue compared to competitors is displayed in Figure 9.2.)

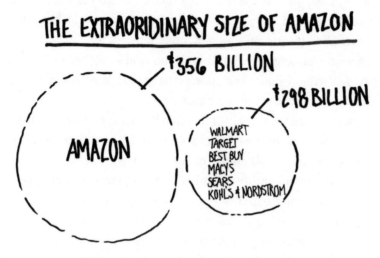

THE EXTRAORIDINARY SIZE OF AMAZON

$356 BILLION

$298 BILLION

AMAZON

WALMART
TARGET
BEST BUY
MACY'S
SEARS
KOHL'S & NORDSTROM

Figure 9.2 The revenue of Amazon is greater than that of six of their competitors combined.

In fact, if you wanted to assemble a group of companies that when combined would equal the one trillion dollars Amazon was worth, you'd have to add in Costco, Lowe's, Kroger, and Big Lots. Then you'd have to add several of their online competitors, including eBay, Overstock, Wayfair, and CDW. And in the entertainment category, you'd have to add Netflix.

And that still wouldn't be enough to equal the value of Amazon. You'd have to add in a company that competes with Amazon Web Services for cloud computing, Oracle, which by the way is a $200 billion company. All of those companies combined were worth about one trillion dollars—the same amount as Amazon alone!

So why is Amazon such a valuable company? If you were to name one thing that has been the secret to Amazon's success, what would it be? Would it be their unparalleled distribution system? Their lower prices? Their willingness to experiment in many categories and try hundreds of categories and ideas to see what works?

Sure, those are all contributors. Clearly Amazon has demonstrated the value created by operating a truly customer-obsessed business model. Let's face it, Amazon delivers a personalized customer experience that continues to set the bar, not just for all retailers, but for all brands—even those that sell to businesses and not consumers.

But what's underlying all of this? Data. And how they use it. The key to Amazon's trillion-dollar valuation is the unparalleled volume of invaluable data they capture about their customers.

Amazon's ability to deliver personalized experiences is driven by the massive amount of data, touchpoints, and interactions Amazon has on their customers. At the heart of this experience lies a cache of first-party data. Amazon captures hundreds or thousands of data points for every single customer based on what the family buys on Amazon, what questions they are asking Alexa, what songs they add to their playlists in Amazon Music, what they watch on their Fire TV stick, what books and magazines they read on their Kindle, the product reviews they post, what they search for on Amazon (even if they don't end up purchasing the product from Amazon), and more.

Can you imagine having this kind of understanding of 300 million customers, including 90 million of your most loyal and profitable customers who are willing to pay an annual fee to unlock additional value from their relationship with you? Imagine how you could customize messages and products with that data. If you're an Amazon shopper, then you know how Amazon effectively personalizes offers and communicates using the treasure trove of data they have about you.

Now you might be thinking that Amazon (along with Facebook, Google, and Apple) are the only companies capable of building this kind of rich data that enables 1:1 marketing and engagement on steroids. Not true.

Every brand can and should build their own treasure trove of first-party data. It is truly the foundation of becoming a 1:1 marketer. The next chapter covers how to do that and how you'll want to enrich your first-party data with second- and third-party data.

2. AN IDENTITY GRAPH: THE PIPING THAT MAKES 1:1 MARKETING POSSIBLE

The second thing you'll need to be a successful 1:1 marketer is an identity graph, along the lines of the graphic shown in Figure 9.3. Mastering identity is your key to the personalized, relevant engagement that builds your brand and drives relationships with your audiences of one at scale. And believe it or not, you can use many of the same techniques to build what Amazon has built as the ultimate identity graph.

Figure 9.3 The identity graph links data from a variety of sources to create a profile of your prospect or customer.

Simply put, an identity graph creates the linkages between your customers, their personally identifiable information (known as PII in the industry) and their various anonymous digital identifiers, including mobile ad IDs (MAIDs), internet protocol address (IP address), and other information.

You may sometimes hear the term device graph, which is similar but not the same. Typical device graphs are simply groupings of device IDs associated with anonymous persons instead of PII, so they lack the addressability and the tie to purchase and other data.

When you can connect the dots between your brand and your customers—who they are, how they think, where they go, what they buy, and how to reach them—you can effectively accomplish 1:1 marketing. Think of an identity graph as the "connective tissue" between your customers, what you know about them, what others know about them, and the devices where they can be reached.

With all of this info captured in a single database you own, you can target customized messages to your customers, combining a nearly unlimited wealth of information. What's more, you can reach them anywhere and everywhere—their mobile phones, tablets, desktop computers, laptop computers, connected televisions, and more.

IN A NUTSHELL

An identity graph is a way to combine data about your prospects and customers with the device identifiers where they can be reached into a single, tangible piece of information that can then be used to launch and deploy campaigns.

---

3. THE 1:1 MARKETING PLAN: THE STRATEGY AND TACTICS THAT BRING 1:1 MARKETING TO LIFE

So far, we've discussed two out of three things you'll need to be a 1:1 marketer—data and an identity graph. The third item is a 1:1 marketing plan.

You've no doubt heard the timeless adage: if you fail to plan, you plan to fail. That couldn't be truer than with 1:1 marketing. Even if you succeed in amassing a treasure trove of customer data and build a complete identity graph, you still won't be a 1:1 marketer. That won't happen until you revisit how you've marketed in the past and create a plan to transition to the completely new approach of 1:1 marketing.

An upcoming chapter will cover the components of a 1:1 marketing plan in detail. But as you are considering how you amass your first-party data and create an identity graph, you also want to begin thinking about how to leverage those assets to begin marketing to your audience of one. If you think of it as a transformation versus flipping a switch, you'll begin identifying easy wins: things you are already doing that could be made more effective by applying 1:1 marketing techniques.

That's the starting point. Then you can consider new ways of creating dialogues with customers in ways you've never been able to do before. These strategies and tactics require more building, training, and execution than the easy wins.

Throughout the entire transition, you also want to plan for how you will measure the effectiveness of your newly implemented 1:1 marketing efforts and make sure the right data is being captured. Of course, you also have to plan for the data that will be analyzed and reported to the team and your management and how you can use it to help justify the effort and resources involved and to identify progress achieved, as well as areas needing improvement.

What you might gather from this is that becoming a 1:1 marketer is a new path forward, not a project with a defined start and stop. Once you begin to employ 1:1 marketing techniques, you will never stop. In fact, you'll look to continuously improve upon your efforts.

You'll be learning far more from your dialogues with your audience of one than you ever learned from a mass marketing media plan recap. And these learnings will feed and foster new ways you can build the value of your audiences of one by improving the value they are receiving from your relationship together. Think of 1:1 marketing as a virtuous cycle versus a new approach to your marketing plan for the year. With each successive year, you'll find new ways to put your 1:1 marketing efforts on steroids and grow your brand loyalty, frequency, and lifetime customer value.

KEY TAKEAWAYS

Here are some things to keep in mind as you reflect on the concepts in this chapter.

- **What's needed.** There are three things you need to be a 1:1 marketer: customer data, an identity graph, and a 1:1 marketing plan.
- **Data is king.** Data is at the heart of Amazon's success. They understand what their customers buy, what questions they are asking Alexa, what songs they add to their playlists in Amazon Music, what they watch on their Fire TV stick, what books and magazines they read on their Kindle, the product reviews they post, and what they search for on Amazon (even if they don't end up purchasing the product from Amazon).
- **Identity graph.** An identity graph takes first-party data about your customers and combines it with third-party data to create a robust profile of the people who buy your products or services. It differs from an anonymous device graph because it provides insights about people, not just the devices they use.
- **Ongoing process.** Becoming a 1:1 marketer is an ongoing process. Don't expect to flip a switch and suddenly have an entire department, organization, or company become a 1:1 entity. Instead, prepare yourself for an evolution rather than a revolution. It takes time. And the journey never really ends because you'll be in a constant state of learning.

PART

4

PUTTING IT ALL TO WORK

YOU'RE ROUNDING THE BEND!
1:1 OVERVIEW
DIGGING DEEPER
STRATEGIC THINKING
PUTTING IT ALL TO WORK
ADVANCED TECHNIQES

BUILDING AND IMPLEMENTING A MARKETING STRATEGY AROUND YOUR AUDIENCE OF ONE

The 1:1 future will be characterized by customized production,
individually addressable media, and 1:1 marketing,
totally changing the rules of business competition and growth.
Instead of market share, the goal of most business competition
will be share of customer—one customer at a time.
—DON PEPPERS AND MARTHA ROGERS, AUTHORS OF *THE ONE TO ONE FUTURE*

The previous chapter discussed the three things you need to be a 1:1 marketer—data, an identity graph, and a 1:1 marketing plan. This chapter focuses on the 1:1 marketing plan. Later chapters circle back and take a deeper dive into data and the identity graph, but for now, let's talk about how you would go about developing a marketing plan that leverages the 1:1 techniques discussed so far.

As touched on throughout this book, implementing 1:1 marketing doesn't mean you're going to stop what you've been doing and shift gears completely. In fact, the first thing we'd suggest is to keep doing what you're doing while you plot a parallel path for your new 1:1 marketing strategy. Then when you're ready to shift to the 1:1 strategy, you can evolve from your mass marketing approach to the 1:1 approach.

So let's get down to brass tacks and explore in detail how to launch your 1:1 marketing strategy. You return to the familiar framework of Who, What, Where, When, and Why, but shake up the order a bit because you can't really answer the Who of your strategy until you've identified the Why behind it. At the same time, you can't really answer the Why without answering Who. They are like two sides of the same coin: the success of your campaign will depend on who you're targeting, and who you're targeting will drive what you might achieve with the campaign. In other words, if you answer the Why, you'll also answer the Who.

We recommend focusing on a single 1:1 campaign first before you launch into doing multiple campaigns. By starting small, you can learn from your mistakes and make adjustments before moving forward with larger, more complex campaigns.

ANSWERING THE WHY AND WHO

What Do You Want to Accomplish with Your First Foray into 1:1 Marketing?

Most marketers think the easiest way to grow revenues is to focus on acquiring new customers. Actually, the opposite is true—it's easier to grow revenues by getting existing customers to buy again than it is to get a new customer to buy from you the first time. And that's perfect for a 1:1 marketer because the foundation behind your 1:1 campaign is the first-party data you have on your existing customers. So focus on getting existing customers to buy again and use your first-party data (e.g., first and last name, address, email address, spending patterns, etc.) to create a campaign that matches what those customers need.

Chapter 4 talked about the five essential levers you can use to get customers to spend more with you so you can increase customer lifetime value:

1. Get customers to purchase more frequently
2. Get customers to spend more when they do purchase
3. Get customers to remain customers for a longer period of time
4. Get a customer to refer friends
5. Get a customer who has lapsed to come back again

You'll begin your 1:1 strategy by deciding which of these levers you want to pull. And no, unlike dessert, you don't have to choose just one. It's often possible to move multiple levers in a single campaign.

For example, a restaurant chain might implement a strategy to reach past customers who've not visited one of their restaurants in more than 90 days. For some restaurants, like a quick-service restaurant (QSR) whose average customer visits 10 times annually, a customer who hasn't visited in 90 days would qualify as a lapsed customer. But for other restaurants, especially more expensive fine-dining establishments, one visit per quarter could qualify as one of your most loyal customers.

And the offer you present could not only get them to return but get them to spend more than they typically do. For example, in the case of the preceding QSR, perhaps the return promotion offers a compelling 30 percent off their purchase but requires a minimum purchase of $25. If the average purchase is $10, then they would have to spend more to qualify for the discount, which means they would probably bring their friends or family. In the end, for every customer you convince to purchase with the promotion mentioned previously, you'll be (1) getting a lapsed customer to return, (2) getting that customer to spend more when they do, and (3) potentially increasing their overall frequency. That's three of the five levers you've pulled with a single promotion.

That's the first step: identify who and why you are running the campaign. To assist you in this process, here's a simple planning worksheet (see Figure 10.1) to help get a snapshot of your overall campaign.

The 1:1 Campaign Planning Worksheet

WHO You Are Targeting

WHAT Approach You Use to Build Your Message

WHERE You Reach and Engage with Prospects and Customers

WHEN Your Message Is Delivered

WHY You Are Messaging a Prospect

HOW You Measure Campaign Success

©2021 Jamie Turner & Chuck Moxley   Audience of One

Figure 10.1 The 1:1 Campaign Planning Worksheet is a simple document that helps you take a 30,000-foot view of your overall campaign approach.

Start by filling in the two blanks on the worksheet that correspond to the Who and the Why; for example, the following uses the QSR example:

WHO You Are Targeting: Customers who haven't visited the restaurant in more than 90 days. (Use our CRM data to find customers whose last visit was more than 90 days ago.)

WHY You Are Messaging a Prospect: To get our existing restaurant customers to come back again.

Identifying the Who also means you have to start considering realities that will ultimately impact other aspects, such as What and Where. In the QSR example, if you've decided you want to try to get customers who've not been in one of your restaurants in the past 90 days, you also must determine who those people are. Where's the data residing that would tell you who has lapsed?

If your business is similar to a QSR restaurant in how purchase transactions occur, then you may have to start with a subset of customers from whom you have collected PII and thus can target in a 1:1 campaign. For example, QSRs often create loyalty programs that reward customers for every visit. This means a customer must provide PII when joining the program and must identify themselves on each visit to accumulate points that result in rewards, such as discounts or free food.

IN A NUTSHELL

An initial challenge to overcome is to determine the data you will use for targeting and tracking down where the data resides and who has control over it. Many organizations will not have complete purchase data for every customer, so they may have to begin with a subset of customers on whom you've collected personally identifiable information (PII). Oftentimes, this is done through loyalty programs or some other means.

Not every customer participates in a loyalty program, but the QSR marketing team can still develop 1:1 marketing campaigns targeting the percentage of customers who do. And since loyalty members identify themselves at the cash register with each visit, the QSR will know how much the customer has spent since being in the program, when they were last in, and how much on average they spend per visit. That's the essential data they need for launching the lapsed customer campaign.

There are ways a brand can obtain information on and target past customers without having customer data collected by the brand, also known as first-party data, and the later chapter on data discusses those and other strategies. Once you've determined what you want to accomplish and who that's going to impact, you have to determine what data you have or need to acquire to implement the campaign. There's an area on the planning worksheet to note those details (or questions). Identify your data sources and locations earlier in the process since some effort may be required to track down the PII you have on customers, where that data resides (internally or externally), who has control over that data internally, and how you will gain access to that data to implement the campaign.

Now you're ready to tackle the next two questions.

ANSWERING THE WHAT AND WHERE

What's the Message and Method of Reaching Your Target Audience, and Where Will You Reach Them?

With the campaign goal and target audience defined, you are ready to determine *what* message and format you will use when targeting your audience, and *where* you will find your target audience. Once again, these two questions are combined into a single set, because they are highly dependent on each other. When you consider What your message is, you'll find the Where is often answered.

To continue with the same QSR example, the goal of the campaign is to get lapsed customers to return. Now you have to decide what offer and message you want to use when targeting them. The content of the message, such as the specific promotion, is the easy part of the equation. Your goals for the campaign naturally drive what offer and message you have to deliver to accomplish that goal.

Since the customer hasn't been in one of your restaurants in the past 90 days, you have to create an offer so compelling it convinces them to return. In most cases, you won't know why customers lapse. Some may have had a bad experience, although hopefully that's a minority. For a category with relatively frequent purchases of low dollar amounts, such as QSRs, a common reason is because the customer simply didn't think of your restaurant the last few times they chose to eat out. They may have seen more ads from competitors or received compelling discount offers that caused them to choose other establishments for those dining occasions.

You can employ a similar tactic to win them back, by presenting a compelling, high-value offer. If you've been advertising regularly and include promotional offers in your ads, it's likely they saw them, but there was something about your competitor's offer that caused them to go there instead. Using an offer that's better than your typical offer might be enough to entice the customer to come back in.

But that's where the message and offer, the What, naturally leads to Where you are going to distribute those messages and offers. Since it's an especially generous offer, you won't want to distribute it via the mass marketing channels you typically use, such as television or freestanding inserts (FSIs) in newspapers. If you do, you'll be giving the generous offer intended only for the lapsed customer to frequent customers who would have visited your restaurant anyway.

1:1 marketing is particularly effective when you want to extend an extra-generous discount to lapsed customers to get them back in and thus hypertarget the campaign to reach only the lapsed customers. Assuming you have a way of identifying lapsed customers in your customer data, then you have to consider what channels you have to reach them. A few likely 1:1 marketing channels for such an offer include targeted direct mail, email, or text messaging.

IN A NUTSHELL

You may discover that more channels are available for targeting prospects for a 1:1 marketing campaign than you are accustomed to with typical direct marketing campaigns. Your initial campaign can offer an opportunity to test some of the additional channels to see how they perform relative to channels you typically use.

Of course, in the new world of 1:1 marketing, more options are available to you. For example, you can target your lapsed customers via an addressable media channel that offers 1:1 message targeting, such as mobile in-app display or streaming television ads. That ensures only the lapsed customers are given the discount. And with today's digital consumer, who may no longer get the newspaper or pay attention to direct mail, it gives you a way to engage them on the devices they use often. But you will need an already-produced television commercial to append the offer to.

An offer code redemption could prove to be a challenge on TV, since your prospects won't have a way of saving the offer for later redemption in-store or online. A common practice in television is to show a keyword easy-to-recall code, known as a *vanity offer code*, that viewers note and provide later during the purchase.

Another possibility is targeting lapsed customers via online display ads or social media, such as Facebook, Twitter, LinkedIn, and others. Online advertising has some limitations due to the technology used to target ads, which is discussed in a later chapter on digital identity, so be aware the precision of the targeting may not be perfect. This means that some people who are not lapsed customers could receive the offer in error. So, it's similar to the problems with mobile display and connected television, which is that the offer code redemption could prove to be a challenge without providing a mechanism for the user to save the offer for later redemption.

Budget may also influence which channels you can use for this campaign. Determining the acceptable budget is a factor of how many prospects you are targeting and the potential value that getting each customer back represents to your business. While connected television is more expensive than broadcast television on a cost-per-thousand (CPM) basis, it's usually far cheaper than the CPM of direct mail. FSIs fall in between the two. And email and text messaging are typically the cheapest of all.

After considering all of the factors, you should have your message/offer defined and the channels you will use defined. So now add them to the worksheet:

WHAT Approach You Use to Build Your Message: We'll offer a 40 percent discount on purchases of $30 or more.

WHERE You Reach and Engage with Prospects and Customers: We'll use text messaging and email.

Just two factors remain in planning your first campaign: *When* the campaign will run and *How* you'll measure success. Let's tackle the How first, since it is closely linked to the topic just covered, the campaign budget.

HOW TO MEASURE THE SUCCESS OF YOUR 1:1 MARKETING CAMPAIGN

Measuring campaign success is where 1:1 marketing shines, since you can use the same precise 1:1 data you use for targeting to link to the purchase transaction. Remember that for the QSR campaign in this example, you're targeting lapsed customers. And you determined that to identify lapsed customers, you'll have to use the loyalty data you've collected from members of the loyalty club.

To measure campaign success, simply tap into the same data. The simplest measurement will be to use your loyalty and purchase data during the promotional period for the loyalty members being targeted.

People who purchase during the promotion would represent successful conversions, and the total amount of revenue from these customers is the attributable revenue. Dividing the revenue by the cost of the campaign enables you to calculate the return on ad spend (ROAS) from the campaign. (Be sure to check out Chapter 18 on marketing math, which takes a deep dive into the specifics of how to calculate the ROI of a 1:1 campaign.)

Some marketers, though, will note that some of those customers may have possibly returned without receiving the offer; their purchase during the promotional period could have been coincidence. One solution would be to isolate the results to just those customers who redeemed the specific offer code. That would likely filter out customers returning who weren't exposed to the offer but may not be perfect. Errors can be introduced by cashiers who key in the offer without the customer presenting the offer code or customers who returned but fail to mention the offer.

Marketers determined to measure the campaign as precisely as possible can also use proven methodology common in 1:1 marketing: test and control. You will know which consumers were potentially exposed to the offer, based on the direct mail or email list. With digital media and connected television, media providers track each impression served. In other words, you can zero in on who received the ad and then make your calculations based on that information.

You can use a measurement service like Acxiom, NCSolutions, Catalina, Experian, or others that will intercept the impression data and connect it back to your customer data to identify which of your customers were targeted. The same measurement company can take the purchase data derived from your loyalty data and match to the exposure data. They will also calculate the sales from an identical or hold out group who didn't receive the ad. The delta between these two groups allows the measurement provider to measure *incremental* sales lift. In other words, how much *more* did the customers exposed to the offer purchase versus customers who weren't exposed to the offer during the promotional period?

Regardless of the method used to measure campaign success, the key takeaway is that 1:1 marketing gives you far greater ability to measure campaign success than mass marketing methods. Therefore, before you embark on the campaign, you should determine how you intend to measure success. It's especially important if you plan to employ an outside measurement firm, since the campaign must be set up ahead of time to ensure the proper methodology is used to create a control group.

Now add the measurement plan to your worksheet.

> **HOW You Measure Campaign Success:** We'll track our progress by measuring (1) the number of lapsed guests redeeming the offer, (2) the revenue from those transactions, and (3) the cost of the redemptions and the media.

DETERMINING WHEN THE CAMPAIGN WILL RUN

The final *W*, When, is generally a factor of answering all of the other *W*s. Once you know Who you are targeting and have identified the targeting data you will use, created the What you plan to message and the offer, identified the channels you will use to find prospects Where they are, and finalized How you will measure success, you're ready to start the campaign.

Then it's simply a matter of completing the creative development and production, and securing media availability before the campaign begins. The budget generally dictates how long the campaign runs, although competing offers and promotions may also be a factor as well as seasonality and holidays.

Note the campaign timing to complete your worksheet.

> **WHEN Your Message Is Delivered:** Our promotion period will be October 1 through 31. We'll run flights on 10/1, 10/5, 10/12, 10/18, 10/22, 10/28, 10/30, and 10/31.

Now you're ready to embark on your first 1:1 campaign. As noted earlier, working through this process will prepare you for your next campaign and the evolution from mass marketing to 1:1 marketing.

KEY TAKEAWAYS

Here are some things to keep in mind as you reflect on the concepts in this chapter.

- **Start small.** To put 1:1 marketing into practice, begin with a single campaign. Doing so will keep challenges manageable while still allowing the team to work through all of the details that 1:1 marketers have to consider, whether tackling a single campaign or transitioning their entire marketing operation to 1:1 marketing.
- **Follow the framework.** Following the same Who, What, Where, When, Why, and How framework to plan your first campaign.
- **Ask Why and Who.** Answering the Why will also lead you to the Who: the goals of the campaign dictate who you will be targeting, whether new prospects or existing customers.
- **Define What and Where.** Determining the What and Where are also closely linked. Once you know the message and offer, the methods you will use to reach your target audience will become self-evident.
- **Figure out How.** Be sure to determine How you will measure campaign success before launching the campaign, since measurement methodology may dictate how the campaign is set up and completed.
- **Answer the When.** Answering the When is a by-product of answering all of the other questions. The choices you make in audience, channels, message, budget, and measurement will provide the parameters to determine when the campaign launches and how long it lasts.

THE TOOLS IN
THE TOOLSHED

Data doesn't equal intelligence and intelligence doesn't equal success.
—DAVID CHARMATZ, FORMER SVP, STARZ ENTERTAINMENT[1]

So far, this book has covered a lot of information, ranging from strategic insights (as they relate to 1:1) to some of the more tactical information. Before talking about tactics, it's important to understand the tools that are in the toolshed. So this chapter provides information about tools you should consider for your next 1:1 campaign. Not every tool available is included, because that would make the book 1,250 pages long. And nobody wants to read a 1,250-page book unless it's a *Harry Potter*, right?

HOW TO MAKE SURE YOU'RE THE SHARPEST TOOL IN THE TOOLBOX

When you think about it, the most important tool of all is your brain, which is made up of your experience, your hard work, and your smarts. But good 1:1 marketers also have a great set of tools at their disposal. With that in mind, we've come up with a list of the tools you should be familiar with. Table 11.1 will help you understand what each one of the tools can do as it relates to Who, What, Where, When, Why, and How.

Table 11.1   Marketing Tools for 1:1 Marketing Campaigns

SOLUTION	WHO	WHAT	WHERE	WHEN	WHY	HOW
6sense	●	●	●	●	●	●
Acxiom	●		●		●	●
AdQuire	●					
Bombora	●			●		
Cadent	●	●	●	●		●
CallRail						●
Constant Contact		●	●	●		
Demandbase	●	●	●	●		●
Drift	●	●	●			
Eloqua	●	●	●	●	●	●
FollowAnalytics		●	●			
GetResponse		●	●	●		
HubSpot	●	●	●	●	●	●
Intercom	●	●	●			
Leanplum		●	●	●		●
LiveRamp	●		●			
Mailchimp		●	●	●		
Marketo	●	●	●	●	●	●
Metadata.io	●	●	●			●
Mobivity	●	●	●	●	●	●
Nimble	●			●	●	●
Outreach.io	●		●	●	●	●
Pardot	●	●	●	●	●	●
Sailthru	●	●	●	●		●
Salesforce	●			●	●	●
SalesLoft	●		●	●	●	●
SundaySky		●				
Terminus	●	●	●	●		●
Vidyard		●				

6sense

6sense is an account based marketing (ABM) platform that helps B2B organizations achieve predictable revenue growth by using artificial intelligence (AI), big data, and machine learning to optimize campaigns. The platform uncovers anonymous buying behavior, prioritizes accounts and sales and marketing, and enables them to engage resistant buying teams with personalized, multichannel, multitouch campaigns. 6sense even has a patented AI model that can tell your sales and marketing teams the best time to engage with an account.

Acxiom

Acxiom enables one-to-one marketing with a simple approach that connects systems and data to drive better customer experiences for individuals and greater return on investment (ROI) for businesses. With Acxiom, you can target consumers and measure results across all channels and devices—not just digital channels. Acxiom can also help you map out the best engagement journeys by knowing and analyzing the channels a customer prefers. They've been a leader in identity, customer data management, and the ethical use of data for more than 50 years, and Acxiom now helps thousands of clients and partners around the globe work together to create millions of better customer experiences, every day.

AdQuire

AdQuire drives new customer acquisitions and improves customer retention by providing brands with scalable, cost-effective solutions to build out their first-party data set by supplementing what the brand knows about their audience. The platform leverages proprietary technology to understand the audience and makes decisions on displaying the ads that have the highest propensity for engagement. It also captures consumer consent and custom personally identifiable information (PII) data, verifies its accuracy, and transmits the data seamlessly to the marketers' CRM for immediate activation. Brands can also be sure that consumers have confirmed 100 percent opt-in consent of and have interest in the brand, and they own that data outright allowing for long-term remarketing to the individual across channels and devices without the inherent challenge of the short life cycle of a cookie.

Bombora

Bombora provides intent data for B2B sales and marketing. Bombora's data helps sales teams base their outreach on the knowledge of which people are actively researching their products and services. In other words, it lets salespeople know exactly who is visiting their website, how interested they are in what they're seeing, and what products and services have caught their eye. Using this information, marketers can drive more qualified leads through the funnel, and sales teams can prioritize the leads based on actual behaviors.

Cadent

The Cadent Advanced TV Platform is a purpose-built platform created for the evolving world of television. Designed to help at every stage of their customers' workflow—identifying targets, finding supply, analyzing campaigns, fine-tuning for the future—it provides clients the tools they need to make the most of media investments.

CallRail

CallRail lets its customers track calls, manage leads, analyze conversations, and track form fills on websites. With CallRail, you'll know which marketing makes your phone ring. You'll also be able to automate your call transcriptions with AI-powered analysis so you can see what's working and what's not working with your campaigns. Whether you're a brand or an ad agency, CallRail can help you track and manage your campaigns and optimize your results.

Demandbase

Demandbase is an ABM platform that helps B2B marketers identify, win, and grow accounts that matter most. Accenture, Adobe, DocuSign, GE, Salesforce, and others rely on Demandbase to drive their ABM strategy and maximize their marketing performance. (Side note: It's worth mentioning that while doing research for this chapter, one of the authors visited the Demandbase website and was greeted by his company name on the Demandbase home page. That's a terrific example of a 1:1 marketing technique at its best.)

Drift

Drift helps companies engage in real-time, personalized conversations with the right customers at the right time so they can build trust and accelerate revenue. Drift uses conversational marketing and conversational sales to help companies grow revenue and increase customer lifetime value faster. More than 50,000 businesses use Drift to align sales and marketing on a single platform to deliver a unified customer experience where people are free to have a conversation with a business at any time, on their terms.

Eloqua

Eloqua is a software as a service (SaaS) platform for marketing automation offered by Oracle that aims to help B2B marketers and organizations manage marketing campaigns and sales lead generation. The platform offers campaign design, advanced lead scoring, real-time firmographic data, and integrated sales tools to help smooth the flow from prospect to customer. Eloqua can deploy campaigns to mobile devices, email, video, and search results pages.

Email Marketing and Marketing Automation Platforms

There are hundreds of email marketing and marketing automation platforms available to a 1:1 marketer. Some of these include very large and very well-known platforms such as Marketo, HubSpot, SAP, and Salesforce. Others include some of the more nimble contenders including Mailchimp, Constant Contact, AWeber, Campaign Monitor, and others. Most of these tools can help you deploy email marketing campaigns, while at the same time are used to score which of the recipients is most engaged with your brand and what they're most interested in. As with most SaaS platforms, there are a lot of additional features that make each tool unique, so be sure to review them thoroughly to see which set of features best matches your needs.

FollowAnalytics

FollowAnalytics is a new generation of app-centric customer engagement. The company's app builder turns websites into sophisticated mobile applications in minutes, with a publishable app ready within weeks. The FollowAnalytics framework automatically detects, adapts, and continuously optimizes to brands' users in real time. The company also lets its customers integrate the mobile app to current ecosystems without writing a single line of code.

HubSpot

HubSpot is a customer relationship management and marketing automation platform that helps sales, marketing, and customer service work together to manage the customer journey and improve your close ratio. The platform includes marketing, sales, service, and website management products that start free and scale to meet their customers' needs at any stage of growth. Today, more than 100,000 customers across more than 120 countries use HubSpot's powerful and easy-to-use tools and integrations to attract, engage, and delight customers. HubSpot was founded in 2006 and is headquartered in Cambridge, Massachusetts. The company's thousands of employees work across the globe in HubSpot offices and remotely.

Intercom

Intercom is a conversational relationship platform (CRP) that helps businesses build better customer relationships through personalized, messenger-based experiences. It's the only platform that delivers conversational experiences across the customer journey, with solutions for conversational marketing, conversational customer engagement, and conversational support. Intercom powers 500 million conversations per month and connects 4 billion unique end users worldwide across its more than 30,000 paying customers, including Atlassian, Sotheby's, and New Relic.

LiveRamp

LiveRamp is a leading data connectivity platform powered by core identity capabilities and a sophisticated network. The platform enables companies to better connect, control, and activate data to transform customer experiences and generate more valuable business outcomes. LiveRamp's infrastructure delivers end-to-end addressability for the world's top brands, agencies, and publishers. The company prides itself on delivering privacy-conscious solutions that honor practices of leading associations, including the Digital Advertising Alliance's (DAA's) ICON and AppChoices programs, the Interactive Advertising Bureau (IAB), the Data & Marketing Association (DMA), and the Advertising Research Foundation (ARF).

Leanplum

Leanplum is a leading multichannel customer engagement platform that helps forward-looking brands like Tesco and Zynga meet the real-time needs of their customers. By transforming data into an understanding of users' needs and wants, and optimizing engagement campaigns using multiple communication channels, the platform delivers unified experiences that are timely, tested, and relevant—building customer loyalty that fuels business growth.

Marketo

Marketo, which is now part of Adobe, started out as a marketing automation platform. Now that it's part of the Adobe Experience Cloud, it has been supercharged to help marketers drive growth by personalizing complex buyer journeys and by aligning marketing and sales teams across every channel. Marketo's platform is feature-rich and cloud-native with significant opportunities for integration across Adobe Experience Cloud. Marketo's ecosystem includes over 500 partners and an engaged marketing community with over 65,000 members.

Metadata.io

Metadata.io is an ABM platform that helps its clients identify companies to target and analyzes which companies are a best fit for your products and services. It provides an experimentation platform that lets you conduct A/B split tests so you can optimize campaigns. In the end, if you're looking for a platform that helps you acquire and activate leads, then Metadata.io can help you do that.

Mobivity

Subway, Sonic, Dutch Bros., and 30,000 other food service locations rely on Mobivity's sophisticated messaging platform to get customers to come back more frequently and to spend more while they're there. Mobivity's Unified Guest Engagement Platform comprises Unified Messaging, including text message marketing and SmartReceipt™, Unified Offers, Unified Loyalty, and Unified Insights, enabling brands to know what's working and, more importantly, what's not working. By tying every message to an in-store transaction, Mobivity's platform continuously learns over time to begin personalizing offers and message delivery times for each customer to keep and delight subscribers. (Disclosure: Both authors have worked for Mobivity as either consultant or employee.)

Nimble

Nimble helps its customers find prospects, nurture relationships, and close more deals, all without leaving their inbox. If you're looking for an easy-to-use platform that's somewhat more intuitive than Salesforce, then Nimble is for you. It combines the strengths of traditional CRM, classic contact management, social media, sales intelligence, and marketing automation into one powerful relationship management platform that delivers valuable relationship insights everywhere you work.

Outreach.io

Outreach is a sales engagement platform that helps companies increase productivity and drive smarter, more insightful engagement with their customers. Outreach can use buyer sentiment analysis to help sales leaders and their teams optimize content performance in real time based on buyer signals. It also provides in-the-moment diagnostic and coaching tools so reps can be coached and brought back on pace to accelerate revenue goals.

Pardot

Pardot is now part of the Salesforce family. It's a very robust marketing automation platform that can help you run and manage your target market's journey from prospect to customer. With Pardot, you can deploy campaigns and score leads before turning them over to the sales team. The platform uses AI to help you run and manage campaigns that can generate a positive ROI for your company.

Sailthru

Sailthru helps modern marketers at leading retail and media companies build deeper relationships with their customers. Sailthru personalizes individual customer experiences across digital communication channels—in email, on a brand's website, and in their mobile applications. The company's 1:1 relationships with consumers help drive higher revenue, improve customer lifetime value, and reduce churn. Publishers such as the *Economist, Business Insider,* and *Mashable,* and the world's fastest-growing ecommerce companies, including Rent the Runway, JustFab, and Alex and Ani, use Sailthru to help them succeed.

Salesforce

Salesforce is the world's largest CRM platform. It has every bell and whistle you might imagine, which can make it cumbersome for small- to mid-sized organizations to use. (If you're a small or medium-sized business, check out Nimble, listed previously, which might be better suited for you.) Salesforce focuses on helping its customers' marketing, sales, commerce, service, and IT teams work as one from anywhere, so their customers stay happy everywhere.

SalesLoft

SalesLoft helps B2B sales teams close more deals by integrating with your CRM platform. It turns data into easy, actionable, multichannel steps that help your sales team get to "yes" quicker than they have in the past. SalesLoft positions itself as a copilot for your CRM, so it would work alongside your CRM platform to help personalize email, phone, social, direct mail, and video outreach.

SundaySky

SundaySky helps you deliver video-powered experiences at critical moments along the customer journey that engage, educate, and inspire consumers. The platform is used by companies such as Bank of America, MetLife, Staples, UnitedHealthcare, and others. Companies that use SundaySky can increase revenue, reduce costs, lower churn, and generate higher customer satisfaction.

Terminus

Terminus is an ABM platform that gives marketing and sales teams the data they need to understand who their next best customers are, all of the engagement channels they need to get in front of them, and customizable reporting and attribution so they can prove their impact. Terminus uses an embedded customer data platform (CDP), along with first- and third-party behavioral data to provide insights on purchase intent as well as real-time sales alerts.

Vidyard

Vidyard is a platform that helps organizations record and send videos to reach prospects and connect with customers. The platform goes beyond just video hosting and management. Instead, it allows businesses to connect with viewers through personalized video experiences. Customers can also explore analytical insights about their audiences and turn those insights into action through integrations with top enterprise tools. Global leaders and industry pioneers on the Fortune 500 list and beyond rely on Vidyard to power their video strategies and turn viewers into customers.

THE MOST IMPORTANT THING TO REMEMBER ABOUT TOOLS

This chapter provided a list of more than two dozen tools you might use as part of your 1:1 marketing campaign. There are hundreds—well, actually thousands—of other tools you could use to accomplish what you're looking to do. So be sure to do your homework and zero in on the best tool for your specific use.

Why should you do your own homework and trust your own judgment? Here's why—one of the authors had heard great things about Salesforce and decided to get a subscription. But Salesforce is best used by companies with large sales forces. In addition, it's a data-centric platform, so there are a lot of spreadsheet-ish kinds of charts. Salesforce isn't a good match for smaller companies, so the relationship lasted all of about three weeks (sorry, Salesforce). A much better platform for this user was Nimble. It has a modular, visual, easy-to-use dashboard that is perfectly suited for visual learners and for companies that are smaller than the ones Salesforce caters to.

Does that mean that Nimble is better than Salesforce? Not necessarily. It just means it was better for that particular user. The point is this—do your homework, figure out what's right for you, and trust your own judgment. By doing so, you'll be able to put the best tool to work for your business.

KEY TAKEAWAYS

Here are some things to keep in mind as you reflect upon the concepts in this chapter.

- **Know your tools.** Understanding the tools in the toolshed is an important part of becoming a successful 1:1 marketer. There are thousands of tools available to you. These are just a sampling of some of the tools you might consider.
- **Do your homework.** The key to choosing a tool is to do your own homework and to trust your own judgment. If a tool isn't working for you, it's better to switch gears and get a tool that fits your style rather than to live with a tool that isn't a match.
- **Fewer is better than too many.** The most important thing to remember about tools is that they have to be used if they're going to provide value for your company. It's better to have a handful of tools you use regularly than to have too many tools that you don't use enough.

HOW TO TURN CONSUMER PRIVACY INTO A STRATEGIC BENEFIT FOR YOUR BRAND

In my experience as an ad agency owner, people say
they are a little creeped out by ads that follow them around
the internet. But then they put the "creeped out" aside
because hey—there's a deal on kitchen tiles!

—MIKE TURNER, PARTNER/CREATIVE DIRECTOR, RED LETTER MARKETING

Privacy is a funny thing. Not *ha-ha* funny, but *interesting* funny: what people *say* about privacy and how they *behave* around it are two separate things. For example, how many times have you typed your credit card information into an e-commerce site without checking to find out how they're storing your data? Even if you consider yourself a privacy advocate, the odds are you've given your information up freely to e-commerce stores, social media platforms, mobile apps, and other platforms.

As you'll see in the following section (written by two experts on the subject, Laura Bright, PhD, and Karen Wallach, PhD), there's a lot to unpack on the subject. But here's the key thing to remember: how your brand uses privacy isn't something to shy away from. In fact, a global research study conducted by the 60 Second Marketer and GetResponse[1] found that brands that address privacy up front can use it as a differentiator. In other words, consumers respond positively when a brand says, "We respect your privacy and here are the specific details behind how we're protecting your data." The key is not to be afraid of the topic. Instead, you should lean into it (the way Apple does) and use it as a way to build trust with your prospects and customers by using transparent policies and procedures.

THE PRIVACY PARADOX

Did you know that 6 in 10 US adults said they don't think it is possible to go through daily life without having data collected about them by the government or companies?[2] It's true. And if you do research with a typical consumer, they'll say they're concerned about privacy, but then will divulge sensitive or personal information relatively freely.[3] This behavior is commonly known as the *privacy paradox*, which identifies the disconnect between a person's behavior and their stated attitude toward their own privacy preferences.[4]

For example, many people talked about acting on the #deletefacebook movement after the Facebook-Cambridge Analytica data misuse scandal surfaced in 2018.[5] However, reports indicate that it had little impact on actual usage of the social media platform, and 7 in 10 adults currently use the platform regularly.[6] So while many said they would act on their privacy concerns, few actually took the necessary steps to do so. This behavior is consistent with research that repeatedly shows a clear disconnect between a person's intention to disclose personal information and their actual disclosure behavior with personal information.[7]

Much research has explored the disconnect between how people *feel* about a subject and how they *behave* around it. We believe there are three reasons for this:

1. **There's a low likelihood of a negative outcome.** For example, if a data breach is reported but only 10 percent of customers are impacted, the risk is low that it will affect them personally. As a result, people are reluctant to change their behavior and have a low motivation to do so.
2. **Some information doesn't necessarily need to be private.** For example, many people don't think it's a big deal to share some aspects of their personal information (e.g., birthday, email address, favorite restaurant) versus other more sensitive details (e.g., health concerns, prescriptions, bank account data).
3. **The effort needed to engage in privacy protection.** For example, many people have years of photos and easy access to friends with Facebook. While they may not want Facebook to have all of their information, they realize that "quitting" Facebook (or any other social platform) involves a lot of work on their end.

When consumers think about privacy and negative outcomes from a data breach, they'll often consider good behaviors and not-so-good behaviors as coping mechanisms to help manage their anxieties. For example, these behaviors can range from dramatically increasing their level of privacy protection for an online banking website (i.e., adaptive behavior) to not bothering to update their password when one of their social media profiles gets compromised (i.e., maladaptive behavior). These behaviors are greatly influenced by the relationship the consumer has with the company and the level of effort needed to take action to protect their privacy.[8] As you might imagine, these behaviors evolve regularly as industry practices change and consumers are prompted to update their preferences.

SOCIAL EXCHANGE THEORY

Consumers will often give up their personal data if they believe it will result in more relevant ads and product information delivered to them. The relationship between giving up your data and getting personalized advertising matches research on social exchange theory where there is a "cost-benefit" analysis to determine the risks and rewards.

Social exchange theory suggests that many types of relationships, from business to personal, come with levels of expected reciprocity between what you are giving (i.e., money, data, time) and what you are receiving (i.e., coupons, products, customized communication). Importantly, the expectations will change or evolve over time as the parameters of the relationship change. For example, consumers who are normally open about sharing information on a social media platform might decide to change their behavior based on a scandal about privacy or other violations.[9]

Consumers might also oscillate between the perceived benefits and costs of a given situation. For example, consumers may allow an e-commerce provider to keep their credit card on file if it streamlines future checkouts. But they might also be reluctant to share personal information about their family members (e.g., birth dates, clothing sizes, etc.) on the same website.

PRIVACY AS STRATEGY

As consumers become increasingly sensitive about their personal information and the need for privacy protection increases, brands that can compete on privacy may have an advantage over their competitors. This concept of "privacy as strategy" may be extremely beneficial for a brand. Still, it also comes with a heightened sensitivity to backlash when the trust is misconstrued.

If a firm is outwardly communicating that it is working to help consumer privacy concerns, it is also taking on the higher reward for doing it well and the higher risk for being watched more closely.[10] For example, tech giant Apple is known for its consumer-facing communications committed to privacy rights, even kicking off an ad campaign in 2020 on how its iPhone is designed to protect consumer privacy. This has been helpful for overall Apple branding, but in the process, Apple has taken on risk in the event they fail.

Besides the *high risk, high reward* that comes with a privacy strategy, two other factors influence the ability for this strategy to be successful:

1. **Cross-cultural variations.** European and American customers have notable differences in privacy concerns. While Europeans are more privacy-conscious, Americans overall believe that online behavior being tracked is the "price to pay" for discounted or free products and access to social media platforms.[11] For firms doing business across countries, they will need to understand variances in how people feel about privacy in different countries.
2. **Brand reputation.** When consumers no longer see a brand as trustworthy, they can end the relationship and switch to a competitor. So if you're going to collect data from customers, it's important to protect that data carefully. Otherwise, it could damage your reputation and drive customers to your competitors.

CURRENT STATE OF CONSUMER PRIVACY

Online privacy has been a hot topic since the dawn of the internet in the 1990s—however, recent privacy scandals and security breaches have brought this issue to the forefront of the digital landscape. Today, many successful internet companies have business models predicated on consumer data sharing, which in turn allows them to provide more customized services to their users while monetizing those data sets on the open market. This creates a privacy paradox for consumers where they need to share data to receive personalized and relevant content while also being mindful of how their data is being handled by each company.

Most often, companies layer their data-sharing policies into complicated "terms and conditions" agreements that are rarely read by consumers and constitute what some consider one of the internet's big little lies.[12] As such, consumer privacy protection has become a key legislative topic, resulting in new, nationwide privacy laws in many countries—the United States being a notable exception.

The last several years have seen advances in how consumer privacy is handled online and the protections needed to manage the expansive amounts of data being generated by connected devices, wearables, and social media platforms. Yet despite these advancements, consumers still have little knowledge about the amount and type of data being collected from them on a daily basis. In fact, a recent Pew survey that concluded 74 percent of online consumers don't know that the data being collected about them is used to target advertising messages.[13] To this end, consumers know they are under surveillance to some degree by the companies they engage with online and are growing deeply anxious about how their personal data may be used for future economic gains.

As consumers grow more anxious about their data privacy, they'll need to renegotiate their boundaries with technology companies to ensure that they're getting what they want in exchange for their personal data. To help smooth this boundary turbulence, companies will need to be transparent about their data collection and management practices to bolster consumer confidence and trust.

As an outgrowth of these efforts, the General Data Protection Regulation (GDPR) legislation was put into place in the European Union in May 2018 allowing consumers to revoke their consent to data collection at any time as well as the "right to be forgotten" online. Any company that is operating in the European Union and is in violation of these policies can be fined up to 4 percent of the company's annual revenue. To help manage this new policy, many EU companies have hired data protection officers (DPOs) as additions to their C-suite to provide data management leadership from the top down.

Designating a DPO helps build brand trust with consumers as well as create transparency about data management policies and decisions. Unfortunately, the United States has failed to adopt a nationwide data protection plan for consumers and instead is letting states create their own agendas. For now, roughly one-third of US states have adopted some type of data privacy law with the California Consumer Privacy Act (CPPA), passed in 2018 and put into effect in January 2020, being the most stringent statute. This momentum, while trailing at the global level, is steadily increasing state by state in the United States.

Privacy protection will continue to be a moving target for consumers going into the 2020s. While legislation and new privacy regulations will help to combat privacy issues long term, in the short term consumers need to become more mindful of the terms and conditions that they are agreeing to when signing up for online services as well as the value they're engaging in with brands. In many ways, consumers have become the product as their data streams become more valuable and brands have a stronger desire to connect with them—making the prospect of privacy protection even more important. The onus is not all on the consumer, however, as brands and companies also need to take responsibility for providing transparent and easily understandable terms and conditions that allow consumers to understand what is happening with their data, who has access to it, and how it is being used by both companies and third-party vendors.

CONCLUSIONS AND FUTURE OF CONSUMER PRIVACY

In a recent annual report presentation, Facebook CEO Mark Zuckerberg proclaimed that "the future is private"—if consumers and social media companies want to thrive in this new ecosystem, they must learn to easily communicate with one another about their privacy policies and build trust through proper data management.

Consumers are becoming increasingly aware of the exchanges they are making in the online environment, which is making privacy management a detrimental component of the consumer experience. A recent *AdAge* article predicted that, much like other types of online media, legislation will enforce consumer-friendly, privacy compliant personalization on social media platforms.[14] Moving into an increasingly connected future, it will be necessary for companies to become more transparent about their data use policies as well as third parties who get access to their data. These adaptations on social media along with evolving regulations across the online industry will create an open value exchange with users about how their data will be used and shared.

BEST PRACTICES FOR MOVING FORWARD

Here are the best practices to help firms manage data privacy issues:

1. **Decide as a company how you will be mapping the data.** "Data mapping" includes tracing the flow, analyzing the life cycle, and creating safeguards around how data will be handled now and in the future.

2. **Remember that your brand and the consumer are on the same team.** Brands and consumers don't have to be two opposing forces when it comes to privacy. Companies can benefit from data and still be responsible, respectful corporate citizens.

3. **Know how your brand will handle a breach.** While every safeguard may seem like it is in place, even with the best of intentions, a data breach may occur. Be prepared with a plan for how your company will respond both internally and externally—that is, with consumers and the public at large.

4. **Live the values of transparency.** Talk about ways for brands to be transparent with privacy practices and consumer data management. People can reach a point for improved relationships regarding data management practices and privacy concerns.

5. **Treat it as a relationship.** This is an exchange, but it comes with personal considerations that are more than just currency. Don't be too creepy, and don't be too greedy!

KEY TAKEAWAYS

Here are some things to keep in mind as you reflect on the concepts in this chapter.

- **Mindset versus behavior.** What people say about privacy and how they behave around privacy are two separate things. Some of your prospects and customers will say they're very concerned about privacy but will then act in ways that would normally indicate that they're not actually concerned at all.
- **Give and take.** When a customer gives you their data and information, they're doing so with an expectation that they'll get something in return. With that in mind, be sure to promote the benefits of being a registered customer—discounts, special events, members-only customer service portals, and so on.
- **Lean in to privacy.** Research by the 60 Second Marketer and GetResponse indicates that organizations should embrace privacy rather than shying away from it. While there are risks behind promoting your brand's privacy initiatives (i.e., in the event of a data breach), the benefits outweigh the negatives.

SEVEN TIPS AND BEST PRACTICES FOR IMPLEMENTING 1:1 MARKETING IN YOUR ORGANIZATION

Innovation means replacing the best practices
of today with those of tomorrow.
—PAUL SLOANE, AUTHOR OF 25 BOOKS ON INNOVATION,
LEADERSHIP, AND PROBLEM SOLVING[1]

While the process of implementing 1:1 marketing will never be identical at any two companies, there are some best practices we've learned over the years of helping multiple companies implement 1:1 marketing that can help you successfully navigate the process.

BEST PRACTICE #1: "PERFECTION IS THE ENEMY OF PROGRESS"

That's a quote from Winston Churchill.[2] And it's true for marketers implementing 1:1 marketing. As you navigate the process, you may find yourself in debates about the absolute precision of identity matching or a specific approach to measurement. But if you only implement "perfect" solutions in your 1:1 marketing, you risk never actually implementing 1:1 marketing!

One of the authors once met with a client about applying 1:1 marketing. He explained to a brand's marketing team how they could target their competitor's customers, focusing on those spending $200 monthly and then filter further by excluding their own loyal customers. He then showed them how they could measure the actual incremental sales lift generated by comparing purchases made by people exposed to just mobile ads versus those exposed to just desktop ads versus those exposed to just addressable TV ads, and so on. Amazing stuff, not possible 10 years earlier.

But a 20-minute debate among the marketing team ensued regarding the impossibility of a perfect test. They couldn't hypothesize a single method that would ensure a 100 percent pure and perfect read of results, untainted by errant exposure to other ads or contaminated by other factors. Regrettably, that was a brand who couldn't see the forest for the trees and most likely never benefitted from 1:1 marketing.

Here's a dirty little secret about marketing that no one talks about—there is no such thing as perfect when it comes to marketing. Sure, in concept and at a 10,000-foot level, ideas such as having unique conversations with audiences of one can sound like marketing perfection. But at the ground level, where the execution happens, some level of imperfection is inevitable.

Brands sometimes send direct mail pieces to deceased people. Or they may use the wrong name in a personalized email, like the charity that continually sends letters to "Chuck and Charles Moxley" despite the fact that Chuck Moxley *is* Charles Moxley. Or they might send three of the same direct mail piece to the same person. They may even target you for a product you won't ever buy, like the one that targeted Chuck with direct mail promotions for a high-powered wood chopper for cutting felled trees into firewood. Meanwhile, Chuck is a serial do-it-*for*-me kind of guy who breaks out in hives at Home Depot and has not and is not likely to *ever* chop down a tree!

The point is that when you attempt to achieve an exceptional level of precision in your targeting and do it at scale, some level of inaccuracy must be expected. (It's like that old expression: Good, fast, cheap . . . choose two.) But that's OK. What's possible today with 1:1 marketing is still light-years ahead of how mass-marketed ads were targeted and measured in the past. Don't allow your team to set a bar of perfection that will be so impossible to attain it prevents your organization from implementing 1:1 marketing. Better to get started, and continuously improve precision over time.

BEST PRACTICE #2: "FAST IS FINE, BUT ACCURACY IS EVERYTHING"

The beauty of 1:1 marketing lies in its potential to deliver the right message at precisely the right time to just the right person. But it can get pretty ugly when you deliver the right ad to the wrong person. Or a poorly timed ad to the right person. Hence this best practice derived from a quote from Wyatt Earp.[3]

Sure, 1:1 marketing (or any marketing, for that matter) isn't brain surgery. The cost of an errant ad isn't in the same ballpark as a surgeon making a medical mistake. Nevertheless, you should attempt to make as few mistakes as possible, approaching 1:1 marketing with the same desire for accuracy as a brain surgeon. (As it turns out, errors in neurosurgery are more common than you might realize![4])

This tip and the prior tip about striving for perfection aren't in conflict. Rather, they suggest that the more accurate the data powering your 1:1 marketing, the better results you can expect to achieve. Therefore, while data will never be perfect, you should invest time and resources in cleaning up the data you have and keeping it accurate over time. Doing so will maximize the benefits you achieve from your 1:1 marketing.

When you begin to assemble the data you already have in the various silos in your organization, be sure to invest in data hygiene to normalize your data, which will remove duplication and standardize data elements. The investment in doing so will pay huge dividends when you delight your customers with a highly relevant message at just the right time, and they in turn spend more with your company. Employing bad data could instead infuriate or annoy your customers, making them less likely to spend more money with you. (Chapter 15 covers how to assemble and normalize your data in detail.)

Delighting your customers is not the only way investments in accurate data pay off. After all, the moment you deliver the wrong ad to the smartphone, tablet, desktop, or connected television of the wrong person or household, the value of 1:1 marketing goes out the window. And that will cost you money in wasted impressions.

BEST PRACTICE #3: "SUCCESS IS A JOURNEY, NOT A DESTINATION"

Famed tennis professional Arthur Ashe went on to say, "The doing is often more important than the outcome."[5] As noted several times in the book, you won't simply flip a switch and go from being mass marketers to a 1:1 marketer. Not only is it not possible, it's not how we recommend you approach the process. Rather, we recommend you take Arthur Ashe's advice to heart.

The fundamental mind shift required to go from mass marketing to 1:1 marketing requires an iterative process be followed. You will learn things from each step that will make the next step more effective. Just like learning to ski, the falls will teach you what *not* to do next time. Expect to have a few of those aha moments along your journey to 1:1 marketing.

Expect to *crawl* initially, simply employing more precise targeting based on past-purchase data for a new customer campaign. Then after you've mastered crawling, progress to *walking*. That might mean you've consolidated your customer data from across your organization and appended five other data elements to enable greater personalization of messages.

When you've mastered these steps, learnings throughout the process will prepare you to begin to *run* with your 1:1 marketing efforts. Your prior successes in achieving incremental improvements will give you the confidence to attempt more sophisticated approaches, such as using digital creative optimization to identify the most effective ad among a few dozen possible combinations of headlines, images, and offers, or tracking whether or not the people you targeted in the ad campaign actually went to a bricks-and-mortar store to make the purchase.

Besides learning from each step in the process, taking an iterative approach to your process will also improve your chances of getting started. You won't feel like you must wait until you can achieve perfection (best practice #1), instead realizing that "the journey of a thousand miles begins with one step," to quote Lao Tzu.[6] The last chapter, which gives you an action plan to put everything covered in the book into action, gives you steps in terms of this crawl-walk-run philosophy to implementing 1:1 marketing in your organization.

BEST PRACTICE #4: "WHAT GETS MEASURED GETS MANAGED"

This expression is commonly attributed to Peter Drucker, although the originator and accuracy of the statement has subsequently been debunked and even debated.[7] Your company will invest time and money when transitioning marketing practices from mass marketing to 1:1 marketing. At some point, someone (likely the CEO or CFO) is going to ask whether the investment was worthwhile. You don't want to be in a predicament where you can't answer that question.

Therefore, it's critical you establish measurement frameworks up front and ongoing as you put 1:1 marketing into place. Knowing how you plan to measure impact prior to beginning a campaign, process, or plan will undoubtedly impact how you go about implementing it. And too often, if you fail to plan up front for measurement, you may find yourself in a situation that won't permit results to be measured afterward.

For example, say you've decided to change your approach with television from mass marketing to 1:1 marketing. With mass marketing, you buy based on demographics, the daypart, and the TV program. But with 1:1 marketing, you use connected television to serve ads to just the households likely to buy your product based on past-purchase data. A valuable benefit of 1:1 targeting is the ability to also measure incremental sales lift from a campaign. But to measure incremental sales, you have to be able to compare subsequent purchases from two groups of people: those who were exposed to the advertising during the campaign and an otherwise identical group who weren't exposed to the ad during the campaign.

A common method is to remove a subset of your targeting audience prior to the campaign beginning. This group is the *control* group who won't see the ad because the ad platform doesn't even receive those households in the targeting audience file. At the end of the campaign, you can use impression data to know which households in the targeting file were exposed to the ad. These are called the campaign's *test* group. Now you can compare sales from the test group versus the control group and measure incrementality.

Our recommendation is that you consider measurement in everything you do and think about how you can prove the value of the investment you are making in each tactic. While you don't have to measure *everything*, you should measure enough things in your 1:1 marketing efforts to justify the effort and expense down the road. Doing so will also help you secure additional funding in the future to continue to improve and refine your 1:1 marketing efforts.

BEST PRACTICE #5: "YOU CAN DO ANYTHING AS LONG AS YOU HAVE THE PASSION, THE DRIVE, THE FOCUS, AND THE *SUPPORT*"

The key word in this quote from musician Sabrina Bryan[8] is *support*. If you are tasked with leading your company's efforts in transitioning to 1:1 marketing, you will need buy-in from others along the way. Not only is buy-in from your leadership critical, since they are key to securing the funding and resources you will need, but you'll want to get buy-in from everyone involved in the process.

It's been noted several times in this book that many of the practices behind 1:1 marketing are counterintuitive to people who've spent decades practicing traditional mass marketing. You will make progress faster if you can help people involved understand how and why the paradigm has shifted in the last decade and at minimum obtain tacit agreement. Otherwise, you risk them potentially blocking or undermining your process by questioning the wisdom in the path you are pursuing. Especially if they carry clout with executives that rank higher than you in your organization.

Don't assume that because 1:1 marketing makes complete sense to you that it makes sense to others involved in the process. Be sure to present the rationale along with the plan and the expected benefits, and continually check in and assess each participant's mindset throughout the process.

And returning to best practice #4, measuring impact throughout the process will help you in getting buy-in for future steps. While 1:1 marketing may not seem intuitive initially to some people, it's hard to argue with data that proves afterward a positive impact from changing how you buy media or otherwise market your company's products and services. Having the ability to show team members the data that proves 1:1 marketing outperforms mass marketing will go miles toward changing rigid mindsets anchored in historically proven practices.

BEST PRACTICE #6: "ANY SUFFICIENTLY ADVANCED TECHNOLOGY IS INDISTINGUISHABLE FROM MAGIC"

When you implement 1:1 marketing effectively, many in your organization will perceive that you are creating magic. The magic, as this quote from science-fiction writer and futurist Arthur C. Clarke[9] suggests, comes from the proper implementation of technology. And implementing the right technology to power your 1:1 marketing efforts will require your company to spend money.

As you build out your 1:1 marketing plan, be sure to budget adequately for licensing and implementing the technology you will need. You should budget for technology to compile, centralize, and manage your customer data effectively. Budget for technology to normalize, append, and otherwise enhance your data to better target and personalize messages. Budget for the technology you will need to plan, deliver, and measure messages and campaigns across all of the devices your customers use. Budget for technology to manage the process of implementing 1:1 marketing, including project planning and collaboration between teams and team members.

The necessary investment in technology may be more than you initially expect. If you can't secure adequate funding for everything you have planned, create a crawl-walk-run plan that implements the technology in phases that might take several years. Start with process and foundational technology to master your data, and move on to additional technologies that let you implement and manage campaigns. Save investments for technology to measure campaign impacts, and report on the results as your third wave of investment.

That doesn't mean you don't measure results or implement campaigns prior to investing in the technology. Rather, look for opportunities to initially license the technology as a service provided by partners, and use more core technologies such as spreadsheets while you are building your programs. Doing so may cost more over time and limit some of your results and output, but in the end the results you begin achieving earlier will provide the support you need for investing larger amounts in technology over time.

BEST PRACTICE #7: "THERE'S A FINE LINE BETWEEN SUPPORT AND STALKING, AND LET'S ALL STAY ON THE RIGHT SIDE OF THAT"

When caller ID, the ability for phone systems to transmit the phone number from which a call is being placed, rolled out in the late 1990s, service providers who were early adopters tried to use caller ID to personalize inbound phone calls with customers. When customers called from the phone number associated with their account, instead of the impersonal approach of asking for a name and address to look up the customer record, the company could simply greet the customer by name.

It turned out, though, that having a customer support rep greet you by your first name when you call the 800 number creeped customers out.

How did you know it was me? How do you know my name? Companies quickly learned that asking customers for their name, despite the fact that the customer's name and address is displayed on the agent's screen when the phone is connected, resulted in a better customer experience. Next time you call your utility or credit card company, notice that as you state your name and address you don't typically hear the operator typing on his or her keyboard. That's because they are simply verifying the information displayed on their screen.

The quote earlier from Joss Wheden,[10] the American screenwriter and director who cowrote and directed the horror film *The Cabin in the Woods*, sums it up nicely for 1:1 marketers. The line between personalizing messages, precisely targeting ads, and being creepy is surprisingly easy to cross. This means sometimes you may not want to reveal all you actually know about a prospect or customer. Like in the earlier case with the utility company not revealing they already know who you are.

Many people believe that Amazon's Alexa and the Facebook app on their phone are listening to every conversation even when the devices haven't been alerted.[11] And many people are convinced the ads they see are a result of some private conversation they had the other night with their spouse. (Qualitative research conducted by one of the authors with graduate students at the University of Texas indicates that this isn't the case—yes, the smart speakers are listening to you, but they're not collecting data about your conversations until you alert the device.)[12]

As a 1:1 marketer, it's incumbent on you to not further the inherent distrust that advances in technology are fostering by carelessly using the data you amass on customers. You also need to evaluate every opportunity for precision targeting against a backdrop of whether consumers are likely to be creeped out by the tactics you employ. Sowing distrust is unlikely to build the type of 1:1 long-term relationship you are seeking through 1:1 marketing.

An agency approached one of the authors' previous company with a precision targeting request. The agency wanted the company to build an audience of people who worked at warehouses and distribution centers for several large e-commerce retailers, so they could target them with ads for their tax-preparation-service client in January when the e-commerce companies were known to distribute W-2 forms to employees for tax preparation.

Because the turnover rate for employees who work at such facilities is high, identifying the audience of current and former employees would require watching signals over many months. The advertiser wanted the company to provide the agency with the mobile ad IDs from those devices seen throughout the year to target them with ads.

The company declined the request, not because it was illegal but because it was simply too creepy. The company's internal mantra was to not ever do anything so creepy that the company ended up in a *Wall Street Journal* article on privacy. That's a good approach for any 1:1 marketer to consider before attempting to go to extremes to precisely target or message audiences: if this technique were to become known, is there a risk my company could end up in a story on the front page of the *Wall Street Journal*? If so, then your idea is too creepy to pursue.

KEY TAKEAWAYS

Here are some things to keep in mind as you reflect upon the concepts in this chapter.

- **Don't prioritize perfection over progress.** Don't wait until you can devise an absolute perfect approach to your 1:1 marketing. There simply is no such thing as perfection in marketing, and you risk getting stalled and never actually implementing 1:1 marketing. Instead, devise your best plan and pursue it, increasing accuracy and performance over time.

- **Do prioritize data accuracy.** The best approach to 1:1 marketing goes out the window when you deliver the right ad to the wrong person, or the wrong ad to the right person. Invest in data hygiene and normalization not only when initially assembling your customer data, but over time as data is updated and more data is added. Not only will you save money by not spending money on wasted impressions, but you'll create a better experience for your customers.

- **Take a "crawl-walk-run" approach to implementing 1:1 marketing.** Start with simple tactics and iterate over time, instead of attempting to flip a switch from mass marketing to 1:1 marketing. You'll learn from each tactic along the way that will improve the next step. Plus, taking the crawl-walk-run approach lets you start sooner and iterate over time.

- **Measure everything.** Or at least measure the key things. This will help you understand the impact of implementing 1:1 marketing and help justify the investment in resources when asked down the road. Just remember to plan up front for measurement to ensure processes and campaigns are created in such a way they can be easily measured.

- **Gain support from your peers and superiors throughout the process.** Resistance to change is normal, so be sure you are marshalling support for the changes at the beginning, during, and throughout the process of implementing 1:1 marketing in your organization. It may require extra effort in helping others understand the benefits of changing your approach to marketing, but it will help ensure efforts aren't slowed or stopped due to resistance.

- **Budget for investments in technology.** The techniques described in this book are made possible by technology. 1:1 marketing requires technology at every step in the process, so be sure to understand what will be needed and incorporate that into your budgeting process. If you can't secure adequate funding for all of the technology needed up front, stage your project plan to allow for investments over multiple years.

- **Don't be creepy.** The power of 1:1 marketing is diminished when customers are creeped out over the techniques and messaging you employ. Be smart about what should and shouldn't be revealed in your marketing efforts. It's OK to use data to be remarkably targeted and relevant in your messaging and timing, without letting the customers see behind the curtain. Creeping your customers out won't result in the long-term, profitable relationships you are seeking from highly personalized and relevant marketing.

YES, B2B MARKETERS CAN ALSO BE 1:1 MARKETERS

> To be successful and grow your business and revenues,
> you must match the way you market your products with
> the way your prospects learn about and shop for your products.
> —BRIAN HALLIGAN, COFOUNDER AND CEO, HUBSPOT[1]

If you're a B2B company, you're probably wondering if 1:1 marketing is even a possibility for you. A lot of the examples used in the book are B2C case studies. And let's face it, if you've been working in B2B for a while, you realize that the quantity and precision of data for businesses is not like the seemingly limitless data available for B2C marketers.

Don't worry. Both authors of this book have worked for and with numerous B2B businesses over the years. (In fact, Chuck has headed marketing for multiple B2B software as a service [SaaS] companies over the past couple of decades.)

B2B marketers can absolutely leverage 1:1 marketing.

Sure, 1:1 marketing in a B2B world is approached differently than in the B2C world, from the data you use to basic concepts like how purchase decisions occur. But not only is it possible for B2B marketers to use elements of a B2C approach; we also believe every B2B marketer should be leaning into the 1:1 marketing movement and applying these techniques to their campaigns. In some ways, 1:1 can be even more valuable for B2B marketers than for B2C marketers.

UNDERSTANDING THE FACTORS THAT SEPARATE B2B 1:1 MARKETING FROM B2C 1:1 MARKETING

How business purchases are made is distinctly different from how consumer purchases are made:

- **More people.** Consumer purchases often are made with just one or two decision makers involved, but that's rarely the case with business purchases. Most business purchases involve multiple decision makers, influencers, evaluators, and negotiators who must all come to agreement before a purchase can be made.
- **More risk.** That's because consumer purchases generally affect only a person or at most a single household. Bad consumer purchases, such as choosing not-so-tasty bargain brand mac 'n' cheese, generally result in short-term, relatively minor problems (trust us, we've made that mistake). Business purchases, on the other hand, impact entire departments or companies, and can significantly impact business outcomes. Making a bad purchase decision in the business world can result in the loss of people's jobs or entire company fortunes.
- **Bigger investment.** Most household purchases involve small amounts, often less than $100. Businesses routinely make purchases costing thousands, hundreds of thousands, or even millions of dollars.
- **Considered purchase.** Consumers often make impulse purchases, such as which fast-food restaurant to grab lunch from or buying a clearance-priced blouse while browsing in a store. Few business purchases are impulse purchases. Nearly all business purchases

require extensive research, evaluation, and even reference checking before they can be completed.

These differences result in far-longer purchase processes for businesses, often lasting many weeks or months. Decisions can take circuitous routes, stall, suddenly increase in speed, and sometimes end unexpectedly without a purchase. It's not surprising then that the role of marketing and how 1:1 marketing techniques can be applied are radically different from consumer marketing.

IN A NUTSHELL

While there are many differences between how businesses and consumers make purchases, there are a few similarities, especially since people are involved in both. B2B marketing can benefit from 1:1 marketing, perhaps even more than consumer marketing.

However, not everything about business purchases is different from consumer purchases. They do share some commonality, including:

- **B2B is people, too.** In the end, businesses don't make purchases; people do. They may be spending the company's money and purchasing products and solutions that impact the corporation, but it still requires that the people involved make the decision to buy.
- **Emotional purchases.** Despite the rigor around business purchases, in the end, the people involved can still buy for emotional reasons and justify their purchases with logic, just like they do when making consumer purchases.
- **Personalized experiences.** Business buyers and influencers prefer personalized experiences and conversations, based on their specific business, industry, and the role of the person involved, instead of being blasted with mass marketing messages.

In the end, smart B2B marketers realize that their customers, just like consumers, represent a lifetime value that can be far greater than what they gain from the initial purchase. And just like with B2C selling, it costs far more to acquire new customer than to get current customers to spend more, buy more frequently, refer friends, or remain a customer longer. And that's why 1:1 marketing is just as important for B2B marketing as it is with B2C marketing.

Ultimately, though, how you implement 1:1 marketing in a B2B world is radically different. Let's use the same Who, What, Where, When, Why, and How framework to examine how 1:1 marketing can be applied to marketing to businesses.

WHO YOU ARE TARGETING

Targeting prospects in the business world requires a two-step process. To know which people to target, you have to first determine which companies to target, since the decision makers and influencers ultimately are making purchases on behalf of the company they work for. And while more people are involved in B2B purchase decisions than B2C purchases, there are far fewer businesses than there are consumers in the United States. In fact, the US population in 2019 was 328 million people,[2] but there were only 32.5 million businesses.[3]

And while millions of consumers could buy a single company's products, very few businesses market a product that is purchased by millions of businesses. Businesses are generally limited either by geography (e.g., a local company that provides office cleaning services) or because the product's or service's value proposition applies to only a subset of companies (e.g., a company that sells industrial steel shelving).

Smaller companies purchase far fewer products and solutions than large enterprises. In fact, 76 percent of the 32.5 million US businesses have zero employees,[4] meaning they are sole proprietorships or single person LLCs. This leaves fewer than eight million businesses in the United States purchasing the majority of B2B services and products.

But targeting the businesses your company would sell to can narrow even more, since few solutions apply to businesses of all sizes. Take accounting software. The accounting software that a business with $3 million in sales uses is not the same accounting software used by a company with $100 million in sales. In the end, it's not unusual for a business to have a solution or product that would be of interest to just a few thousand companies, or in some cases, a few hundred companies.

This is why many B2B marketers have transitioned from traditional broad marketing approaches to a concept called account-based marketing (ABM). In ABM, prospect targeting is organized around accounts (or businesses) that are likely to buy a particular product or service. Marketers start by identifying the ideal customer profile (ICP)—what are the characteristics of a business that make it a particularly ideal prospect? Characteristics may be firmographic, such as the revenue, number of employees, location, or industry. They may also be more situational-based, such as companies that sell a particular type of product, have a certain average purchase amount per customer, or compete with many other companies.

IN A NUTSHELL

ABM is the application of 1:1 marketing to B2B selling, starting at the business (account) level and working down to the individuals at the business involved in purchase decisions. By first identifying the prospect accounts that match your product's ICP and the roles/titles involved in the purchase decision, a B2B brand can identify the audiences of one—the decision makers and influencers involved in the purchase decision—to target with messaging that results in in 1:1 conversations.

Once you identify the hundreds or thousands of ideal businesses that are prospects for your company, you then need to determine what roles within the company are likely to be involved in the purchase decision. It could be people within a business unit (e.g., solvents), in certain depart-ments (e.g., marketing or engineering), at a certain seniority level (e.g., vice president and above), or with certain titles (e.g., chief financial officer).

Once you have your target companies and people/roles defined, you can begin to practice 1:1 marketing. Many companies compile informa-tion about businesses, including firmographic, technology solutions the companies currently use, products people inside the company are cur-rently researching, budgets for certain categories of products, and more.

Similar to 1:1 marketing to consumers, it's critical for B2B marketers to compile a master database of the companies they wish to target, and ideally the people in those companies that will be involved in the purchase decisions. And because purchases are more complex, involve more steps and people, and last longer with many conversations and meetings during the purchase process, most B2B companies use customer relationship management (CRM) software, such as Salesforce or Nimble. This allows them to collect additional information with each interaction and conver-sation, to better understand the needs of the buyers, the purchase process, and the current stage of each purchase opportunity.

All of this information is inherently collected on a 1:1 basis, associ-ated with each company and the person at the company involved in the purchase process. And because a single company's purchase process can last for weeks or months, it's not unusual that during the process some of the people involved leave the company and replacements are hired. When this occurs, the seller may have to restart the process with the new people involved. Thus CRM solutions are critical to effective 1:1 B2B marketing, tracking all of the information and history of interactions with business contacts, ensuring that the right information is delivered at the right time to the right person.

WHAT APPROACH TO USE

Because B2B purchases can last much longer and involve a far more complex process than consumer purchases, messaging tends to be more complex since the type of information needed varies by person/role as well as the stage of the purchase. Treating each purchase maker and influencer as an audience of one enables you to create personalized messages that create conversations with all of the people involved and at every stage in the purchase process.

For example, the message and language included in an email, letter, or ad to a CEO, CFO, a manager in the information technology department, and a director of marketing *should* be dramatically different to be effective. They each have different priorities, value different aspects of a product when considering a purchase, and serve in different roles within the buying process. Each purchase decision may have researchers, evaluators, negotiators, purchase managers, influencers, and decision makers.

Furthermore, the information buyers need during the initial awareness and knowledge stages will be different in later stages in the purchase process, such as the liking and preference stages. Early-stage messages are likely to be focused on driving awareness of a specific brand or product and helping prospects understand the problem your product can solve. Later-stage messages need to provide more detail and information, including information such as technical specs, capabilities, and pricing.

IN A NUTSHELL

When approaching B2B marketing with 1:1 marketing approaches, identifying the message to send to prospects is driven by a combination of the prospect's role in the company and the current stage in the purchase cycle. B2B marketing technology solutions make it possible to customize hundreds of different messages for everyone involved in the purchase process.

With the additional complexity, numerous people involved, and extended length of B2B purchases, a common approach is for B2B marketers to create a library of informational content that helps educate people throughout the purchase process. The goal of the B2B marketer is to provide the right information they need at each stage in the purchase. Content can be packaged as emails, infographics, comparison worksheets, eBooks and guides, technical white papers, webinars, and more.

And because most of these are delivered and accessed via digital means such as websites, landing pages, and emails, engagement data and signals are collected along the way by marketing automation software, such as Marketo, Eloqua, and HubSpot. Marketing automation software syncs with the company's CRM and enables marketers to send targeted emails to prospects and track what content they engage with and for how long. Capturing this information at a 1:1 level helps marketers and salespeople know which prospects are engaging with content, evaluating solutions, and at what stage they are in the buying process.

Another technology that has gained popularity in B2B marketing is chatbots. Chatbots, from companies such as Drift and Intercom, are placed on B2B websites to intercept visitors and engage them in conversations. Known as conversational agents, chatbots employ natural language processing and artificial intelligence (AI) to interpret responses from prospects visiting the website. Once they understand what the prospect wants, they can provide answers by accessing information from the company's knowledge base.

With information synced to CRM and marketing automation solutions, playbooks can be developed to create different conversations and paths for different customers. They can even identify people returning to a website and refer to the visitor by name or mention their company. The playbooks can also determine how to direct the prospect, connecting them to a human being to further facilitate a personalized, one-to-one conversation.

Thanks to a multitude of B2B technology solutions, sophisticated B2B marketers can truly create and manage thousands of 1:1 conversations with customers to move them through the purchase process. Buyers receive the right information and education at just the right stages and can complete a complex purchase transaction highly satisfied. With the advent of technology, business buyers often prefer to control the process and conduct research and information exchanges without actually talking to or visiting with a salesperson.

The same technology can be used after the purchase to help ensure the customer is successfully onboarded (which can be a challenge with technology purchases, where implementations can take weeks or months), remains satisfied, and continues learning about additional features and solutions available. In the same way a consumer marketer increases the lifetime value of customers over time, B2B marketers can employ 1:1 marketing techniques and messaging to cause current customers to spend more, increase frequency of usage, refer other businesses, extend the lifetime of the customer, and even bring back past customers who left.

WHERE YOU REACH AND ENGAGE WITH PROSPECTS AND CUSTOMERS

Options for B2B marketers to reach decision makers and influencers used to be limited. Broadcast and print methods were available to larger advertisers, but to target business buyers, they would typically choose television networks watched by businesspeople, such as CNBC and Fox Business. Print advertising would target business publications, like the *Wall Street Journal*, *Fortune*, and *Forbes*, or more niche industry trade publications for the industries being targeted.

The only 1:1 options were direct mail and cold-calling, whether in person or by phone. While you can still use those today, many more options are available for the same reason there are more consumer options for 1:1 marketing: the growth of internet usage on laptops and smartphones. You can now digitally target the specific people you are looking for by using platforms that can match business data to digital signals. For example, you can use the IP address tied to a router specific to a particular business to reach people accessing the internet from that business location.

With the increasing popularity of ABM, a number of advertising and marketing solutions have been developed to reach the right decision makers and influencers in B2B purchase decisions via digital advertising.

With ABM SaaS solutions from companies like Demandbase, Terminus, and Metadata.io, B2B marketers can reach prospects with ads via social networks (e.g., LinkedIn, Twitter, Facebook) and via DSPs that serve ads across thousands of websites.

And much like 1:1 audience targeting in consumer marketing, these solutions allow B2B marketers to reach specific buyers or select roles, functions, and seniority level in targeted companies, regardless of the website or app the person is using at the time the ad is delivered. So instead of purchasing a print ad in the *Wall Street Journal* because it's read by business buyers, brands can instead deliver ads to the right people or roles within the specific companies that match their ICP. It's equivalent to B2C 1:1 marketing where you can target specific households based on their previous purchase behaviors.

> **IN A NUTSHELL**
>
> Numerous B2B marketing technology solutions enable 1:1 marketers to reach all of the people involved in purchases with the right message, using a combination of email, digital ads, phone calls, social media networks, and direct mail.

You might be wondering if streaming or connected television options would enable targeting of business users. In theory, it could be done. At minimum, advertisers can purchase ads on business networks such as CNBC and Fox Business, but limiting impressions to a much more precise location, such as just certain cities or even just specific zip codes. While in theory it would be possible to link data to specific households to target business buyers, the challenge lies in the fact that few if any B2B data sources tie a business user to their home address. They are far more likely to be able to tie the user at an office address, but few people stream television programs from their offices.

WHEN YOUR MESSAGE IS DELIVERED

The timing of messages with businesses may be impacted by seasonality and/or sales processes. But in the business world, seasonality has less to do with the weather outside or holidays; rather, seasons are based on periods of times when businesses budget and make purchases. Most businesses establish budgets at the beginning of the year, which means sellers often want to be in contact with decision makers and influencers early in the year as they begin spending their budgets, or even during the previous quarter when budgets are being established. Some businesses require departments to use their entire budget before the end of the year or lose any unspent dollars, which can result in last-minute purchases at the businesses' year end.

Outside of seasonality, timing of messages is driven by where in the sales cycle the purchase decision is at the time the message is delivered. And since every prospect's purchase process could be at a different stage, employing 1:1 marketing and mapping messages to current stage by prospect enables you to deliver the right message at just the right time to hundreds or thousands of prospects. As long as you have a system and method for tracking each prospect's current position in the sales funnel, you can make sure you're delivering a relevant message that will answer the questions they have at that particular stage and help advance the process to the next stage.

IN A NUTSHELL

Timing of 1:1 messages in B2B selling is dictated by a combination of budgeting cycles and where in the sales process each message occurs. Marketers can use B2B marketing technology solutions not only to capture the signals that will identify where the prospect is in the sales funnel, but also to deliver the right message during each step.

B2B marketers often employ sales enablement solutions to more precisely time and personalize messages that create 1:1 conversations with B2B prospects. Sales enablement solutions help the sales organization understand their buyers, communicate with buyers, adapt messages, and ideally engage in conversations that help answer questions and address concerns buyers have, ultimately moving the purchase to a successful close.

Solutions such as Outreach.io and SalesLoft help sellers engage consistently throughout the buying process using a sequence of touches by phone, email, direct mail, and social messages. Because many interactions occur digitally, signals such as an email being opened or a recipient clicking on a link to a website can be used to personalize and even change the next step in the sequence. And in situations where the purchase is delayed or cancelled, these sales enablement solutions allow the marketer to place prospects into a "nurture" sequence that periodically sends an email from the sales rep or sales development rep (SDR). Sequences can also trigger the SDR to periodically touch base via phone. When the purchase process resumes or the prospect begins a new purchase process, it helps ensure that prospects recall your business and have someone reach out to pick up the prior conversation.

WHY YOU ARE MESSAGING A PROSPECT

Much like consumer 1:1 marketing, the Why can be answered by looking at the goal for that message. But with many more buyers and steps in the purchase process with B2B marketing, you will set specific goals or objectives for the communication at each step in the process. For example, a cold-call email or phone call has the objective of making the prospect aware of your product or service. If they happen to be in market for such a solution, the prospect will engage with your sales team to learn more. Meanwhile, a follow-up email thanking the prospect for meeting to demo your solution and pressing for next steps has the goal of moving an opportunity forward toward the close.

Additionally, you want to have a number of ongoing marketing programs to maintain awareness with all prospects, positioning your company as a leader in your respective market. For example, you might produce a monthly email newsletter or periodic webinars to make people aware of new products, features, and case studies from current customers successfully using your product. These campaigns may have fewer specific objectives, although since you are still delivering communications via 1:1 marketing, you will know how many and which customers are engaging with the content, including reading the email and clicking through to additional resources on your website.

In the end, most marketing departments practicing 1:1 marketing develop playbooks with a specific set of communications and steps for each prospect. It's common to develop personas for each of the roles involved in the purchase decision. A persona describes a fictional character with specific characteristics of the people in that role, describing their challenges, pain points, stressors, and desires when purchasing products in your category. You can then develop playbooks for each persona you will engage with during the sales process, with a preset sequence of communication and engagement steps that will be executed using your marketing technology stack to deliver the right message at the right time in the most effective format.

IN A NUTSHELL

B2B marketers often identify different objectives for each communication in each step, as well as overall objectives for entire campaigns. In the end, all of the steps are working together to drive more sales at the highest velocity possible.

Finally, like consumer marketing, even businesses that practice 1:1 marketing will still employ some marketing practices that aren't 1:1 in nature. For example, running ads or conducting a webinar in partnership with a trade publication is inherently not a 1:1 form of media, since targeting is merely limited to the readers of the publication. And that audience will likely include some people who aren't prospective buyers or influencers for your product.

However, with the ability to use technology to implement 1:1 marketing with prospects once they become known to you, B2B marketers place even greater emphasis on using mass marketing methods to drive people to download a piece of content or participate in a webinar the marketing team develops so the person will provide personally identifiable information (PII) that lets you begin a 1:1 conversation with the prospect.

HOW YOU MEASURE CAMPAIGN SUCCESS

Given the number of various touchpoints in 1:1 marketing campaigns for B2B marketers, there are multiple ways to measure campaign success. Of course, in the end, like consumer marketing, success ultimately equates to revenue: How much revenue did the campaign result in compared to the cost to obtain that revenue? With the previously mentioned technology solutions available to B2B marketers, all of the activity is easily tracked back to the people involved in the purchase decision and linked to the opportunities that close as won business.

The problem in B2B marketing is that with the sheer number of people involved and multiple touchpoints, it can be challenging to tie a specific touchpoint to an opportunity closing. In other words, it's the culmination of the many touchpoints and 1:1 engagements that ultimately results in closing sales. The most sophisticated marketing organizations apply multitouch attribution (MTA) to try to determine the relative impact of every engagement, but it's not easy and requires a certain amount of guesswork. Most organizations simply calculate a customer acquisition cost (CAC), based on the cost of marketing and sales attributed to driving sales.

Additionally, 1:1 B2B marketers will also use metrics such as open and click rates to measure effectiveness of specific communications at each step in the process. The more sophisticated sales enablement and marketing automation solutions enable A/B split testing of messages at each step, allowing marketers to isolate variables such as headline, image, and copy length to identify which performs better.

IN A NUTSHELL

In the end, a B2B company's 1:1 marketing will be judged on how efficiently those efforts drove closed sales opportunities, most often by calculating CAC compared to the cost of the marketing effort. But metrics are also evaluated at every step to continuously optimize marketing efforts.

The most sophisticated solutions, including Outreach.io, use AI to determine the sentiment being expressed in every interaction, allowing for more precise analysis and optimization. For example, instead of just identifying that the prospect responded to an email, Outreach will decipher the difference between the prospect writing "tell me more" and "please stop emailing me, I'm not interested."

KEY TAKEAWAYS

Here are some things to keep in mind as you reflect upon the concepts in this chapter.

- **1:1 is for B2B.** 1:1 marketing is a powerful technique for both B2C and B2B organizations, although differences in how business purchases are made versus consumers purchases will dictate different approaches.

- **Account-based marketing.** In B2B marketing, where a finite number of companies are likely buyers of a particular product or service, ABM is employed. With ABM, marketers start by identifying the prospective businesses, or accounts, that match the ICP for the product being marketed. They then identify the roles involved in the process and that provide a starting point for identifying the audiences of one they need to reach with 1:1 marketing efforts.

- **Target market.** Messaging in 1:1 marketing for B2B marketing is driven by who in the purchase process is being targeted and what stage the purchase process is in at the time of the engagement.
- **B2B solutions.** Technology solutions enable targeting of each persona involved in the purchase process with digital ads, emails, direct mail, and phone calls. Most B2B marketers also use mass marketing approaches to drive prospects to engage with the brand and provide their contact info, enabling ongoing 1:1 exchanges.
- **Timing is important.** Timing of messages in a B2B 1:1 marketing campaign is most often driven by budgeting cycles. Technology solutions make it possible to time the ideal message to arrive at the ideal time, based on where the prospect is in the buying process.
- **Purchase cycle.** Objectives for B2B 1:1 marketing efforts ultimately tie back to sales, something that often is easier to do in a B2B selling situation versus consumer marketing, thanks to a slower, more involved purchase process involving multiple people.
- **Metrics.** Similarly, 1:1 campaigns in B2B are ultimately measured by how efficiently they drive customer acquisition, by taking the revenue generated and dividing it by the CAC. Additionally, metrics can be evaluated at every step in the process to continuously optimize each step.

PART

5

ADVANCED
TECHNIQUES

YOU'RE A ROCK STAR! (YOUR PARENTS ARE SO PROUD.)
1:1 OVERVIEW
DIGGING DEEPER
STRATEGIC THINKING
PUTTING IT ALL TO WORK
ADVANCED TECHNIQES

DATA IS THE NEW OIL THAT KEEPS 1:1 MARKETING RUNNING SMOOTHLY

The world's most valuable resource is no longer oil, but data.
—*THE ECONOMIST*, MAY 6, 2017[1]

In 2006, Clive Humbly, UK mathematician and architect of the Tesco Clubcard, made the now notorious statement, "data is the new oil," comparing the nature of raw, unrefined data to oil. A May 2017 article in *The Economist* expounded on the idea. The author noted that new commodities lead to lucrative, fast-growing economies that eventually draw the attention of antitrust regulators worried about who can control their flow. The article compared oil, the new commodity a century ago, to data, the "oil of the digital era," and called for the titans of data—namely Google, Amazon, Facebook, and Microsoft—to be broken up.

As discussed in Chapter 9, Amazon's most valuable asset—and the most valuable asset for many companies—is customer data. For many years, companies that sold primarily to consumers put little emphasis on the value of customer data. Most manufacturers sold their products through a two- or three-step distribution system that created a chasm between them and the consumers who purchased their products.

Over time, manufacturers realized that not having a direct connection to customers and their data put them at a disadvantage. Understanding the demographic makeup and other characteristics of their buyers was challenging. Knowing what products and features would appeal to customers required expensive research. Even uncovering the problems buyers experienced using their products could be a challenge, since the information arrived filtered through one or more parties between the company and the customers.

This is how warranty registration cards came to be. Let's face it, you have plenty of ways to prove you bought a specific product, including purchase receipts and manufacturing dates stamped onto products. The manufacturer doesn't really need you to register the product to ensure your eligibility to receive product repairs, replacement, or service in the future.

But companies realized that if they alarmed consumers into completing and mailing warranty registration cards out of fear of not being eligible for service, they would obtain the names, addresses, phone numbers, and other valuable information from the people who buy their products. And it gave them a database of consumers they could use then to market replacement parts and additional services beyond the initial product purchase.

Thanks to e-commerce and other technology advances that have removed layers between consumers and companies selling products, most companies have ways to obtain customer data today. And over time, amassing a treasure trove of customer data provides immense value for companies. It's also vital for adapting from mass marketing methods to marketing to audiences of one.

As discussed in Chapter 9, customer data is one of the three key foundational elements of 1:1 marketing. Let's review the various types of customer data and each one's role in powering your conversations with your audiences of one. Customer data falls into two primary categories:

1. Essential data brands collect from their customers
2. Additional data you can obtain from other companies that will enhance the relevance of your messaging

You likely have some of this data already, although few brands have amassed both data types at a scale and in a form that would enable them to power advanced 1:1 marketing programs. Chances are if you already had this data available to power your marketing, you would be an accomplished 1:1 marketing practitioner and wouldn't be reading this book!

But that's OK. As noted earlier, implementing 1:1 marketing is a process and a journey. We'll discuss some of the challenges of assembling customer data in a way that makes it readily accessible by your marketing efforts and explain how to acquire missing data for each type you need to transition your marketing to the 1:1 marketing promised land.

And Chapters 16 and 17 will talk about the technological and process challenges you're likely to face in bringing all of this customer data together in a way that can power your 1:1 marketing, along with a blueprint for how to tackle those challenges and build the critical repository of customer data 1:1 marketers need.

ESSENTIAL DATA BRANDS COLLECT FROM THEIR CUSTOMERS

If data is the new oil, then what data you collect and how you collect it is critical to effective 1:1 marketing efforts.

Customer Contact Data

At a minimum, you should have basic customer contact data: name, address, email, phone number(s). These are necessary for reaching your customers whether by mail, phone, email, mobile messaging, or other methods. This info also can be used to target digital ads to your customers. You may not have every contact method for every customer and will need to fill that in over time. The more elements you have for each customer, the better chance you have of being able to communicate with that customer, especially in an era where people move and change contact info frequently.

Contact data is also required for building an *identity graph*, a topic covered in Chapter 16. Data elements that enable you to identify a person are referred to as *personally identifiable information*, or PII. Some brands simply don't know who their customers are and have little or no PII on their customers; this is especially true of brands that sell their products through distributors and not directly to their customers.

But that model is rapidly changing. Even packaged goods companies, a category that has historically sold only through distributors and retailers, are starting to sell direct to their consumers. For example, people craving chips or perhaps a flavor of Cheetos they can't buy in their local grocery store can purchase them at Snacks.com, a direct-to-consumer (DTC) website launched by PepsiCo's Frito Lay. With distribution centers located throughout the United States to supply local grocers with their products, Frito Lay is able to promise orders will arrive in three days or less. And imagine the rich repository of customer data that Frito Lay is building, especially on their most loyal customers who are willing to bypass the convenience of the local grocery store to stock up on the products they love and use most.

Purchase History

The second type of essential data you should have for each of your customers is a history of their purchases. Ideally, you will be able to match customers and every product and service each has purchased over time, including date of purchase, item(s), amount paid, payment form, location of purchase, and expiration data (if applicable).

Purchase data is critically important in 1:1 marketing because it gives you a starting point for your communications. For example, after the initial customer purchase, you can use 1:1 marketing to help the customer feel good about their purchase and reinforce the value they receive from the item or service they purchased. 1:1 marketing can help customers maximize value from their purchase, feel valued as a customer, and encourage them to buy additional products or services that will help them get greater value from their initial purchase.

You can also use 1:1 marketing to encourage satisfied customers to tell friends and acquaintances (and thanks to social media, even people they don't know) about your brand and how great your products are, which will cause others to make purchases. And in an era where product research and satisfaction can be obtained by any consumer with a few clicks, you want to leverage customers to help boost your company's and product's ratings and give other people confidence to buy your products. In fact, you can use 1:1 marketing to encourage customers to tell you when they aren't satisfied or have issues with your product, and how you can make it right.

All of these customer communications are highly dependent on knowing when and what a customer purchases. Plus, knowing a customer's past purchases enables future communications to be more relevant. The historical purchases of a customer can be a highly reliable predictor of other products they might buy in the future.

For example, consider a hotel chain, like Hilton, that offers multiple brands that cater to various types of travelers. Past hotel stays can serve to predict future stays customers might make. By knowing that a customer often stays at their Waldorf Astoria brand of upscale hotel but hasn't stayed at one of Hilton's other luxury brands such as LXR and Conrad, they can target offers for each of these other brands to secure more of the Waldorf Astoria's luxury hotel stays throughout the year.

Similarly, Hilton offers several budget-friendly hotel brands, including Hilton Garden Inn, Hampton, and Tru. For a customer who regularly stays at Hampton hotels, but hasn't stayed at the other two brands likely to appeal to this same value-minded traveler, Hilton can present a compelling discount to try the other brands and deepen the traveler's loyalty to Hilton. Over time, 1:1 marketers begin to build segments of customers based on past purchases that receive messages about other products and services the company offers that are likely to appeal to these same buyers.

Depending on how you sell your products, you may have limited historical purchase data for your customers or won't be able to match purchase data to specific customers. For example, quick service restaurants (QSRs) like McDonald's or Subway historically have had little information about their customers given the high frequency of small purchases, many of which have been paid for with cash. If this is the case with your brand, you want to employ many of the same practices QSR brands use to build customer data.

For example, many of the largest QSR brands have created loyalty programs for their most frequent customers, rewarding them with points for each purchase. The incentive to earn a reward or discount incentivizes frequent guests to download a company's app, sign up for email and text offers, and ensure that every purchase they make is captured—even if paid for with cash—to ensure they receive their frequent guest points and rewards.

Frequent buyer programs give brands a way to chain together all of the historical purchases a customer makes. And because valuable PII is captured during the process of registering the app or signing up for rewards, they now have contact information for their customers that can be used to power 1:1 marketing. And while they won't have purchase and even contact information for every customer who visits one of their restaurants, they will have it for the most loyal customers, the ones for whom 1:1 marketing will prove most effective and valuable.

If you have limited ways to capture customer purchase data, consider developing a similar program. While such programs can be costly, including the rewards earned by customers such as free food, the value of being able to implement 1:1 marketing with your most profitable customers typically far outweighs the investment in rewards infrastructure and incentives to capture the data.

ADDITIONAL DATA THAT YOU CAN OBTAIN FROM OTHER COMPANIES

The types of data we classified as "essential customer data" is known in the industry as first-party data. First-party data is defined as the information you obtain directly from your customers, including their contact info and purchase history, and is the most valuable data you can collect. The importance and value of amassing first-party data from your customers cannot be overstated. As noted in Chapter 9, the first-party data amassed by Amazon is the ultimate driver of Amazon's trillion-dollar valuation. When you collect enough data about your customers, the value that first-party data represents can be added as a line item on your company's balance sheet.

The second type of data, data that is worthwhile to collect about your customers, is compiled by other companies and must be purchased or licensed for use. Investing in this data enables the 1:1 marketer to personalize communications and more precisely segment customers into categories that will improve the relevance of the messages you send.

Additionally, this data provides a view into customers that tells you exactly how, when, and what you should communicate, a hallmark of 1:1 marketing. Having this data helps the customer feel like you really know who they are, what they care about, and value their time enough that you only promote the products, services, and benefits they care about.

Data about your customers that you obtain from other companies falls into two categories: second-party data and third-party data. We cover both and how you can use these to target and personalize your 1:1 marketing efforts.

Second-Party Data

Second-party data refers to the exchanging of first-party data between two companies. The practice began many years ago when catalog marketers realized that their most valuable customers often purchased from other catalog marketers that weren't directly competitive. For example, a company that sells jewelry might discover that their customers also purchase electronics from another company's catalog.

Catalogers began to trade data with other noncompetitive catalogers to acquire prospect data for people likely to make a purchase. Each company would share its customer list with the other company, governed by a written agreement that the data would only be used to prospect for customers for the trading partner's catalog. Second-party data is an inexpensive way to obtain target prospects; typically, neither participant charges the other partner. Each company's first-party data represents the value exchanged in the quid pro quo transaction.

If you've ever ordered a product from a catalog, you may have noticed that you begin receiving catalogs from other companies you've never done business with. That's a result of the companies creating a second-party data exchange.

Over time, independent data companies formed to create and manage unified cooperative databases between many companies, where each company would contribute the PII and purchase data of their customers to the cooperative database. The more data a company shared, the more data they could obtain from the centralized database as long as it was contributed by other, noncompetitive companies. The arrangement allowed each marketer to grow their customer base and better understand purchases prospects make with other companies. With this understanding, they could personalize their 1:1 marketing to be more effective and grow their own first-party data set.

Third-Party Data

As direct marketing grew in popularity, companies emerged to try to satisfy direct marketers' thirst for more data to better target direct mail programs. These companies don't have a direct relationship with consumers, but rather aggregate and amass data from other companies that do have direct customer relationships to build extensive consumer profiles.

For example, Acxiom is a leading compiler of consumer data that tracks more than 11,000 data attributes on more than 2.5 billion people in more than 60 countries. It's partnered with thousands of companies who share the first-party data they collect from their customers with Acxiom. Acxiom takes the other company's data and attaches it to its massive consumer identity graph, making it available for other companies to license while carefully protecting consumer privacy.

Examples of the types of data that third-party data companies compile on consumers include financial, purchase, demographic, psychographic, behavioral, and more. For the companies that share their first-party data with third-party data companies in exchange for usage fees, it provides an opportunity to further monetize one of their key assets—the data they acquire and maintain about and from their customers—increasing the value of their first-party data.

You can enrich your customer data with third-party data to better understand and personalize communications to your customers. For example, going beyond the purchase data you collect to attach purchases your customers make from other brands or in other categories can allow you to adjust offers and messages. Take a QSR brand like Subway. Imagine if they could append their customer file with data amassed through credit card companies that would help them flag customers who spend more at competitive QSRs, such as Jimmy John's and Firehouse Subs. They could then give those customers a larger-than-normal discount to convince them to increase their visits to Subway at the expense of competitors.

DEVELOPING A DATA STRATEGY

While most brands have customer data, they often fail to establish a formal data strategy. A data strategy is an overarching approach and plan for consolidating the data they collect on consumers and making it accessible to teams within the company and vendors outside the company who are conducting marketing efforts, while protecting customer privacy and the assets they've created from their customer data.

If your company doesn't have a data strategy, the desire to implement 1:1 marketing can also be the impetus for establishing a defined data strategy. A core component of a data strategy is establishing a *single source of truth*: a centralized repository that contains one authoritative copy of all crucial customer data.

Unfortunately, many companies instead build numerous separate silos of disparate customer data over time, with different departments collecting specific pieces of data about customers that don't get shared with other departments. For example, a retailer might have customer and purchase data from purchases made in its stores separate from the customer and purchase data resulting from purchases on its e-commerce site. Additionally, it may maintain a third database of customer data through the company's customer service or tech support department, collected when customers contact the company to resolve problems with the products they purchased from the retailer.

Companies often outsource some functions to external vendors, such as call centers and warranty providers. As a result, these other companies may maintain customer and purchase data on their own servers, separate from the data maintained by the retailer on its own servers.

To effectively implement 1:1 marketing, bringing all of these separate data silos together to create a single consolidated view of the customer is critical. After all, if there are purchases or service incidents from customers who aren't included in your data, you risk targeting customers with offers on products they've purchased previously. Or you may target them with an upgrade promotion for a product they've repeatedly had problems with and are attempting to resolve.

For larger companies, such an undertaking can represent a massive effort involving dozens or hundreds of people. If so, you should consider conducting simultaneous processes: one for establishing a data policy and creating your company's single source of truth, and another to begin to implement 1:1 marketing based on the data you have ready access to. As noted in Chapter 13, 1:1 marketing often requires a crawl-walk-run approach. Taking this approach with the daunting task of consolidating your data and establishing a single source of truth can allow you to begin iterating on your 1:1 marketing strategy far sooner than it will take to solve decades of data hubris within a large, distributed organization.

IMPLEMENTING DATA HYGIENE AND NORMALIZATION

As you catalog the customer data distributed throughout your organization and attempt to consolidate it into your company's single source of truth, you will be challenged with data accuracy and inconsistency. Names and addresses are entered with typos and other mistakes. Addresses may be abbreviated inconsistently across databases, making it difficult to identify and combine the same customer's data from multiple sources into a single record. The process of taking inconsistent data about the same customer, modifying it, and bringing it together into a single, clean customer record is known as normalizing.

Fortunately, numerous companies can help you with the process of deduping, cleansing, and normalizing your data. Companies use algorithms to uncover inconsistencies and match what appears to be two different customers into a single customer record. The US Postal Service licenses its address data to many companies, who use it to standardize addresses to ensure direct mail pieces are properly delivered.

Large third-party data and identity companies, like Acxiom, have developed methods of tracking changing information on consumers, including address changes, telephone number changes and additions, and even name changes, such as when a person gets married and takes their spouse's last name. If you don't know that Mary Jones married Thomas Smith and now goes by Mary Smith, you may treat Mary as two different people, potentially targeting her with competing offers and sending multiple pieces to multiple addresses.

Specialized data companies and service providers are using artificial intelligence (AI) and machine learning to normalize messy data collected from multiples sources to create a single usable database from which companies can glean meaningful insights. Mobivity, for example, helps restaurant and retail chains who collect purchase data across hundreds or thousands of points of sale normalize their messy point-of-sale (POS) data into a single usable data set.

Think about the inconsistencies in purchase data that results from a large franchised QSR chain. First, because locations are operated by hundreds or thousands of different franchisee owners, many QSR chains use multiple POS systems throughout their systems. Getting the systems to talk to each other and share data can be a challenge.

But the bigger challenge is inconsistency introduced by the people involved in the process. POS systems often require menus to be updated at the local store level. Can you imagine how many ways a menu item such as a fried chicken sandwich can be spelled and abbreviated by thousands of different store managers, who often are in a hurry when updating the store's POS terminals?

And then there's the inaccuracies introduced by the cashier, who is often a part-time teenage employee who may receive limited training on the POS system. Discounts are often applied by the cashier pressing one of several different discount keys, each intended for a different discount offer or type. Cashiers press the wrong discount key, especially if the resulting discount amount is the same, literally thousands of times daily in large QSR chains.

In the end, the cascading effect of consolidating POS data from multiple POS systems across thousands of store locations, inconstancies between stores in how the POS is set up, and mistaken key presses by cashiers results in a mess of unusable data. Without the ability to normalize and clean up the errant data, the QSR chain can't accurately understand what products are being sold in different stores and regions and which promotions are driving profitable increases in purchases.

Mobivity ingests the data at every terminal across thousands of different locations and uses AI and machine learning trained by hundreds of millions of transactions to clean up inconsistencies and create a single, normalized data set. The marketing team can then use that to analyze sales and promotions and gain insights into how to optimize media spend and promotional offer strategies to drive profitable sales increases.

THE 1:1 FRAMEWORK

The 1:1 framework is designed to help you gain a better understanding of the complexity and precision of various 1:1 techniques. Take a look at Figure 15.1 to gain a better understanding where each of the techniques discussed in this chapter would fall on the framework.

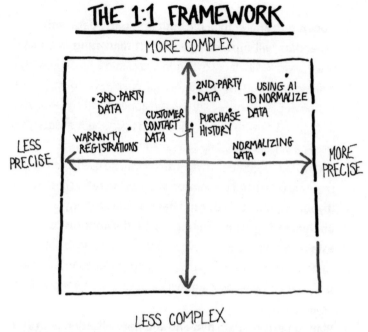

THE 1:1 FRAMEWORK
MORE COMPLEX

- 3RD-PARTY DATA
- WARRANTY REGISTRATIONS
- CUSTOMER CONTACT DATA
- 2ND-PARTY DATA
- USING AI TO NORMALIZE DATA
- PURCHASE HISTORY
- NORMALIZING DATA

LESS PRECISE ← → MORE PRECISE

LESS COMPLEX

Figure 15.1   The 1:1 framework is designed to help you understand the complexity-versus-precision equation for different kinds of campaigns.

KEY TAKEAWAYS

Here are some things to keep in mind as you reflect upon the concepts in this chapter.

- **First-party data is one of your company's most valuable assets.** The data you collect from and about customers represents strategic value to your company, value that can be leveraged through 1:1 marketing. The more PII you can collect on your customers, the greater your ability to reach them with messaging and ads. Combining detailed purchase data with your PII gives you the ability to inform and personalize your 1:1 marketing efforts.

- **Appending and enhancing your first-party data with other data will supercharge your 1:1 marketing.** You may want to work with friendly partners to create a second-party data exchange arrangement that will enable you to grow your customer base. Meanwhile, you can append and enhance your first-party data with a nearly unlimited assortment of data from third-party data companies to expand the insights you have about your customers. These insights can be used to more precisely target and personalize your 1:1 marketing efforts.

- **If your organization doesn't have a data strategy, implementing 1:1 marketing can be the impetus to establish one.** A critical component of a company's data strategy is to create a single source of truth for your customer data, by consolidating customer data scattered throughout the organization.

- **Plan to perform data hygiene and normalization with your customer data.** Most organizations have inconsistencies and inaccuracies in their customer data, especially when aggregating multiple sources of customer data scattered throughout the organization. Cleaning up the data and normalizing it will be a critical step in implementing 1:1 marketing. Without doing so, you are likely to end up with poorly personalized and targeted 1:1 marketing efforts.

IDENTITY: THE LINCHPIN
OF 1:1 MARKETING

Google will know that you are hungry for sushi before you do.
—BEN KUNZ, VP, MEDIASSOCIATES[1]

Chapter 9 told you there are three key components required to be a 1:1 marketer. We just covered the first one—the data you need to amass and normalize to power personalization. This chapter covers the second essential component—an identity graph.

As a reminder, an identity graph enables you to combine data about your prospects and customers into a single data set that can be used to launch and deploy campaigns. Perhaps it's not clear why an identity graph is a foundational element of 1:1 marketing.

Chapter 1 introduced the idea of the *addressable consumer*. With the majority of consumer consumption of media, entertainment, news, and education taking place on computers, smartphones, tablets, and connected televisions, and all of those devices being connected to the internet, it opens new possibilities of reaching consumers across all the devices they use. And as pointed out earlier, that's because the internet assigns unique addresses to each wireless network and to many devices, much like your home address makes it possible to reach you via direct mail.

To understand the critical role of an identity graph in achieving 1:1 marketing, let's start with a brief history of how ads have been targeted online for several decades. And more recently, how evolving stances on consumer privacy by governments and technology companies are changing the game for everyone targeting consumers via the internet. All of this explains the critical role of an identity graph for 1:1 marketers.

ALL DIGITAL ADVERTISING ISN'T TRULY ADDRESSABLE ADVERTISING

In the early days of digital advertising, *digital* meant reaching people on their desktop and laptop computers. While each website and internet access point has a unique address, computers do not. There isn't a unique identifier tied to a computer that would tell you which of the 200 computers in your office or the 5 computers in your household is being used by whom.

Instead, when online display advertising first became possible in 1995, it was made possible by a technology called a "cookie," which is simply a small file stored on the computer by a web browser that contains information about the user. Digital cookies were not created originally for the purpose of targeting ads, but rather to serve users' interests, such as maintaining their preferences and login data so they didn't have to sign in each time they visit a website. Once signed in and a cookie is saved to the user's computer, settings will automatically change to match their preferences each time they visit the website.

IN A NUTSHELL

Digital cookies are small files stored on a website visitor's computer that lets the website recognize the user when they return and personalize the user's experience while using the website.

But advertisers quickly determined that cookies could also serve their interests by storing information about the user that could later be used for targeting ads, such as websites visited or items previously shopped for. By dropping a cookie when a person visits a site, they could then be retargeted with ads related to the site they visited.

Everyone has experienced the phenomenon of shopping for an item, like shoes, and then suddenly being targeted with ads for shoes on every website you visit for days after that initial shopping visit. That's because your browser dropped a digital cookie or breadcrumb that is then used to tell the ad server you appear to be in the market for shoes. Therefore, the website is going to show you an ad for shoes. (Too often long after you've purchased the shoes you were originally shopping for!)

To be clear, cookies contain only information that visitors provide or can be inferred by their browsing history, such as sites they visit, their internet's connection location, type of connection, and type of device they are accessing. As noted earlier, cookies originally were used to store user preferences and login information, such as an email address. Users provided this information because they received a benefit in return—saving time, preventing them from having reset their preferences with every visit to a brand's website. By providing personally identifiable information (known as PII in the industry), websites would be able to identify users based on that PII.

And because the consumer and the website have a direct relationship (the consumer registered for access to content on the website), this type of cookie is known as a *first-party cookie*. The term *first-party*, used throughout the book, refers to the fact that the company collecting the information has a direct relationship with the consumer providing the information. And as noted in Chapter 15, first-party data is the most valuable data a brand can collect. This means first-party cookies are also extremely valuable for the brands that create their own pool of cookies.

As the online advertising market exploded, various companies were founded to broker and sell advertising on other companies' websites. These sites would drop a cookie that they could use to track consumers across sites and continually target with ads. These companies didn't generate revenue from consumers, but rather from businesses who want to advertise to consumers, such as in the retargeting example earlier.

> **IN A NUTSHELL**
>
> First-party cookies are created and maintained by a website you have a direct relationship with. When you register for access to a website and provide PII such as a name and email address, the website recognizes you every time you visit the website, by accessing its first-party cookie stored on your computer.

These sites didn't have a direct relationship with the consumer; their relationship was with the websites that let them create cookies for their users. This type of cookie was known as a third-party cookie since it wasn't owned by the site the consumer visited but rather by an unrelated *third party* (the company selling advertising).

In fact, most consumers didn't know that the website they visited was selling access to visitors to these advertising companies and letting them create cookies on their computers. It happened in the background, and some websites had partnerships with dozens of companies who dropped cookies on users' computers, often without their knowledge.

To recap, companies that sell advertising across many websites partner with websites to drop cookies on the computers of users who visit those websites. Because the advertising company doesn't have a direct relationship with consumers and is trading on the relationship the website has with its visitors, these cookies are called third-party cookies. Most users didn't even know the cookies were being created and their browsing activity was being tracked across websites.

COOKIES, LIKE MOST METHODS IN ADVERTISING, WERE NEVER ABSOLUTE OR PERFECT

Despite their popularity and universal acceptance by advertisers, digital cookies are not and never were a perfect method. First, cookies are exclusive to the browser that created them. A person using both Microsoft Edge and Google Chrome on a single computer appears to be two different people to the advertiser.

Second, cookies aren't persistent. They expire over time. And that means the user can no longer be identified and targeted once the cookie goes away, until a new cookie is created on the user's next visit to that website. The continual expiration and regeneration of cookies easily confuses ad servers, tricking them into identifying one person as multiple people.

Disappearing cookies also creates breaks in historical tracking, often preventing advertisers from linking new advertising impressions delivered to one person to past advertising impressions delivered to the same person. This can result in serving too many ads to some people and too few to others. It also prevents accurately attributing campaign performance to the ads delivered to each person who ultimately makes a purchase or otherwise completes the desired action the campaign was designed to achieve.

Third, the explosive growth of third-party cookies began to slow down the performance of websites, with some web pages accessing and updating dozens of cookies with each visit. Users began to notice, and so did the companies operating the websites people were visiting. The last thing a publisher wanted was to create a poor user experience, so leading publishers began to limit the number of third parties with which they would contract and allow to create cookies.

Moreover, publishers began to realize that amassing a treasure trove of PII represented the new oil of the digital world, adding exceptionally high value to the party that collected it. Companies like Facebook and Google grew to valuations that dwarfed traditional companies, like airlines, auto manufacturers, and retailers, despite the fact that traditional companies incurred much higher costs of goods—the cost of building an automobile is exponentially greater than the cost of creating and hosting a web page.

> ## IN A NUTSHELL
>
> Cookies had inherent issues that limited their usefulness. Each browser creates unique cookies, which means a single person can have multiple cookies for the same website. Cookies aren't persistent and expire frequently, which means preferences and tracking is lost periodically and has to be re-created. Finally, overuse of third-party cookies began to slow performance on websites, creating a poor user experience for website visitors.

But digital companies simply needed to attract an audience; the actual cost of providing services was relatively low. This point wasn't lost on digital publishers, who began to limit or even refuse to share PII with third parties that were building their own business value by monetizing the audiences that publishers were investing in to cultivate.

Fourth, once people started understanding the idea that websites were creating a "digital footprint" of them through the use of cookies, they grew concerned about their personal data being accessible to companies or bad actors with whom they had no relationship. Initially, most people didn't realize that when they visited a publisher's website, such as their favorite news channel, for example, dozens of companies unrelated to that channel were dropping cookies and using that visit to target ads to them on other websites they would later visit. As these practices came to light—in part because people started getting ads for products on other sites for many days after their initial shopping visit and it creeped them out—it created an uproar over consumer privacy.

In response, browser companies created security controls to ensure users' personal data is encrypted and difficult to gain access to unless the website owner has a direct relationship with the user. What's more, browsers began to give users control over the use of their cookies, allowing them to prevent cookies from being created and deleting cookies already stored on their computer periodically. When cookies are deleted, the user then "disappears" to advertisers, and all prior interactions and data are gone and can't be linked to future activities from that user.

IN A NUTSHELL

The biggest challenge with third-party cookies was the inherent concerns about consumer privacy, especially since few consumers understood that cookies were tracking them and targeting them with ads across websites. As consumers became aware of their use, a backlash resulted against the use of third-party cookies.

Eventually, privacy concerns resulted in sweeping governmental regulations across the globe in a drive to give consumers control over how their internet browsing activity and other data are shared. The European Union enacted the General Data Protection Regulation (GDPR) in May of 2018. GDPR requires users' consent to having their data stored by websites and also restricts the transfer of personal data outside the EU and EEA areas.

More regulations followed, with the California Consumer Protection Act (CCPA) going into effect in January 2020, with a similar goal of protecting consumer privacy and requiring consumer consent to store cookies. You've no doubt noticed the little pop-up window whenever you first visit a website that asks you to accept its use of cookies. This prompt is required by the new regulations.

Regulation signaled the beginning of the end for third-party cookies, but other factors resulted in the final two nails being hammered into the third-party-cookie coffin.

First Nail: Cookies Crumbled in a Mobile World

Surprisingly, these challenges weren't the biggest assault on the effectiveness of cookies. The explosive adoption of smartphones and tablets was. That's because many mobile browsers don't support cookies, and cookies created by mobile browsers that do support them are even less persistent than desktop cookies, often lasting less than a week.

Smartphones and tablets also multiplied the number of different devices a single person could be using, and since cookies are unique to each device and each browser on the device, a single user could now be represented by a dozen or more different cookies, further challenging an advertiser's ability to accurately target a single individual.

But there was a silver lining to the explosive use of mobile devices. Unlike computers, each mobile device is assigned a unique ID. Originally, the unique device ID (UDID) was passed to the apps that people used on their mobile devices. That device ID could then be used to target an ad to a specific device for ads displayed while using mobile apps.

IN A NUTSHELL

Mobile devices, including smartphones, tablets, and e-readers, each have a unique identifier referred to as a MAID. Unlike cookies, MAIDs are persistent for the life of the device and cover an entire device, including all browsers and apps. MAIDs were a game changer in making consumers addressable to marketers employing 1:1 marketing, especially with the rapid mobile adoption by consumers and shift of media consumption to mobile devices.

Early on, device manufacturers, including Apple and Google, realized that allowing the UDID to be visible and shared for advertising purposes presented identity risk for users. A new unique device ID was created, called an advertising ID, as a unique but anonymous ID that resolves to a single smartphone, tablet, or e-reader. Mobile advertising ID (MAID) is a generic term that each operating system named differently: Apple called its ID an ID for Advertisers (IDFA) and Google called its ID the Android Advertising ID.

Knowing the MAID for a specific device enables targeting ads to that device regardless of how the device is accessing the internet or from where. It transcends the network to identify the specific device. Unlike cookies, which expire frequently, ad IDs are persistent IDs that never change. That persistent nature made them ideal as a method for tying people to their mobile devices and being able to target ads once you could identify the person whose device the ad ID belongs to.

The ad ID (see Figure 16.1) is passed from the device to apps used on that device, but it is not passed to a web browser. This means ads appearing in apps can be targeted using ad IDs but ads on web browsers cannot. Therefore, ad targeting when someone is visiting a website from a

Figure 16.1 A MAID can be uploaded to an app server, which then allows 1:1 marketers to target those individuals. But a MAID is not uploaded via a mobile website, which means that 1:1 marketers can target that household (based on IP address) but not that specific individual.

web browser on a mobile device can only be as granular as the IP address. Third-party companies attempting to identify a specific device via mobile web have generally employed a form of probabilistic modeling, known as fingerprinting, that yielded mixed results in accuracy and eventually fell out of favor.

And finally, with devices used for streaming content, including Roku, Apple TV, and Google Chrome devices, many are creating their own unique IDs, which enables identifying some specific streaming devices. But those manufacturers often limit those device IDs' visibility for ad targeting, and there are many streaming devices for which there is no unique ID, such as DVD players, game boxes, cable set-top boxes, and laptops connected to a TV via wireless or HDMI cable. As a result, identifying streaming devices is typically accomplished via the IP address.

IN A NUTSHELL

Streaming television providers, such as Roku and Apple TV, have created their own unique identifiers. But because of limited scale of any single player in connected television, the ubiquitous IP address has become the de facto standard for connecting consumers with internet-connected television devices. In other words, marketers can reach consumers on streaming television using device IDs or IP addresses, but the IP address is more common because of its greater scale.

The Second and Final Nail: Browser Companies Ending Support for Third-Party Cookies

Firefox, an open-source web browser created by the Mozilla Foundation, and Safari, Apple's web browser, both began blocking third-party cookies to protect user privacy several years ago. But since the two browsers' worldwide share of the browser market is less than 25 percent,[2] it did not have a major impact on ad targeting via third-party cookies.

However, Google announced that it will no longer support third-party cookies starting in 2022. And that is a big deal, since Chrome controls more than 60 percent of the worldwide browser market share.[3] With more than 80 percent of browser usage not supporting third-party cookies, the advertising industry has come to accept that third-party cookies will no longer be available as an ad-targeting technology.

To make matters worse, Apple also announced that it will require users to proactively consent to having their MAIDs used for advertising targeting and has since issued software updates requiring user opt-in. Frankly, a change as significant as eliminating support for the primary identity method for targeting online ads—one that has been the de facto standard for more than 25 years—and then requiring consumer opt-in for the de facto standard for mobile ad targeting for the past decade, has thrown the industry into chaos as key players scramble to come up with alternative solutions. Many advertisers believe few consumers will consent to tracking,[4] and that would limit the ability for brands to reach consumers using the MAID. And initial opt-in rates suggest they have reason to be concerned.

Apple's moves are seen by many as collateral damage from the war between Facebook and Apple, whose business models and fundamental principles of consumer privacy are in direct conflict. Based on testing, Facebook estimates that Apple's new policies could reduce revenue on Facebook's Audience Network by more than 50 percent.[5]

Many in the digital advertising industry are concerned that the elimination of support for third-party cookies, despite alternatives being developed by multiple players and consortiums, will challenge 1:1 advertisers in reaching customers with ads across third-party websites at any meaningful scale, negating the value.

LEVERAGING THE POWER OF IDENTITY RESOLUTION IN THE CONNECTED WORLD

What? Didn't we start this chapter by talking about the opportunity brands will have getting their message in front of addressable consumers? And now we've told you about regulations, browser restrictions, and smartphone manufacturer privacy controls that might appear to eliminate the ability to reach addressable consumers across their devices. Will it even be possible going forward?

Absolutely. Don't let the technical opportunities and challenges of connected devices cloud the picture for what this means to brands desiring to connect with their audiences of one. The new connected consumer creates more opportunity and potential for 1:1 targeting than ever before, and it's readily available to any brand willing to invest the effort and resources to create and manage their own identity graph.

And that's the key: brands have to invest in building an identity graph that maps consumers between their data and their devices. Fortunately, first-party cookies will still be supported, and brands can use their own first-party cookies as well as other identifiers in their own identity graph. Furthermore, many companies are developing alternative identifiers that will be viable for targeting and reaching consumers across their devices, even after user consent mechanisms go into effect.

Chad Engelgau, CEO of Acxiom, explained, "A brand's ability to create an identity graph and then connect that identity graph to other identity graphs that are proactively being created in the ecosystem and doing so in a privacy compliant way makes 1:1 marketing possible." Acxiom is one of a number of companies that are helping brands build and manage identity graphs powered by first-party cookies. Chad doesn't believe that the industry changes are bad news and actually sees potential upside for 1:1 marketers, stating "It's a really exciting time, and we are absolutely out there, constantly promoting the need for brands to create a first-party identity graph to solve for 1:1 marketing."

Engelgau went on to say, "While third-party cookies have offered scale, there has been a question of accuracy given all of the challenges with cookies (noted earlier). In reality, over the last 20 years, it's quite possible that marketers have been spamming people because identity is not being applied effectively. With first-party cookies replacing third-party cookies and other methods being put into place, there will be greater levels of more targeted audiences available, so your media buys won't be as large but they're probably going to be as effective or even more effective."

Engelgau also believes the industry changes and brands taking ownership of their identity will help brands prove the efficacy of their advertising dollars.

"Because you own your identity graph, you will now be an active participant in the measurement of paid media," he explained. "You will have greater transparency on the performance, which again will create benefits for the brands in achieving greater efficiency, and for us as consumers because we're going to get a lot fewer ads that are redundant or not relevant."[6]

IN A NUTSHELL

Brands can reach addressable consumers across all of their devices thanks to the ability to create and own their own first-party cookies and identifiers, ultimately building a custom identity graph to power the brand's 1:1 marketing efforts.

We've also talked about the opportunity to reach consumers while watching television via connected televisions. "When it comes to connected TV and Over-the-Top Television (OTT), Apple simply does not pull the strings the way it does with mobile. Apple doesn't have a monopoly on TV, nor does it have the same audience scale or high-value demographic reach with Apple TV as it does with the iPhone,"[7] noted Tim Jenkins, executive vice president of Cadent, a company powering the evolution of TV brand advertising by connecting brands with national TV audiences across cable, broadcast, and OTT. Since the IP address is the primary identifier used to target users in connected television, brands will continue to have the ability to reach their customers while watching streaming television.

Bottom line? Your customers are now fully addressable across their devices. This will be a game changer for many brands that leverage the ability to know and connect with their buyers and prospects in ways never before possible. In the long run, this can contribute to a brand's market value in the same way companies like Google, Apple, and Amazon have benefitted.

By knowing your customers and prospects (thanks to the rich data sets available, in addition to their own valuable first-party data) and being able to reach them across all of their connected devices, a brand committed to connecting with their audiences of one can achieve levels of 1:1 targeting never before possible. Marketing budgets become war chests to engage with customers and prospects in deeper, more meaningful ways that ultimately win a greater share of their wallets. The level of deep insight available from having this level of connectivity with customers will impact all aspects of product and value delivery, from determining what products and services customers want to driving sales faster and more predictably than ever before.

So how does a brand create its own customer identity map? That's covered in the next chapter.

KEY TAKEAWAYS

Here are some things to keep in mind as you reflect upon the concepts in this chapter.

- **Cookies were originally created to enable personalized experiences on websites.** When a user registers for a website, and provides PII, the website saves a small file called a first-party cookie to the user's computer. When the user returns to the same website in the future, the user's preferences can be retrieved from the cookie and the experience personalized. First-party cookies are still used today and can be used by a brand to deliver ads to their own customers and website visitors.

- **Advertising companies created a different kind of cookie to track users across websites and target them with ads.** Companies partnered with websites that let them drop a cookie for each visitor to the website. These cookies could be used to target advertising across websites. Since the advertising company didn't have a direct relationship with the consumer, these cookies were called third-party cookies. They are no longer supported by browsers and are being deprecated as a consumer targeting method.

- **Each mobile device has a unique identifier called a MAID and it is a persistent identifier for the life of the mobile device.** Being able to map your customers to MAIDs enables connecting with them whenever they are consuming content on a mobile device. Device manufacturers are starting to require opt-in for every app for the MAID, which could limit their usefulness in tracking consumers across apps.

- **Brands can connect to their customers across their addressable devices by building a customer identity graph.** An identity graph maps people, their devices, and the data about them. Brands can create their own first-party identity graphs, and that enables them to recognize consumers across their devices. By connecting a brand's identity graph to identity graphs being created by other providers, a brand can reach its customers and prospects across devices and apps with 1:1 marketing efforts.

HOW TO CREATE AND
MANAGE YOUR IDENTITY GRAPH

Be yourself. Everyone else is already taken.
—OFTEN ATTRIBUTED TO OSCAR WILDE, AUTHOR AND PLAYWRIGHT[1]

The last chapter talked about why identity resolution is a foundational element for all 1:1 marketers. This chapter covers the specifics of how a brand can create an identity graph by mapping its customer data to the consumers' devices and digital identifiers.

Doing so unlocks the ability to reach your customers with a personalized message on any of their connected devices. More important, by creating and managing your own identity graph, you can reach the same people on the same and other devices more consistently. In other words, you can stay connected with your audience of one across any device (email, direct mail, desktop computer, smartphone, tablets or connected television) and any ad platform (Facebook, Google, Amazon, Yahoo, USA Today, or thousands of others).

Of course, titling a chapter "How to Create and Manage Your Identity Graph" assumes you know what other options are available to you besides creating an identity resolution. So let's start by answering the question of what options you have if your goal is to be able to deliver personalized messages to your customers across any of the devices they use.

Chapter 9 established that 1:1 marketing requires three things:

1. Customer data
2. Identity graph
3. 1:1 marketing plan

For this discussion, we're going to assume you have ample customer data and you've developed a plan to begin engaging your audiences of one with personalized messages.

Now, you're ready to start delivering messages to your customers. You should have contact information for your customers within your existing customer data. Contact information includes personally identifiable information (PII) such as email addresses, phone numbers, and home address.

To launch your campaign, you'll rely on business partners to actually connect the message to a customer, whether that's a direct mail house that prints the address on the envelope and mails it, or a social media platform like Facebook or Twitter delivering an ad on their channel. The partner will use the customer data that you provide them to target your customer with your ad. In other words, you're saying, "Here's our customer data. Now, please go out and use our data to target our customers via direct mail, online display, paid social media, marketing automation, etc."

You have two options for connecting the PII from your customers to the audiences they can reach via their platforms:

1. You can have a direct match between your first-party data and the targeting platform.
2. You can use your custom identity graph to translate your customer data to the platform's audience IDs.

These two approaches might seem like they're the same thing, so let's dig in a little bit and explain the differences between the two.

DIRECT MATCH WITH YOUR FIRST-PARTY DATA TO A TARGETING PLATFORM

The easiest method for targeting your customers is simply sending a copy of your customer file to a platform that can use it for targeting your customers with messages.

For example, you can send your customer file to a direct mail house that will print addresses on envelopes and send personalized printed messages to your customers via mail. Or you can upload your customer file to Facebook, LinkedIn, Google, or other demand side platforms (DSPs). Or you can upload it to an ad platform you use to place ads across exchanges of thousands of DSPs, such as The Trade Desk (see Figure 17.1). They'll match your first-party data to their identity resolution, and anyone that matches can be targeted with digital ads.

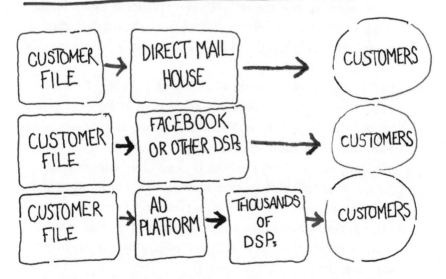

Figure 17.1 Think of the direct match approach as something similar to making chicken soup—there are plenty of different recipes for chicken soup, but in the end, they all lead to the same final result.

There are several benefits to this approach:

- **It's easy.** You simply email or upload your customer file to the platform.
- **It's targeted.** The targeting list for that campaign reflects up-to-date customer data since it reflects a complete data set at the moment it is exported for uploading to the targeting platform.
- **It's cost efficient.** Ad platforms, like Facebook, don't typically charge an advertiser fee for onboarding their customer data, so it's a low-cost option.

But there are some drawbacks:

- **Data security.** You are forced to share your prized and confidential customer data with every ad platform you want to run campaigns with.
- **It's labor intensive.** The process of exporting your customer file and uploading it to the targeting platform must be repeated with every campaign you run and with every platform. (Some brands employ a third-party onboarder, who can onboard the same file to multiple ad platforms and thus require just one file upload for each campaign.)
- **Lack of transparency.** Some ad platforms, including Facebook, won't share impression data with advertisers after the campaign, leaving you dependent on the platform's campaign measurement to validate the value of each campaign.
- **Matching issues.** Every platform is using its unique methodology for mapping your customers to their devices, which can result in different matching results between platforms. For example, the same device could be matched to two different people or households with two different platforms if either platform's matching logic is faulty.

CREATING YOUR CUSTOM IDENTITY GRAPH

The other option is for a brand to develop its own custom identity graph based on its first-party data. You will partner with an identity resolution platform that specializes in building custom first-party identity graphs, like Acxiom or Infutor. Through identity resolution, the partner will optimize and resolve all data points (online and offline) to create a custom identity graph with a consistent and persistent 360-degree view of individuals and their relationship with brands.

IN A NUTSHELL

When you want to reach your customers across their digital devices, you either have to send your customer data to platforms that can reach consumers with digital ads or create your own identity graph. With your own identity graph based on your first-party data, you need only provide digital ad platforms with the anonymous digital identifier for the customer's device.

Your identity graph maps all known anonymous digital identifiers for each consumer. This enables you to push a file of anonymous digital identifiers directly to the publisher. The publisher receives anonymous digital IDs that they can use to target your customers on their platform, but unlike sending your customer file directly to a DSP, they won't have any visibility or access to your customer data. You maintain ownership of your customer data throughout the process.

Most identity resolution companies can also help you build and manage your first-party cookie pool, which will be especially critical going forward as third-party cookies go away. Your identity resolution partner will map your first-party cookies to their referential identity graph. They will partner with other referential identity graphs plus media partners to enable mapping of your first-party cookies with these other graphs, extending your ability to reach consumers across all of their devices and on whatever apps and websites they use. All without the need for using third-party cookies.

This method requires more effort and up-front cost. You have to work with an identity resolution platform to build out the mapping of customer data to all of the possible digital identifiers that publishers and ad platforms use to target those customers. However, once the initial mapping is completed, an ongoing, automated process can be put into place to continually refresh the customer file and digital IDs, since both data sets change often.

Brands who plan to transition to 1:1 marketing and will be communicating frequently with customers will be best served by investing the time and resources into building a custom identity graph. The benefits far outweigh the initial and ongoing investment.

Why Create a Custom Identity Graph?

Creating your identity graph, versus relying on onboarders or sending your customer file directly to DSPs, provides several competitive advantages including:

Ensures Consistency in Targeting and Measurement

Because onboarders and DSPs often use different methods for mapping people and their devices, the accuracy of the mapping varies widely between platforms, which is a big problem for a 1:1 marketer. No matter how sophisticated you are in personalizing a message to a customer, it's useless if you've connected the wrong device to the wrong person.

Relying on each DSP to map your customer data to their identity resolution will result in inconsistencies into which customers actually receive a message. You think Customer A is the one being targeted, but the DSP may have mapped Customer B's device to Customer A. You will be none the wiser that the mismatch occurred, since you have no way of validating another platform's mapping accuracy.

For example, you may think you are talking to a 32-year-old male who buys premium food products but may actually be talking to a 62-year-old woman who lives on a pension and buys generic brands. And if you're using purchase data for closed-loop sales lift measurement to evaluate campaign performance, the wrong device mapped to the wrong person could result in a person in the control group being counted in the test group, muddling measurement results and potentially even causing the campaign to appear to produce a negative sales lift.

Conversely, if you are creating your own identity graph, you will perform all of the mapping of the devices to people. Even if during that process the identity resolution platform you rely on has the wrong device mapped to a person, that will be applied consistently throughout all campaigns and on every DSP since they are simply targeting the device ID you tell them to target. Your results will be consistent across campaigns, and you can rest assured that the same people are being targeted during the campaign.

Frees You from the Restrictions of Walled Gardens and Other DSPs

When you own your identity resolution, you can activate media on any platform of your choosing, based on your consistent, validated methodology for mapping people to devices. If you aren't satisfied with a platform or aren't getting the data you need for measurement, you can easily move to another platform with minimal effort. You aren't beholden to any one social media platform or DSP for targeting and measurement, instead remaining in control of both.

Furthermore, with recent headlines about some of the behemoth platforms allowing data to be shared with questionable entities without user or marketer knowledge, managing your own identity graph reduces the risk of your customer data ending up in another entity's possession. Instead of sharing your prized customer data to publishers (e.g., Facebook Custom Audiences), you build your own custom audiences using your first-party data plus second and third-party data and only send publishers and DSPs the anonymous identifiers they need to deliver the ad to the target audience via their platform. Your data never leaves your control.

Enables Cross-Screen, Cross-Publisher, Closed-Loop Measurement

Publishers and DSPs need only provide you with the digital IDs that were targeted with ads during a campaign for you to enable what marketers often call "the Holy Grail" of digital advertising: cross-screen, cross-publisher closed-loop measurement. The identity platform you partnered with to build your identity graph can convert anonymous digital IDs to the person IDs used by the measurement vendor you choose for them to complete a single measurement study based on all the impressions delivered during the campaign across a multitude of DSPs using the same methodology and data set.

HOW TO CREATE AND MANAGE A CUSTOMIZED IDENTITY GRAPH

Creating and managing a customized identity graph involves the following steps:

1. Consolidating and normalizing your customer data
2. Appending and enriching your customer data for targeting
3. Mapping your customers to their digital identifiers
4. Creating a mechanism for creating and sharing targeting segments with DSPs
5. Developing a process for ongoing refreshing of your identity graph

We'll cover each of these involved steps in its own section.

Step 1: Consolidating and Normalizing Your Customer Data

The first step in building an identity graph is identifying all of your customer data, which often is stored in multiple silos across an organization. Additionally, you must normalize and consolidate your customer data into a single data set. This process was covered in detail in Chapter 15 on data.

Step 2: Appending and Enriching Your Customer Data for Targeting

Once you've pulled together all of your customer data, eliminated dupli-cates, and have a clean set of customer data, you'll be ready to overlay your customer data with additional data to help you better target and personalize messages to customers. In Chapter 15, we covered in detail all of the various types of data and data sources you can use to enrich your understanding of customers.

Over time you want to invest in acquiring the second- and third-party data sets that provide valuable insight into your customers and give you the ability to segment your customer database into smaller, related groups of customers that have certain criteria. For example, a restaurant such as Chili's might want to overlay demographic information to identify households with two or more children; these people are more likely to be interested in family value packs, versus unmarried people who will find an email promoting dinner for four of little value. Conversely, they can target unmarried members of their frequent diner program with cocktail events happening at the restaurant.

You can start simple and expand your use of outside data over time. Each data set you license costs money, and you have to make sure you have a strategy for effectively using the insights from its data to improve your marketing effectiveness to justify the cost. Say a vendor of third-party data charges you five cents per customer for their data. If you have one million customers, that data costs $50,000. That sounds expensive, but if you use that data to drive an incremental $300,000 in sales by better targeting an offer and personalizing the messaging in a way that causes more customers to purchase, then it's money well spent.

Don't be afraid to iterate over time by using additional data sources and trying different targeting ideas and personalization tactics, testing whenever possible (e.g., conducting A/B split testing of offers, messages). In the earlier Chili's example, they could overlay competitive purchase data with their customer file, tagging customers who visit their competitors' restaurants regularly.

> **IN A NUTSHELL**
>
> Enhancing your first-party data with second- and third-party data provides a richer view of customers, and enables more precise targeting and personalization of messages and offers.

By identifying customers spending heavily at competitors, Chili's could test higher value offers with these customers than they offer regular customers, and then measure sales lift over time to see if they are able to convert some of those purchases away from competitors.

As long as you can measure the effectiveness of the data you overlay and produce a profitable return on your marketing spend for those customers, the sky should be the limit on what data you overlay.

Step 3: Mapping Your Customers to Their Digital Identifiers

With your customers consolidated into a single repository and your data appended, the next challenge is reaching your customers with your messages.

If you're sending direct mail, all you need is a mailing address. You can send that to a direct mail fulfillment house and it can print and mail your pieces. Similarly, if you want to send emails to your customers, you simply need to have their email addresses and you can upload a message to an email sending platform and send the campaign.

If you want to reach your customers with a digital ad when they are on a social media platform, such as Facebook or Twitter, or on any app or website that sells advertising, then it's not quite as easy. The identity resolution platform maps your customers to their digital identifiers using their identity graph comprising digital identifiers mapped to hundreds of millions of people and households. You send the anonymous digital identifiers for the people or households you want to reach with a campaign to the ad platform delivering the ad.

As discussed in an earlier chapter, digital identifiers differ based on the device a person is using. Someone using an app on their mobile phone or tablet has a mobile ad ID (e.g., MAID) assigned to that device. Someone visiting a website from their laptop computer will have a cookie and/or IP address associated with them. If you are trying to reach someone with a commercial while they watch a television show on one of the hundreds of streaming platforms available, then they will be tied to their IP address. In some cases, they also have a device assigned by the streaming app such as Roku, which uses what they call a Roku ID to identify the device accessing their platform, whether it's a Roku Stick, Roku Box, or other device.

The identity resolution platform you work with also has amassed as many pieces of PII as possible for each consumer. This gives them the best chance of being able to map digital and device IDs to as many of your customers as possible.

For example, you may have email addresses for all of your customers but phone numbers for only 30 percent of your customers and home addresses for only 20 percent of your customers. By providing all of these data points to the platform, they will map the maximum number of customers to the maximum known digital identifiers possible, allowing you to reach the majority of your customers with a 1:1 marketing message. The platform can also help you fill in the missing pieces of data, making your first-party customer data more complete.

IN A NUTSHELL

Identity resolution platforms can help you fill in missing pieces of customer data, including home addresses and phone numbers.

There are numerous identity resolution platforms. Choosing the right one can be a challenge, because they often use different methods for building their identity resolution. Different methods yield different levels of accuracy and scale. Many identity resolution platforms use registration data that consumers use to log into various websites and apps as one way to accumulate PII mapped to a digital identifier, such as a MAID. While this can provide a high level of accuracy, there are challenges with using email as the PII for mapping consumers to their digital identifiers (see the following section, "Which PII Is Best?").

To increase the number of customers they can match with, some identity resolution platforms may use one of many methods of probabilistic modeling to infer the digital identifiers that belong to a customer. This method involves a certain amount of guesswork and by its nature is less accurate than a method that uses registration or login data. In the end, most identity resolution platforms employ a combination of deterministic and probabilistic methods, and often let you establish an acceptable threshold of confidence scoring for matching. (For a discussion about evaluating identity resolution platforms based on the method they use, see the upcoming section "Scale Versus Accuracy.")

Which PII Is Best?

The reality is few companies succeed in capturing every type of PII for every customer. This is especially true if customers conduct business with you in different ways (e.g., online versus telephone versus in person). It may also depend on how you deliver products; if you fulfill products or services electronically, you may never have a reason to obtain a customer's home address. But if you have to deliver a product, such as a large appliance, to a customer, then you must have their home address or at least the address where they want the appliance delivered.

So which type of PII offers the best match rate? Generally speaking, home address is the most persistent and accurate PII available for consumers. That's because the US Postal Service provides methods for continually updating home addresses as people move, new homes are built, street names change, and so on. Most companies use those tools to periodically update their address file. It's also the most persistent because most people have just one home address and they don't move that often (on average about once every seven years).

Contrast that with phone numbers. Many people have only a mobile phone today. But many households still have a home phone. Plus, people might choose to give you a work phone number when purchasing with your company, especially if they are having goods shipped to their office instead of their home. And each member of the household has their own mobile phone number. Plus, phone numbers change over time.

Even more challenging is email address. Most people have on average six email addresses! If that sounds crazy, consider your own situation: Do you have a personal email address? A work email address? A family email address? Perhaps one for a hobby you participate in? Or one you use for job searching?

The other challenge with email addresses is that the average email address is valid for only three years. Remember that old Yahoo email address you used 10 years ago but failed to update with companies you did business with back then? What about the email address from the last job (or two) that is still associated to your record in multiple companies' databases?

IN A NUTSHELL

Home address represents the most persistent, least frequently changing PII you can use for matching your customers to their digital identifiers.

Most identity resolution platforms maintain multiple pieces of PII and often maintain a history of prior phone numbers, email addresses, home addresses, and even prior names (such as a maiden name). Not true if you are matching to a single ad platform, like Facebook. Inevitably, some records will simply fail to match. For example, a person might have used one email address to sign up and register with a company and a different email address when they purchased products from the company. Unfortunately, that failure rate can be as high as 60 percent with some files!

If you have a way to collect multiple email addresses from your customers over time, you'll want to associate as many email addresses as possible to each customer record to maximize your chances of being able to map them to their digital identifiers. And if you have a reason to obtain home address, that will improve your match rate greatly with the identity resolution platform you use.

Scale Versus Accuracy

When evaluating identity resolution platforms, you have to evaluate each on a number of factors. The two most important factors are the scale of their identity graph and the accuracy of their mapping of consumers to their digital identifiers.

Limited scale hinders your ability to conduct 1:1 marketing with the majority of your customers. Match rates can be surprisingly low, with smaller identity resolution platforms capable of mapping to less than 20 percent of your customers. That means you achieve 1:1 marketing across their digital devices with just one out of every five of your customers.

Most companies won't consider the value of communicating effectively with a fraction of their customers to be worth the effort of implementing 1:1 marketing. Furthermore, to accurately measure campaigns based on closed-loop metrics, such as in-store sales, scale becomes critical since the actual incidence of purchase is a fraction of people exposed to the advertising; too few purchases prevents closed-loop measurement.

Like accuracy, the scale at which identity resolution platforms are able to accurately map customer data to digital IDs also varies greatly from one vendor to the next for the same reasons that accuracy varies. It's not unusual to see scale differences between vendors of five times.

The balancing of scale and accuracy is a challenge for every identity resolution platform. For a platform that focuses on accuracy, the goal is to use a method that would be classified as deterministic. In the marketing world, deterministic methodology is defined as a data set of people who have provided some form of PII that can be connected to at least one digital identifier. The largest identity resolution platforms offer large-scale deterministic matching.

The other methodology for matching instead uses modeling and behavior to infer a connection between a consumer and their digital identifiers. This methodology is referred to as probabilistic, in that a certain amount of guesswork must be employed during this process of inference.

The upside is the ability to achieve tremendous match scale because they are limited only in being able to see enough devices to which they can apply the modeling techniques.

> **IN A NUTSHELL**
>
> Most identity resolution companies use a combination of deterministic and probabilistic methods of identity resolution to balance matching accuracy with scale.

You will likely find that most identity resolution platforms combine both deterministic and probabilistic methods for building their identity graphs. This is necessary to balance between scale and accuracy. In evaluating vendors, you want to understand clearly how they have built their identity graph and what percentage is based on deterministic versus probabilistic methods.

To evaluate and measure both scale and accuracy, you should consider running a test of any identity resolution platform you are considering. Some marketers use a "truth set" to test and evaluate. This often takes the form of customer data validated to a home address, such as a retailer who ships product to customers purchasing on their apps and can match a MAID to a home address. You can do a simple truth set evaluation by providing the anonymous IDs to the vendors you want to test and asking them to return the home address to which they've assigned them.

If you don't have a truth set, then you can run test campaigns with multiple vendors using the same target audience and evaluating at the end how many total households and IDs they found in their mapping process, how many target households they reached during the campaign, and what the comparison metrics between them were.

Metrics can be as simple as click-through-rate or more sophisticated, such as buyers and incremental dollars generated. This last factor—incremental dollars generated—will be the most telling when determining accuracy. Obviously, the more correctly the campaign is delivered against the target household, the higher the results should be (because you wasted fewer impressions on the wrong people, etc.).

Be sure when evaluating identity resolution platforms that they built an identity graph. Unfortunately, many companies promote their identity graph, but a thorough investigation will uncover that they are simply licensing someone else's identity graph. For example, they may have licensed LiveRamp's identity graph. Simply ask (and probe) to make sure they built their own identity graph and make certain you understand exactly how they built it. If you aren't satisfied with their answers, look to other vendors who can tell you precisely how their graphs are constructed.

Step 4: Building a Mechanism for Creating and Sharing Target Segments with DSPs

Now that you have your customers consolidated along with their digital identifiers, you are ready to begin outputting files of target customers to DSPs to begin running campaigns. You need to have your data in a platform that allows you to query the data based on any combination of data fields to create segments of customers to message. You also need to pull in any data that will be used to personalize those messages.

Chances are if you employ a data platform to assist you with the process of consolidating, deduplicating, and normalizing your customer data, they will offer a self-service platform that will enable you to query the data and share data files with DSPs. As noted earlier, this could take the form of a customer data platform or something similar. You need someone trained on your team to run queries and perform analysis.

Keep in mind that if you also want to measure your campaigns based on purchases and other online and offline activities, you need a way to bring exposure data back into your platform or a measurement platform to perform the measurement study. Exposure data is simply a list of the digital identifiers for which a campaign ad was displayed.

Typical measurement studies compare the purchases of those exposed to an ad to the purchases of people identical to the targeted group who weren't shown the ad during the campaign. This second group is known as the control group. For example, if the study shows that the control group purchased 20 percent less than the exposed group, then the incremental sales lift would be 20 percent for that campaign.

Most DSPs will share the exposed IDs with the advertiser during or after the campaign, especially if the process is automated. Not all social platforms are willing to share exposure data with the advertiser after a campaign, so be sure you know what the policies are of the platforms you choose before placing the campaign. And with the advent of first-party cookies, those can now be inserted into the digital ad at the time of delivery, allowing you to get impression data directly from the ads versus having to receive impression data from the ad platform.

Digital IDs need to be converted into customer IDs to account for the same customer seeing the ad on multiple devices. The identity resolution platform you use can perform the conversion to enable a closed-loop measurement study.

Step 5: Developing a Process for Ongoing Refreshing of Your Identity Graph

The final factor to consider is how you will ensure your identity resolution remains current. Customers come and go, they move, they get rid of old devices and buy new devices. You must establish a process to ensure that all of these changes are reflected in your identity resolution, or your 1:1 marketing campaigns will become less effective over time.

Most identity resolution platforms have a standard process and mechanism for refreshing the mapping of digital identifiers to customers on a periodic basis. We recommend that the refresh occurs no less than monthly and preferably weekly, since customer data and digital identifiers become outdated very quickly.

By refreshing your file regularly, you can be confident that when you embark on a new campaign and create a targeting file from your customer data, the digital identifiers you send are accurate and complete. Having up-to-date mappings improves any DSP's ability to deliver a campaign in full against the estimated impressions.

KEY TAKEAWAYS

Here are some things to keep in mind as you reflect upon the concepts in this chapter.

- **When you want to reach your customers across their digital devices, you have two options.** Upload your priceless customer data to each ad platform on which you want to run. Or build your own first-party identity graph that you control. The second option lets you control your customer data and only provide platforms with anonymous digital identifiers for the consumers you want to reach.
- **Building your own identity graph requires investment but pays huge dividends.** When you employ your own identity graph, you ensure consistent targeting and measurement across every platform, since identical identity resolution is being applied to every campaign. It also frees you from the limitations and loss of control walled gardens and DSPs introduce. And perhaps most important, it allows you to conduct cross-screen, cross-publisher campaign measurement to know the precise impact of your advertising dollars.
- **You must partner with an identity resolution company to build your own first-party identity graph.** Identity resolution companies help you match your first-party data to all of the anonymous digital identifiers used by your customers. They can also help you fill holes in your first-party data, adding home address and phone numbers to records with only email addresses, for example. Finally, they can help you build and manage your own set of first-party cookies, solving for the loss of third-party cookies and allowing for direct campaign measurement.

FUN WITH ROI CALCULATIONS—EVEN IF YOU'RE NOT A MATH WHIZ

There are three kinds of people—those who are good
with numbers, and those who aren't.

—ANONYMOUS

Here's one of the great things about the world we live in—it's entirely possible to measure the return on investment (ROI) of your 1:1 marketing campaign.

If you're thinking, "Well, of course I'm going to do that," remember this—that wasn't always easy to do. In fact, back in the *Mad Men* days of the 1950s and 1960s, the idea of genuinely measuring the ROI of an ad campaign was a pipe dream. If you tried to correlate a bump in revenues to a campaign you ran, you would quickly find a lot of other people were claiming rights to the sales bump—the sales team, the PR agency, the retailers, or even the new whiz kid in the finance department. During that era, measuring the ROI of a mass marketing campaign was nearly impossible (unless you ran a direct mail campaign, in which case you could measure the results, but for our purposes here, we're talking about traditional TV, radio, print, and outdoor campaigns).

The good news is that it's now possible to connect the dots between a 1:1 marketing campaign and the revenue (or more important, the profit) that the campaign generated. This chapter is designed to start with relatively simple calculations and then get into more and more complex calculations as we go along. With that in mind, we've divided the chapter into two sections. The first section shows you a relatively easy way to calculate your ROI. You'll need to know some basic math for that calculation, but it's well within your abilities.

The second section dives into some more advanced calculations. These are also within your abilities, but you'll need to put your thinking cap on. We discuss something called lifetime value (LTV) and then use the LTV calculation to help you calculate your ROI in that section. Both of those concepts will help you do a more accurate ROI calculation.

Simple ROI Calculation	**Advanced ROI Calculation**
Perfect if you are:	Perfect if you are:
• In a hurry • Terrible with math • OK with a less-than-ideal answer • Making your calculation on a back of a napkin	• Detail-oriented • Pretty good with math • Need a specific, bulletproof answer • Making a presentation to your CFO

So . . . let's do this, shall we?

THE EASY (BUT IMPERFECT) WAY TO CALCULATE YOUR ROI

The easiest way to calculate the ROI of a marketing campaign is to take the sales growth, subtract the marketing cost, and then divide by the marketing cost. In plain English, that means you find out how much your sales increased in dollars during your campaign. Then you take that figure and subtract the amount you spent on the campaign. Finally, you take that answer and divide it by the amount you spent on the campaign.

Doing the calculation this way, you can get a simple, back-of-the-envelope understanding of whether or not your marketing campaign grew your revenue. Here's what the formula looks like:

(Sales Growth – Marketing Cost) / Marketing Cost = Simplified ROI

In this example, if sales grew by $1,000 during the month of March and the marketing campaign cost $100 during the month of March, then the simple ROI is 900 percent.

$$(($1{,}000 - $100) / $100) = 900\%$$

That calculation is pretty straightforward, but it makes a big assumption—that the total month-over-month sales growth is directly attributable to the marketing campaign. But sometimes sales are growing organically on their own. For example, if sales are growing by 4 percent per month over the past 12 months, then your ROI calculation for the marketing campaign should strip out 4 percent from the sales growth.

Here's how the formula looks when you strip out the 4 percent organic sales growth:

(Sales Growth – Average Organic Sales Growth – Marketing Cost) /
Marketing Cost = ROI

So let's do an example using the preceding formula. Let's say that your company averages 4 percent growth per month and you run a $10,000 campaign during the month of March. The sales growth for that month is $15,000. Remember, 4 percent of that growth is organic, so you have to strip out the 4 percent (which is $600).

$$($15{,}000 - $600 - $10{,}000) / $10{,}000 = 44\%$$

A 44 percent return on your marketing investment is pretty substantial. For your business, your results will probably be much lower, but by using the preceding formula, you'll be able to do a relatively easy calculation that will give you a pretty clear understanding of your marketing ROI.

A MORE COMPLEX BUT MORE ACCURATE WAY TO CALCULATE YOUR ROI

Before going on to the more complex calculation, there are a few things to remember about any marketing investment. For starters, the impact of your marketing campaign builds over time.

Say you've invented a new energy drink and you start advertising on January 1. The first ads you run in January are going to have much less impact than the ads you run in July because the ads in July will be building on the awareness from the previous six months. In similar fashion, the ads you run in December will have more impact than the ones you ran for the previous 12 months for the very same reason. We call this the snowball effect (see Figure 18.1).

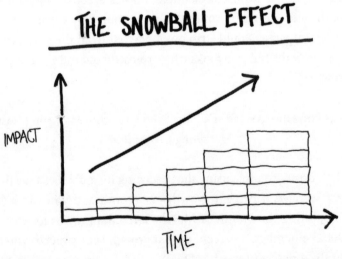

Figure 18.1 If you run a campaign consistently and at a certain level of frequency, the impact of your ads increases over time because consumers become more familiar with your brand.

We know the CEO of a Paris-based software as a service (SaaS) company that started to experience rapid growth after being in business for eight years. The growth was phenomenal, so we called the CEO to find out what he was doing to experience such a rapid rise in sales. Since it was a metrics-based company that closely tracked the ROI of its paid search, online display, and paid social media campaigns, we were eager to hear about the company's ROI.

"I still lose money on every campaign we run," the CEO told us. We were a little taken aback by that, so we kept listening. "We track the campaigns closely and follow the customer as they go from initial click through final purchase. When we do that, we're still in negative ROI territory. But we're also aware that each customer we gain refers us to their friends and associates, so there's added value to the sale that's not in the calculation. We also only use the first-year revenue gained in the calculation. We don't include the revenue from the customer in year two, year three, and so on."

That's a great example of why there are some gray areas in any marketing ROI calculation that you do—there are variables and nuances that aren't always captured by a mathematical formula.

Now let's move on to the more advanced way to calculate marketing ROI. As mentioned, the advanced calculation includes concepts like LTV and a few other things, so let's dive into that calculation right now.

We'll start with a simplified version of LTV and then move on to the ROI calculation. Here's the formula for a simplified version of LTV:

The price of your product/service
× how many times your customer buys it in a year
× how many years they'll be a customer
= Simplified LTV

As an example, let's say the average price for a Comcast subscription in Kansas City is $100 per month. You would expect 12 repeat purchases every year. And the average customer stays with you for three years.

So the simplified LTV in the Comcast version is:

$100 × 12 per year × 3 years, which equals $3,600.

But that formula for LTV uses *revenue* instead of *profit* for the calculation. That's OK for a basic calculation, but there are better, more accurate ways to do the math. In the more accurate version of LTV, you factor in several key data points:

- The profitability of each sale
- Your retention rate (i.e., the likelihood your customer will remain a customer from one year to the next)
- The discount rate (i.e., the time value of money; in other words, the fact that $10 earned today is worth more than $10 earned 5 years later because of inflation and other things)

Using the Comcast example, our data points might look like this:

Total number of customers at the beginning of year 1 = 1,000
Average purchase price = $100 per month
Net profit per purchase = 20%
Number of repeat purchases = 12
Average retention rate = 80% (and then everyone quits after year 3)
Discount rate = 10%

Let's dig into the preceding terms so we're clear on what they all mean.

When we say that the net profit per purchase is 20 percent, we've already accounted for all other costs. For example, if we charge $100 for our product, and we make $20 in net profit, that means we've already included the overhead (e.g., labor, office space, etc.), the cost of goods sold (e.g., cable, trucks, etc.), taxes, interest, and even the acquisition cost (e.g., the cost of running ads to acquire that customer). In other words, you would sell your product for $100, then pay for everything required to make that product, and then have a $20 bill to stuff in your pocket at the end of the day. Make sense?

The discount rate represents the opportunity cost of using the money for marketing instead of using it in other ways. For example, if you had $500,000 to spend on your Comcast marketing campaign for Kansas City, you would have to account for the fact that, alternatively, you could invest that money in other investments in the company and make, say, a 10 percent return on it.

To understand why we have a discount rate, pretend for a minute that you're the CFO of Comcast. Your job, your salary, and even your bonus are tied to one thing—how you invest Comcast's money. If you have $500,000 to invest, and you could get a 10 percent return by putting it into the stock market or a 5 percent return by putting it into marketing, then the smart thing to do would be to put it into the stock market, right?

While the preceding scenario oversimplifies things, the discount rate gives smart numbers people (like the CFO) a way to account for other investments they could make with that money. In other words, the discount rate levels the playing field in a way when you're thinking about where to invest capital.

Now let's put on our thinking caps (Figure 18.2) and kick up the financial discussion a notch.

THE PROVERBIAL THINKING CAP

Figure 18.2 The next section is a breeze . . . if you're a math major. For the rest of us, we'll need to put on our thinking caps.

In Table 18.1, you'll see a term called *net present value* (NPV), which is the number you arrive at when you use the discount rate to calculate the value of your money over time. The NPV gives you the accurate dollar value of your investment.

Take a spin through the following numbers. They might be a bit confusing at first—that's normal—but we'll talk about them afterward so we can be sure we're all on the same page. Also, it might help if you just review the "year 1" numbers at first. Be sure you have a handle on that column before diving into the other columns. If you do that, it'll be much easier to follow along.

Table 18.1   Lifetime Value per Customer Factoring Net Present Value

COMCAST KANSAS CITY EXAMPLE CALCULATION			
	YEAR 1	**YEAR 2**	**YEAR 3**
Total Customers	**1,000**	1,000 × 80% = 800	800 × 80% = 640
Average Yearly Revenue per Customer	**$100 × 12 = $1,200**	$100 × 12 = $1,200	$100 × 12 = $1,200
Average Net Profit Per Customer	**$1,200 × 20% = $240**	$1,200 × 20% = $240	$1,200 × 20% = $240
Discount Rate	**1**	1 + 10% = 1.1	1.1 + 10% = 1.2
Yearly Net Profit	**1,000 customers × $240 per customer = $240,000**	800 customers × $240 per customer = $192,000	640 customers × $240 per customer = $153,600
Yearly Net Profit at NPV	**$240,000**	$192,000 ÷ 1.1 = $174,545	$153,600 ÷ 1.2 = $128,000
Cumulative Net Profit from 1,000 Customers at NPV	**$240,000**	$414,545	$542,545
Total LTV per Customer at NPV	**$240**	$480 ÷ 1.1 = $436	$720 ÷ 1.22 = $600

OK, now that you've looked at the numbers in the chart, let's do a quick recap and then plow ahead:

- Over the past few paragraphs, we discussed the fact that the starting point for all ROI calculations is customer LTV.
- LTV is the total amount of profit you'll generate from your customers over the course of their engagement with your brand.
- So if you had 1,000 customers and your annual profit is $240 per customer, your total profit would be $240,000.

That's pretty straightforward, right? Hang on a second. It gets a little more complicated:

- To accurately calculate the LTV over time, you have to use the discount rate to represent the opportunity cost if you used that money elsewhere.
- The NPV is a way to use the discount rate to account for the fact that $1 in year 1 is worth less than $1 in year 2. In other words, if you have $1 today, that dollar is only worth about 97 cents next year because of the 3 percent inflation rate.
- In the preceding example, if you generate $240 in net profit per customer, and you keep that customer for three years, the cumulative net profit is *not* $720 (i.e., $240 × 3 = $720). Instead, it's $600 because of the NPV calculation.

Now that we've calculated our net profit per customer and used the discount rate to arrive at the NPV, we need to talk about a few other things:

- For starters, every year, we lose 20 percent of our customers. (That's OK, we didn't like those customers anyway. Kidding!)
- Since we lose 20 percent of our customers, our annual net profit drops by 20 percent. That has to be factored in each year.
- So if we start with 1,000 customers, then drop to 800 in year 2, and drop to 640 in year 3, that impacts our cumulative net profit. Instead of our cumulative net profit for 1,000 customers being $240,000 × 3 = $720,000, it's $542,545 because we lose 20 percent of our customer base every year.

Now go ahead and revisit the chart and study the numbers again. If you're like most people, you just skimmed the chart the first time, so go back through the chart and run down each column, making sure you understand each concept before moving on to the next item in the chart.

More Fun with Math

Once you've done that, we're going to throw another concept at you, which is this—cost per acquisition (CPA, sometimes called *customer acquisition cost* or CAC). CPA is exactly what it sounds like. It's how much it costs you to acquire one customer. Let's say you spent $300,000 in advertising to acquire 1,000 new customers. If you looked at just the first column in the previous chart, you would see that you generate $240,000 in net profit from those 1,000 new customers in year 1.

But wait . . . that would mean you spent $300,000 to generate $240,000 in net profit. That doesn't make any sense, does it?

No, it doesn't. But if you take into consideration that those 1,000 customers will generate profit for your company in year 2 and year 3, suddenly the calculation makes sense. In fact, by the end of year 3, the customers who are still with the company have generated $542,545 in net profit for Comcast. So a $300,000 marketing investment in year 1 generates $542,545 in net profit by year 3 (and that's including the discount rate, which factors in the time value of money).

In the end, if you spend $300,000 to acquire 1,000 new customers, then your cost per acquisition is $300. When you look at the last row and the last column of the chart, you'll see that your LTV on a per customer basis is $600. So you're spending $300 to make $600 in net profit. That's an ROI of 2:1—in other words, you make $2 in profit for every $1 you spend.

Not bad for a day's work.

IN A NUTSHELL

The concept of LTV is best used for products or services that have predictable recurring revenue. For example, monthly lawn service, monthly cell phone service, or a monthly consulting fee works great. It's a little harder (if not impossible) to calculate the LTV for a consumer packaged goods product.

If You're Like Most People, You'll Need to Revisit This a Few Times for It to Sink In

There are *three* kinds of people—those who are good with numbers, and those who aren't. If you're in the second category, don't be freaked out by all of the math we just threw at you. We've found that if you revisit the concept a few times, it all starts to sink in and make sense. So don't give up!

OK, let's talk about one last concept that's important. It's called attribution modeling and it's essentially a way to assign value to each interaction that happened along the way. In the previous example, the prospective Comcast customer took this course of action:

1. They clicked on a Comcast paid search ad.
2. They clicked on a Comcast banner ad.
3. They clicked on a Comcast Facebook ad.
4. Finally, they typed the Comcast URL into their browser and ordered the service.

The question is how do you decide which of the four interactions was responsible for the actual sale? Was it the paid search ad? The banner ad? The Facebook ad? The final visit to the Comcast website? In most cases, there's no way to decide which single action resulted in the sale, so you have to designate an attribution model to assign value to each step in the process.

There are a lot of different attribution models, but the five most common can be seen in the Table 18.2. Take a spin through the chart and see

Table 18.2 Attribution Model Comparisons

ATTRIBUTION MODEL	HOW IT WORKS	PROS	CONS
First Touch	Assigns 100% of the credit to the first touch point	Simple and easy to calculate	Gives too much credit to first touch and zero credit to other touch points
U-Shaped	Assigns 40% of the credit to the first and last touch points. Remaining 20% distributed evenly.	Some argue that first and last touch points are most important	Can undervalue key touch points, especially during long sales cycles
Linear	Every touch point is given equal credit	Easy to calculate	Undervalues the important touch points. Overvalues less important touch points.
Time Decay	Bulk of credit given to last touch points	Easier to calculate	Might overvalue last touch points
Last Touch	Assigns 100% of the credit to the first touch point	Easier to calculate	Gives too much credit to last touch point and zero credit to other touch points

which one is a fit for your business. Spoiler alert—you'll probably want to avoid first touch and last touch attribution, since those two models tend to overvalue the first and last interactions the prospects had prior to purchasing the product or service.

Let's Do a Final Recap

OK, we've covered a lot of really important concepts in this chapter. We discussed LTV, studied a chart with a lot of calculations around LTV, took a look at CPA, discussed calculating the ROI, and then discussed attribution modeling.

If you'd like to take a deeper dive into the math behind marketing, you might read Guy Powell's book *Marketing Machine: The Secret History of the Future of Marketing (ROI)*. And if you'd like to understand broader financial concepts, be sure to visit Investopedia.com, which is a well-structured and well-written website that takes a deep dive into a range of financial concepts.

OK, now that we've done all that, let's move on to the next chapter, shall we?

KEY TAKEAWAYS

Here are some things to keep in mind as you reflect on the concepts in this chapter.

- **Simplified versus complex ROI.** The simplified version of ROI is fine if you're at lunch with a friend and want to do a quick, easy calculation on the back of a napkin. If you're heading into a meeting with your CFO, you want to do the more advanced calculation.
- **Lifetime value (LTV).** This is an important concept to understand. If you have a product that's a recurring revenue product (e.g., life insurance, cable service, lawn care service, etc.), LTV is relatively easy to calculate. If you have a consumer package goods product, it's a little harder to calculate, since people might buy your product for a year, then stop buying it, then start buying it again five years later. So it's best used for recurring revenue products and services.
- **Attribution models.** We also discussed attribution models, which help you assign value to each engagement the prospect has with your brand over the course of your campaign.

PUTTING IT
ALL TOGETHER

Humans make decisions based upon logic and feelings, and your feelings
are informed by your experiences. Therefore, if your experience sucks,
then they won't buy your product. But if they have a great digital
experience, they feel like you're awesome and they buy your product.

—SIMON BERG, CEO, CEROS

We've covered a lot of ground over the past 18 chapters, haven't we?
There's a lot to digest here, so let's do a quick recap of some of the key
concepts we've covered throughout the book. Then we'll give you with a
step-by-step action plan to help you crawl, walk, and then run with your
next 1:1 marketing plan.

One of the things we've touched on frequently is that becoming a 1:1
marketer isn't about adopting a technology as much as it's about adopting
a mindset. Moving from mass marketing to 1:1 marketing isn't a destination as much as it's a journey. In other words, if you're a 1:1 marketer,
you'll be in a constant state of improvement as you learn new things and
incorporate new techniques. There's no end point to 1:1 marketing, just
a series of events that build upon one another. It's a good idea to keep all
that in mind as you move forward.

You'll also want to remember that traditional mass marketing prioritizes reach and recall, whereas 1:1 marketing prioritizes reaching just the right people with the right message at the right time. 1:1 marketers aren't interested in reaching large audiences. In fact, in many cases it's the opposite—we're interested in reaching smaller audiences. But since those audiences are highly targeted and have a propensity to buy your products or services, they're more likely to buy, so you actually increase the power of your budget by decreasing the number of people you target.

Traditional mass marketing campaigns are limited in their targeting precision because traditional broadcast media don't know who actually is reached by a campaign. But now that virtually all media provide addressable options (where individual consumers are reached on a 1:1 basis), campaigns can be hypertargeted using data that is closely linked to a consumer's likelihood of purchasing a specific product or brand. Data such as past purchase data, attitudinal data, historical location data, and more can be used.

The creative and message options in traditional mass marketing campaigns are also naturally limited. But when individual consumers are reached based on data tied to them, then ads and other messages can be personalized to make the campaigns more relevant. And in nonbroadcast methods, ads can be built dynamically. Various elements, such as the headline or visual, can be changed based on the recipient. This presents game-changing opportunities for marketers to transition from blasting the same messages to the most consumers to delivering unique messages to each audience of one.

Traditional mass marketing focuses on reaching people based on broad measures, such as demographics, and by buying television shows people in the target market are more likely to watch. But 1:1 marketing focuses on reaching the right consumers, based on who they are and what's known about them, using data such as customer data or past purchase data. Therefore, while 1:1 marketers want their ads to run on high-quality content, in the end, they don't focus on where the ad runs as much as who the ad is shown to. It really doesn't matter what show, website, or app the person is on at the time the ads are served; it only matters that the message is seen by the person they want to reach.

Timing of mass marketing campaigns is usually governed by general timeframes, such as dayparts or seasons. But 1:1 marketers know that where a person is and at what time the message is delivered can have a big impact on the effectiveness of the message. Therefore, they use the more precise methods of 1:1 marketing to carefully time specific ads to certain people at a precise time with the message most likely to resonate, such as an ad for warm soup just before lunchtime when the weather outside is cold.

GOALS AND OBJECTIVES OF A 1:1 CAMPAIGN

The goals of marketing programs and campaigns have a big impact on how they are built, especially in 1:1 marketing. While mass marketers tend to focus more on customer acquisition, 1:1 marketers take a more holistic approach and often focus as much if not more effort on increasing the value of their customers over time versus trying to get new customers. Even within customer campaigns, 1:1 marketers know they have multiple ways to increase lifetime value and apply different techniques, targeting, and methods based on the specific goal of each campaign.

Mass marketers tend to focus on short-term results, but 1:1 marketers are more likely to take the long view to marketing, seeking to increase the value of customers over time. They are also more likely to measure metrics that directly relate to the bottom line, such as sales. Mass marketers tend to measure less granular metrics, such as how many people their ads reach and how often, which typically don't directly correlate to sales or profit.

Remember, no company can flip a switch (like in Figure 19.1) and go from being a mass marketer to a 1:1 marketer overnight. And some marketers use multiple techniques, turning to mass marketing for customer acquisition and 1:1 marketing for increasing the value of customers.

With all that in mind, let's take a look at the action steps that are involved in becoming a 1:1 marketer. We've divided the process into three

Figure 19.1 Becoming a 1:1 marketer takes time. You can't simply
flip the switch. Instead, you have to continuously work to move
from mass marketing to 1:1 marketing.

stages, which we're calling crawl, walk, and run. Many people will start in
the crawl stage and move up to walk, and then run. Others will start in the
walk or run stages. No matter what stage you're at, it's all good because
each of us is on our own journey, right?

One thing to keep in mind before we dive in: the steps we've outlined
are the basic, fundamental steps. This is not intended to be an all-inclusive
set of steps. Instead, it's designed to provide a framework on how you can
move forward. The nuances and complexities of your 1:1 campaign go
much deeper than these steps—we're just trying to point you in the right
direction so you can get started.

BEFORE YOU LAUNCH YOUR 1:1 CAMPAIGN

The foundation for any successful 1:1 campaign is . . . c'mon, you know the answer. We've talked about it a lot throughout the book. Go ahead, say it. The foundation for any successful 1:1 campaign is . . . ?

Did you say *data*? If so, then you're absolutely correct. The foundation for any successful 1:1 campaign is data. So the first thing you need to do is to audit, normalize, and consolidate your data. Here are the steps to do that:

Step 1: Audit your data. Figure out where all your data is and start the process of doing an inventory of what kind of data you have and where it's located. This can include your CRM data, warranty data, purchase data, e-commerce data, marketing automation data, and just about any other kind of data that helps you understand your customer.

Step 2: Normalize and clean up your data. Part of the process here is to clean up your data, which means you'll eliminate information that is duplicated in your various sources. Acxiom is the big player in this space. They do a lot more than just normalization and cleanup work, so keep them on your radar screen for a lot of things. But if you're interested in normalizing and cleaning up your data, you'll be in good shape with Acxiom, LiveRamp, Experian, Neustar, Segment, or other identity resolution companies.

Step 3: Map your customer data to their anonymous digital IDs. When you want to reach your customers across all of their devices, including computers, smartphones, tablets, and connected televisions, you need to know the anonymous digital identifier tied to that device. That's another area where identity resolution companies can help. They have created their own referential identity graphs with every known device ID for hundreds of millions of consumers and can map them to your first-party data. When it's time to run a campaign, you simply provide the anonymous IDs you want to reach to any ad platform, protecting your customer's privacy and your valuable first-party data security.

OK, now that you've taken care of your data, let's go through the crawl, walk, run action steps.

ACTION STEPS FOR THE CRAWL STAGE

In this stage, we're going to assume you're already doing some fundamental things in the 1:1 arena such as segmenting your marketing automation lists, personalizing the messages, and perhaps even scoring the leads that come through your marketing automation platform.

You'll recall in a previous chapter that we discussed an example with Nike running shoes. The example showed how you can segment lists, geo-target people in those lists, develop personalized campaigns for those individuals, and track whether or not they ultimately made the purchase. It was a relatively fundamental version of 1:1 marketing using marketing automation, but it lays the foundation for understanding some of the essential components of a 1:1 campaign, primarily in the use of data to segment, personalize, track the results, and calculate the ROI.

One thing we'd like you to remember about the Nike example—and this applies to all the examples we share with you—is that it's one thing to *understand* the concept of 1:1 marketing, and it's an entirely different thing to *put it into action*. Putting something into action takes discipline and follow-through, so don't try to tackle everything all at once. Instead, learn the ins and outs of a case study, embrace it, and then execute it for your business before you move on to the next level.

A quick side note on the issue of execution and why it's so important. One of the authors remembers seeing a speech by a young person who had had a lot of success with a website that focused on the unique attractions in each of the 50 states. During the speech, the young CEO discussed why they were getting millions of views on their site each month after being in business for only a few years. It was an impressive accomplishment, but here's the deal—the CEO didn't have any secret sauce or insider technology that the people in the audience didn't have. The tips and techniques she shared were the kinds of things that most people who had done their homework would already know about. The difference was that this very impressive young CEO executed each of the tips with focus and intensity. She didn't perform at 75 percent or even at 85 percent. Instead, every tip and technique she was using was executed flawlessly at 100 percent. And the result was that her web traffic went through the roof.

The point is that most of our success in marketing (and in life) doesn't come from some secret technology or insider technique. Instead, *it comes from better execution.* Here's an example of why better execution is a difference maker whether you're in marketing or not. When you think about it, just about any restaurant can make a chicken sandwich, but there's a reason that Chick-fil-A makes more per restaurant than McDonald's, Starbucks, and Subway combined . . . despite the fact that Chick-fil-A is closed on Sundays.[1] It's because of the way Chick-fil-A executes every step of the process. How they run their restaurants is science bordering on art. And it explains why there's a line of customers around the block every day at lunch.

OK, so now that we're all on the same page about the importance of execution, let's discuss a step-by-step plan on how to execute a 1:1 campaign in the crawl stage. The easiest way to do that is to turn to a demand side platform (DSP) like The Trade Desk, Facebook, Google, and others.

All DSPs work with multiple data providers who have reams of data and analytics that can provide you insights into who might buy and (in some cases) when they're most likely to make a purchase. This is a pretty straightforward campaign, and any marketer can just work with a DSP to create this kind of campaign.

To take things up a level, you can provide your customer data to the DSP and use it as a suppression list. This means they have a list of people who have a propensity to buy your product or service, but they're deleting (or suppressing) the people on your list who are already your customers. That way, you're not sending ads to people who already buy your product or service.

The flip side of that equation is that you can have the DSP target *only* your customers. For example, you might decide you'd like develop a campaign designed to cross-sell your existing customers. A cross-sell is where you get people to add on to their order—"You bought golf clubs from us; would you also like to buy our golf shirts?" Alternatively, you might decide that you'd like to upsell existing customers. An upsell is where you get people to buy a better, more expensive version of your products or services—"Last year, you bought our beginner set of golf clubs. Would you like to upgrade to our premium set this year?"

In the end, the crawl stage of a 1:1 campaign is relatively easy because you're relying on other companies to do some of the heavy lifting. So if you're wondering how to kick off a relatively simple 1:1 campaign, then the action steps we've outlined here are just your ticket.

ACTION STEPS FOR THE WALK STAGE

Once you're comfortable with the steps outlined in the crawl stage, then you're ready to take the leap to the walk stage. This isn't a big leap forward, so if you're comfortable with what we've talked about so far, then you'll be able to do this step pretty easily. The primary thing you're going to do at this stage is append third-party data to your first-party data so it provides a more nuanced profile of your customers and prospects.

Let's pretend for a moment that you're the marketing director for Holiday Inn. You have data on your Rewards customers that's pretty robust—you know their home addresses, you know how frequently they stay at your hotels, you know if they're budget travelers or premium travelers, and you know a bunch of other stuff that gives you a pretty nuanced view of your existing customers. But let's say that you, as the marketing director, decide that you want a more detailed understanding of your customers. After all, if your Rewards members stay with you, on average, five times each year, who's not to say that they don't spend the night in your competitors' hotels 10 times each year, right?

Well, there's a way to append your data and find that out. You can get overlays that provide a much richer view of your customer. For example, you might find out that a certain segment of your customers that travel 12+ times a year on business stay at a Holiday Inn 6 times a year, which means you're missing out on another 6-plus potential stays from those customers. That's revenue that should be yours, right? Wouldn't it make sense to develop a campaign specifically designed to get your existing customers who travel frequently to increase the number of stays at your hotels?

That would be relatively easy to do. And the starting point is what we've talked about here, which is to take your existing customer data and then have it appended by Acxiom or another company so you can use that nuanced view of your customers to design better campaigns. Once you have the new appended customer segment, you can work with a DSP and other third-party platforms to deploy the campaign so it's hitting the right customers with the right messages at the right times.

There are other ways you can execute this kind of campaign, too. For example, say you have customer data from warranty cards. It's pretty straightforward data—name, address, and product serial number. But if you append that data with household income (HHI), then you have a better understanding of your customers. Based on that new information, you might develop promotions targeting different segments with different kinds of offers. In its simplest form, you would take the people in the bottom 50 percent of HHI and deploy campaigns to them that would entice them to buy the discount product or service offering you provide. Then, for the segment who earn in the top 50 percent of HHI, you would develop a separate campaign that features the premium products and services.

In the preceding example, if you were a mass marketer with budget allocated for TV, you would execute a simple campaign by choosing a daypart (e.g., Thursdays between 9:00 p.m. and 10:00 p.m.), and a TV show watched by people who have the same demographics as your existing customers. But as a 1:1 marketer, you know there's a huge amount of waste by running a campaign that way, so instead of simply running TV ads based on dayparts and the demographics of the viewing audience, you decide to use that budget for a 1:1 campaign using addressable TV, direct mail, and online display. Since you have the data about your customers and you know which customers are in the top 50 percent of HHI and which customers are in the bottom 50 percent of HHI, you can deliver separate campaigns designed to appeal to the personal needs of each customer segment.

Now that we have an understanding of the walk stage of a 1:1 campaign, let's move on to the run stage.

ACTION STEPS FOR THE RUN STAGE

To launch more advanced campaigns, you want to do everything we've discussed in the crawl and walk sections earlier, but you also want to kick it up a notch. This is done by incorporating transaction data into your data mix. In other words, you can connect the dots between the campaigns you run and the actual results online or in a bricks-and-mortar store.

As you know, there's plenty of transactional data available to marketers. And since you're in the run stage of a 1:1 campaign, you've created an identity graph that provides a near real-time understanding of your prospects and your customers. Your identity graph gives you a 360-degree view of your customers and their purchases. The identity resolution company that helps you build your identity graph can also help you create and manage first-party cookies on your customers.

As an example, say you're Apple and you've developed a new product. The product is called the iTracker, and it's a large, wall-mounted display designed for health-conscious consumers who want to participate in interactive exercise programs. The iTracker has resistance bands attached to the sides so users can do resistance training, but it's also designed for live, interactive high intensity interval training (HIIT) sessions that monitor your health in real time via your Apple watch. The iTracker is an expensive product—say it's $4,500—and there's a good profit margin tied to it, assuming the campaign works. With a profit margin like that, you have plenty of room to develop a 1:1 campaign that would drive sales and have a healthy ROI.

In this example, you would use everything you've learned in the crawl and walk action steps, but then kick it up a notch by tracking whether or not the campaign you ran generated a sale either online or, more important, at the bricks-and-mortar Apple store. In other words, since you're doing a sophisticated 1:1 campaign, you can use your identity graph and first-party cookies to connect the dots between the sale at the Apple store and the specific ads you ran targeting the people most likely to buy the new iTracker.

This kind of campaign can be run by just about any company with customers who have a high LTV. The higher the LTV, the more likely this kind of campaign will work. After all, the more data overlays you do and the more nuanced the targeting, the more expensive it is to run the campaign, so you have to have a pretty robust LTV for all this to work perfectly. The automobile industry, the pharmaceutical industry, some electronics companies, a lot of B2B companies, and plenty of other industries with a good LTV are excellent candidates. But you won't know if a 1:1 campaign is right for your product or service unless you test a few campaigns, so why not give it shot? It's not that hard. Really.

THE 1:1 FRAMEWORK

The 1:1 framework (see Figure 19.2) is designed to help you gain a better understanding of the complexity and precision of various 1:1 techniques. Take a spin through the following graphic and gain an understanding of where each of the techniques discussed in this chapter fall on the matrix.

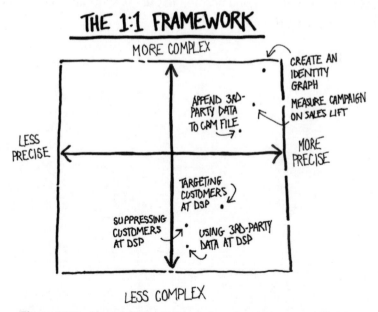

Figure 19.2 The 1:1 framework is designed to help you understand the complexity versus precision equation for different kinds of campaigns.

This helps you get a sense of the complexity and precision each of the techniques can bring to your next 1:1 campaign.

WRAPPING UP WITH THE MOST IMPORTANT MESSAGE IN THE BOOK

As we round the bend on the journey we've had together, we'd just like to revisit a topic we discussed earlier in this chapter—successful 1:1 marketing isn't about reading this book and simply understanding the concepts. Instead, it's about reading the book, understanding the concepts, and *executing the plan*. If you execute the plan properly and then test your campaigns along the way so you can continuously improve the results, you'll be a 1:1 rock star. And that's everything we intended for this book—to turn you into a 1:1 rock star.

Enjoy the journey ahead. You now know more about marketing (and more specifically, about 1:1 marketing) than most other people around you. That puts you in a pretty good position to call the shots and get stuff done.

Go get some stuff done.

ACKNOWLEDGMENTS

This book wouldn't have been possible without the help of so many experts who shared their insights and their written contributions.

Dr. Laura Bright at The University of Texas at Austin and Dr. Karen Anne Wallach at The University of Alabama in Huntsville both contributed one of the most important chapters in the book, the chapter on privacy. They're two of the nation's leading experts on the subject, and we appreciate their expertise and insight.

Guy Powell also contributed to the book and helped review the chapter on calculating the ROI of a one-to-one marketing campaign. Guy is the author of *Marketing Machine: The Secret History of the Future of Marketing (ROI)* and *The Post-Covid Marketing Machine: Prepare Your Team to Win.*

Francheska Rossi, a recent graduate of Emory University, was a very capable researcher and contributor for our chapter on the tools of the trade.

We would also like to thank Casey Ebro, Amy Li, Patricia Wallenburg, Kevin Commins, and the rest of the team at McGraw Hill. Honestly, you have been a joy to work with. You have been responsive, helpful, and inspiring in so many ways, it's hard to count.

Brent Khun and Maribett Varner were an inspiration to both of us for their humility, brains, and talent.

We would also like to thank those who read the manuscript and provided early reviews for the book. They include Doug Busk, Doug

Dichting, Kirsten McMullen, Desmond Martin, Professor Jagdish Sheth, Michael Brenner, Bart Casey, Emily Justin-Szopinski, Ayman Itani, Emeric Ernoult, Dr. Reshma Shah, Erik Qualman, Carrie Schonberg, Jacques Meir, Gary B. Wilcox, Siddharth Taparia, Dave Kerpen, Robert T. Chin, Ravi Raman, Ric Moxley, and Frans Mahieu.

And, of course, we would like to acknowledge Don Peppers and Martha Rogers, both of whom got the one-to-one marketing movement started with their pivotal book, *The One to One Future*, so many years ago, and graciously offered to write the Foreword for this book.

Jamie: I would like to thank my wife, Dayna, and our children, McKensie, Grace, and Lily, for being some of the most centered, kind, and bighearted people I know.

Chuck: I would like to thank my wife, Janice, and daughter, Gabriella, for their sacrifices while I worked many nights and weekends on the book. A special thanks to Earl Hogan, one of the smartest and most experienced people I know in direct marketing and a mentor to me when creating the One2One Marketing division at ad agency Barkley shortly after *The One to One Future* was published.

NOTES

Foreword

1. Don Peppers and Martha Rogers, *The One to One Future*, Crown Business, 1993.

Chapter 1

1. https://www.analyticssteps.com/blogs/how-disney-uses-behavioral-analytics-customer-experience.
2. https://optinmonster.com/ecommerce-personalization-examples/.
3. https://blog.wishpond.com/post/115675437776/marketing-personalization.
4. https://www.internetworldstats.com/emarketing.htm.
5. https://99firms.com/blog/how-many-email-users-are-there/#gref.
6. https://www.pewresearch.org/internet/fact-sheet/mobile/.
7. https://www.pewresearch.org/internet/fact-sheet/social-media/.

Chapter 2

1. https://www.prweek.com/article/1582002/read-marc-pritchards-landmark-speech-creating-new-media-supply-chain.
2. BMO Capital Markets.
3. MoffettNathanson.
4. The Nielsen Company, February 2020 Nielsen Total Audience Report.
5. The Nielsen Company, February 2020 Nielsen Total Audience Report.
6. Cordcutting.com Subscription Mooching & Streaming Media Report, May 2020.
7. Forrester Research, April 2015, *Wining in the Age of the Consumer: Embrace Four Imperatives to Transform Your Company for Customer Obsession.*

8. Catalina, Inc. 2015 Mid-Year Top 100 Brands Performance Review.

9. NCSolutions, 2020, *Loyalty in the Time of COVID: Why Branding and Targeted Advertising Matter More Now Than Ever.*

10. https://www.pymnts.com/news/retail/2020/pg-pepsi-and-other-cpg-brands-continue -push-toward-direct-to-consumer-sales/.

11. Forrester Research, September 2020, *Vast, Fast, and Relentless: The Future of How People Buy.*

12. Pew Research Center, survey of US adults conducted June 4–10, 2020.

13. Ragan's PR Daily, *Organizational Responses to Black Lives Matter*, July 2020.

14. *Eat This, Not That!*, June 18, 2020.

Chapter 3

1. 4INFO case study, May 2017.

2. Metadata.io, 2021.

Chapter 4

1. 4INFO was acquired by Cadent in January 2020.

2. 4INFO case study, May 2017.

3. Direct quote from an interview with Dennis Becker, CEO of Mobivity.

4. IAB case study, https://www.iab.com/insights/mobile-location-use-cases-and-case -studies/.

Chapter 5

1. https://www.linkedin.com/pulse/content-marketings-data-driven-mandate-rob-o -regan/.

2. https://hbr.org/2014/10/the-value-of-keeping-the-right-customers.

3. Acxiom case study, https://www.acxiom.com/resources/case-study-heathrows -customer-experience-took-flight/.

4. LeadsRX case study, https://leadsrx.com/project/b2b-voip-services-case-study.

Chapter 6

1. https://www.linkedin.com/pulse/marketing-funnels-can-give-you-funnel-vision -tom-fishburne/.

2. Lavidge, Robert J., and Gary A. Steiner. "A Model for Predictive Measurements of Advertising Effectiveness." *Journal of Marketing* 25, no. 6 (1961): 59–62. Accessed December 29, 2020.

3. https://hbr.org/2020/10/marketers-underuse-ad-experiments-thats-a-big-mistake.

4. Sean Ellis and Morgan Brown, *Hacking Growth* (Crown Publishing, 2017), p. 9.

5. https://www.youtube.com/watch?v=hGwDMZqFc8o. Accessed December 29, 2020.
6. https://www.youtube.com/watch?v=3dKnW1mbpcc. Accessed December 29, 2020.
7. https://www.youtube.com/watch?v=NR2gH2jTe-U&t=2s. Accessed December 29, 2020.
8. Direct quote.

Chapter 8

1. https://www.smartinsights.com/internet-advertising/internet-advertising-analytics/display-advertising-clickthrough-rates/.
2. https://www.nanigans.com/2017/11/02/why-every-digital-advertiser-needs-to-test-like-a-scientist/.

Chapter 11

1. Direct quote.

Chapter 12

1. https://www.getresponse.com/resources/guides/personalize-and-protect.
2. Ohlheiser, A., "74 percent of Facebook Users Don't Realize the Site Collects Their Interests to Target Ads Pew Survey Says," *Washington Post*, January 16, 2019, https://www.washingtonpost.com/technology/2019/01/16/percent-americans-didnt-know-facebook-collected-their-interests-target-ads-until-pew-asked-them-about-it/?utm_term=.f4007f28ea94.
3. Aguirre, E., Mahr, D., Grewel, D., Ruyter, K. D., and Wetzels, M. (2015), "Unraveling the Personalization Paradox: The Effect of Information Collection and Trust-Building Strategies on Online Advertisement Effectiveness," *Journal of Retailing*, 91, 34–59.
4. Norberg, P. A., and Horne, D. R. (2014), "Coping with Information Requests in Marketing Exchanges: An Examination of Pre-Post Affective and Behavioral Coping," *Journal of the Academy of Marketing Science*, 42, 415–429.
5. Cadwalladr, C., Graham-Harrison, E. (2018), "Revealed: 50 Million Facebook Profiles Harvested for Cambridge Analytica in Major Data Breach," *Guardian*, https://www.theguardian.com/news/2018/mar/17/cambridge-analytica-facebook-influence-us-election.
6. Ohlheiser, A., "74 Percent of Facebook Users Don't Realize the Site Collects Their Interests to Target Ads Pew Survey Says," *Washington Post*, January 16, 2019, https://www.washingtonpost.com/technology/2019/01/16/percent-americans-didnt-know-facebook-collected-their-interests-target-ads-until-pew-asked-them-about-it/?utm_term=.f4007f28ea94.

7. Martin, K. D., and Murphy, P. E. (2017), "The Role of Data Privacy in Marketing," *Journal of the Academy of Marketing Science*, 45(2), 135–155.

8. Petronio, Sandra (2002), *Boundaries of Privacy: Dialectics of Disclosure*, New York: State University of New York Press.

9. Mosteller, J., and Poddar, A. (2017), "To Share and Protect: Using Regulatory Focus Theory to Examine the Privacy Paradox of Consumers' Social Media Engagement and Online Privacy Protection Behaviors," *Journal of Interactive Marketing*, 39, 27–38.

10. Martin, K. D., Borah, A., and Palmatier, R. W. (2016), "Data Privacy: Effects on Customer and Firm Performance," *Journal of Marketing*.

11. https://www.forbes.com/sites/forbestechcouncil/2020/07/29/the-privacy-mindset-of -the-eu-vs-the-us/?sh=1de9e63b7d01.

12. Fowler, Geoffrey A. (2020), "Nobody Reads Privacy Policies. This Senator Wants to Make Lawmakers Stop Pretending That We Do," *Washington Post*, https:// www.washingtonpost.com/technology/2020/06/18/data-privacy-law-sherrod-brown/.

13. Ohlheiser, A., "74 Percent of Facebook Users Don't Realize the Site Collects Their Interests to Target Ads Pew Survey Says," *Washington Post*, January 16, 2019, https:// www.washingtonpost.com/technology/2019/01/16/percent-americans-didnt-know -facebook-collected-their-interests-target-ads-until-pew-asked-them-about-it/?utm _term=.f4007f28ea94.

14. Wagman, M. (2020), "Opinion: No More Excuses—Brands Must Take Control on Privacy Now," *AdAge*, https://adage.com/article/opinion/opinion-no-more-excuses -brands-must-take-control-privacy-now/2264876.

Chapter 13

1. Direct quote.

2. https://winstonchurchill.org/resources/quotes/page/3/.

3. https://www.brainyquote.com/quotes/wyatt_earp_132804?src=t_accuracy.

4. https://www.ncbi.nlm.nih.gov/pmc/articles/PMC4209704.

5. https://www.brainyquote.com/quotes/arthur_ashe_371528.

6. https://www.brainyquote.com/quotes/lao_tzu_137141.

7. https://medium.com/centre-for-public-impact/what-gets-measured-gets-managed -its-wrong-and-drucker-never-said-it-fe95886d3df6.

8. https://www.brainyquote.com/quotes/sabrina_bryan_611182?src=t_support.

9. https://www.brainyquote.com/quotes/arthur_c_clarke_101182?src=t_technology.

10. https://www.goodreads.com/quotes/14318-there-s-a-fine-line-between-support-and -stalking-and-let-s.

11. https://www.nytimes.com/wirecutter/blog/amazons-alexa-never-stops-listening-to -you/.

12. https://60secondmarketer.com/2020/08/06/do-google-apple-and-amazon-listen-to
-my-smartspeaker-conversations-a-qualitative-research-study-by-students-at-the
-university-of-texas-put-this-question-to-the-test/.

Chapter 14

1. *Growth Hacker Marketing: A Primer on the Future of PR, Marketing, and Advertising,*
2013.
2. https:/www.census.gov/newsroom/press-releases/2019/popest-nation.html.
3. https:/www.bizjournals.com/albany/news/2019/04/11/number-of-businesses-in-the
-united-states.html.
4. Ibid.

Chapter 15

1. https://www.economist.com/leaders/2017/05/06/the-worlds-most-valuable-resource
-is-no-longer-oil-but-data.

Chapter 16

1. http://www.thoughtgadgets.com/?author=3&paged=4.
2. https://gs.statcounter.com/browser-market-share.
3. https://gs.statcounter.com/browser-market-share.
4. https://www.cnbc.com/2020/12/15/apples-seismic-change-to-the-mobile-ad-industry
-draws-near.html.
5. https://techcrunch.com/2020/08/27/facebook-vs-apple-ad-tracking/.
6. Chad Engelgau, CEO of Acxiom, in an interview with Chuck Moxley.
7. https://www.adexchanger.com/tv-and-video/the-restrictions-on-idfa-will-shift-mobile
-budgets-to-tv/.

Chapter 17

1. https://checkyourfact.com/2019/08/27/fact-check-oscar-wilde-be-yourself-everyone
-already-taken/.

Chapter 19

1. https://www.entrepreneur.com/article/320615.

INDEX

Page numbers followed by *f* and *t* refer to figures and tables, respectively.

ABOUT THE AUTHORS

Jamie Turner is an internationally recognized author, university professor, and management consultant who speaks about marketing, persuasion, and leadership at events and corporations around the globe. His client list includes The Coca-Cola Company, AT&T, Microsoft, Verizon, SAP, T-Mobile, and Holiday Inn. He was recognized as a top 10 speaker by CareerAddict (along with Ariana Huffington, Daymond John, and Gary Vaynerchuk). He has also appeared in Forbes, Inc., Entrepreneur, Business Insider, and CNBC. And he is a regular guest on CNN and HLN, where he contributes segments on marketing, persuasion, and leadership.

Jamie teaches at Emory University and the University of Texas and has been profiled in one of the world's bestselling marketing textbooks. He is the coauthor of several essential business books including *How to Make Money with Social Media*, *Go Mobile*, and *Digital Marketing Growth Hacks*.

He is the founder of 60SecondMarketer.com and has a YouTube channel that was designated one of "10 Top Business YouTube Channels" in the nation by Wishpond.com.

He is also the cofounder of A School Bell Rings, a nonprofit that improves access to education for impoverished children around the globe.

If you'd like to find out more about having Jamie speak at your next event, visit JamieTurner.Live.

Chuck Moxley is a marketing practitioner with more than 30 years' experience on both the brand and agency sides of marketing. He led brand strategy for many consumer brands while working at several agencies, and has led marketing for numerous business-to-business brands over the past two decades, serving in executive leadership roles.

The One to One Future was published while Chuck worked at a traditional ad agency, inspiring Chuck to build a successful new division of the agency called One2One that focused on database and direct marketing. Chuck used that experience when he went on to cofound three Bay Area technology companies.

Chuck has developed innovative marketing programs for dozens of brands including Chick-fil-A, Lee Jeans, Subway, AT&T, Pepsi, Citgo, NFL, and Sears.

He is one of the nation's leading experts on the convergence of technology and marketing, and speaks frequently at corporations and industry trade organizations on digital marketing, digital identity, and the ethical use of data and its impact on business and society.

To learn about how to book Chuck to speak at your event, visit ChuckMoxley.com.

For more information, please visit audienceofone.website.